ITALIAN CONSTITUTIONAL JUSTICE

IN GLOBAL CONTEXT

Praise for *Italian Constitutional Justice in Global Context*

"This is a very different book—a combination in the best sense of a law book and a book about the law learned and erudite in its descriptive parts, insightful in its analytical part. It is important, because so many will simply be unaware of Italian constitutionalism, its history, institutions, and not least, its jurisprudence. I might say, tongue-in-cheek, that if you read it coupled with Sabino Cassese's *Diary*, you will not need to read much more."

—**Joseph Weiler,** University Professor, Joseph Straus Professor of Law, and
European Union Jean Monnet Chaired Professor, New York University School of Law
European Journal of International Law

"The authors have produced an extraordinary book. It is not by chance that the book has been the subject of great interest from many groups of scholars in Italy, Europe, and the United States. [T]he book is concise, comprehensive, enriched by statistics and good indexes, and well-written. Through frequent and diffuse quotations of the case law of the Constitutional Court (often translated into English for the first time), the book is a window into the whole Italian constitutional system. The book examines the Constitutional Court's historical evolution, its role in adjudicating matters of regional and local government, its interaction with other constitutional bodies, and its relationship with the European Courts."

—**Nicola Lupo,** Professor of Public Law, LUISS Guido Carli University
American Journal of Comparative Law

"[This] book is the first attempt in the Italian scholarly debate to consider the distinguishing features of Italian constitutional adjudication through Italian eyes, whilst at the same time, thinking (and consequently writing) in English so as to render the content accessible to non-Italian readers, by following a deductive and case law-based method, rather than the usual Italian theoretical approach characteristic of most Italian books on constitutional adjudication. [B]y adopting an evolutive historical approach, the authors succeed in demonstrating how it is, thanks to what one might call this 'internal unchosen training' that the court has ended up being better trained and better prepared than other European courts to play a leading role in the current season of cooperative constitutionalism in Europe and, more generally, in constitutional adjudication within the global arena."

—**Oreste Pollicino,** Professor of Constitutional Law, Bocconi University
Common Market Law Review

"The volume essentially provides a generally systematic overall view of the role of the Constitutional Court in Italy. It thus fosters a move away from the fragmented dialogue that has largely characterised the Court to a more open dialogue with the whole community of interpreters of law. In times of fragility and debate regarding the Italian constitutional system, in a period when the Italian constitutional system in general, and Italian constitutional justice in particular, are often at the forefront of controversy, a text of this kind shows its vitality, and in some way contributes, albeit indirectly, to the strengthening of the central role of constitutional justice and the constitutional system as a whole."

—**Gaetano Azzariti,** Professor of Constitutional Law,
University of Rome "La Sapienza"
Italian Journal of Public Law

Italian Constitutional Justice in Global Context

Vittoria Barsotti

Paolo G. Carozza

Marta Cartabia

Andrea Simoncini

OXFORD
UNIVERSITY PRESS

OXFORD
UNIVERSITY PRESS

Oxford University Press is a department of the University of Oxford. It furthers the University's objective of excellence in research, scholarship, and education by publishing worldwide.

Oxford   New York
Auckland   Cape Town   Dar es Salaam   Hong Kong   Karachi   Kuala Lumpur   Madrid
Melbourne   Mexico City   Nairobi   New Delhi   Shanghai   Taipei   Toronto

With offices in
Argentina   Austria   Brazil   Chile   Czech Republic   France   Greece   Guatemala   Hungary
Italy   Japan   Poland   Portugal   Singapore   South Korea   Switzerland   Thailand
Turkey   Ukraine   Vietnam

Oxford is a registered trademark of Oxford University Press in the UK and certain other countries.

Published in the United States of America by
Oxford University Press
198 Madison Avenue, New York, NY 10016

First issued as an Oxford University Press paperback, 2017
ISBN 978-0-19-085972-5 (paperback : alk. paper)

Library of Congress Cataloging-in-Publication Data
Barsotti, Vittoria, author.
    Italian constitutional justice in global context / Vittoria Barsotti, Paolo G. Carozza, Marta Cartabia, Andrea Simoncini.
        pages cm
    Includes bibliographical references and index.
    ISBN 978-0-19-021455-5 ((hardback) : alk. paper)
1. Constitutional law—Italy. 2. Constitutional history—Italy. 3. Constitutional courts—Italy. 4. Judicial process—Italy. 5. Justice, Administration of—Italy. I. Carozza, Paolo G., author. II. Cartabia, Marta, author. III. Simoncini, Andrea (Law professor), author. IV. Title.
    KKH2070.B375 2015
    342.45—dc23

2015013959

Note to Readers

This publication is designed to provide accurate and authoritative information in regard to the subject matter covered. It is based upon sources believed to be accurate and reliable and is intended to be current as of the time it was written. It is sold with the understanding that the publisher is not engaged in rendering legal, accounting, or other professional services. If legal advice or other expert assistance is required, the services of a competent professional person should be sought. Also, to confirm that the information has not been affected or changed by recent developments, traditional legal research techniques should be used, including checking primary sources where appropriate.

(Based on the Declaration of Principles jointly adopted by a Committee of the American Bar Association and a Committee of Publishers and Associations.)

> **You may order this or any other Oxford University Press publication
> by visiting the Oxford University Press website at www.oup.com**

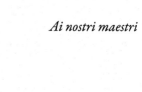

Ai nostri maestri

Contents

Preface

IT IS BY now a commonplace to recognize that the world is currently in a dynamic age of global constitutional dialogue and exchange, with a rich and growing network of interactions among constitutional norms and systems around the world. Comparative constitutional studies have exploded in scope and grown in sophistication, and tribunals around the world are drawing on the practical experience and jurisprudence of their counterparts in other countries. Both scholars and judges now widely read, borrow, and cite the jurisprudence of the high courts of other legal systems. Whatever one might identify and conclude about the causes and consequences of global constitutionalism, as an observable fact it is undeniably a prominent feature of our transnational juridical and political environment in the early twenty-first century.

Given the pervasiveness of this phenomenon, the extent to which the principal sources of constitutional borrowing and comparative dialogue remain dominated by a relatively narrow band of constitutional systems and courts is remarkable. Global constitutional dialogue often appears more like the three- or four-voice Renaissance polyphony of William Byrd motets than the full symphonic chorus embodied in Beethoven's Ninth Symphony. If global constitutionalism is to be an increasing source of the universal understanding and solidarity that the "Ode to Joy" represents, more instruments and voices, representing more fully the breadth and diversity of constitutional systems and traditions worldwide, will need to be added to the score.

Among the more notable voices missing in contemporary constitutional dialogues is that of the Constitutional Court of Italy. Its conspicuous absence is not in any way attributable to a lack of important and interesting aspects of the Court and its work. The Italian Constitutional Court represents one of the earliest, strongest, and most successful examples of constitutional judicial review established in Europe in the last century. Together with the Constitutional Court of Germany, it has served as one of the principal prototypes for later constitutional tribunals in other parts of Europe, from Spain and Portugal in the 1970s and 1980s, to Central and Eastern Europe after the collapse of the communist regimes in the 1990s, to the more recent reform of the French *Conseil Constitutionnel* in 2008. Its value transcends just Europe, moreover: it has a fascinating and instructive history for any country seeking to create and consolidate new institutions and systems of constitutional control; it is distinctive in its structural, procedural, and institutional dimensions; and it has a very well developed and sophisticated jurisprudence, with a unique voice distinguishing it among global constitutional actors, on a broad range of topics from fundamental rights and liberties to the allocations of governmental powers and regionalism.

Although a few great comparative law scholars of an earlier generation, notably Mauro Cappelletti, did briefly shine a brighter light on the Italian Constitutional Court, the growth of comparative constitutional law in general has relied overwhelmingly on the study of systems with jurisprudence and secondary literature available in what has become (for better or worse) the *lingua franca* of global constitutional dialogue: English. Familiarity with the Italian Constitutional Court has been hampered substantially by the very limited availability until recently of English translations of the great majority of its judgments and by the paucity of scholarly literature on it in English. Even though the Court has been making substantial efforts lately to disseminate more of its jurisprudence in English, much that is of potential interest still remains relatively unavailable to a global readership.

Against that background, this book aims to make the Italian Constitutional Court and its jurisprudence more accessible and familiar to scholars and judges engaged in comparative constitutional dialogue. We have sought to do so by providing a broad introduction to the development of the Court, from its formation and early history (Chapter 1) to its growing insertion into the regional European constitutional space (Chapter 7). Chapters 2 and 3 address the Court's structure—a dynamic hybrid of centralized and diffuse judicial review—as well as its judicial processes and its principal patterns of reasoning and methods of interpretation. The remaining chapters delve into several of the most important substantive areas of the Court's case law: rights and freedoms (Chapter 4); the allocation and interrelationship of powers among the branches of government (Chapter 5); and the distribution of authority between the central State and more local entities (Chapter 6). In conclusion, we try to identify some of the most salient themes that make the Italian Constitutional Court an interestingly distinctive and important contributor to our understanding of constitutional law and politics in the global context in which we find ourselves today.

In order to accomplish these goals, we have made several very deliberate methodological choices. The first is to present the Court primarily through a selection of its most significant features, cases, and themes, rather than by trying to be exhaustive in covering every aspect of the Court's jurisprudence. Second, although there are inescapably many evaluative judgments that the authors have made in the process of selecting, describing, and analyzing the significance of the Court's cases, the aim of the book is not in the first instance to be a critical evaluation of Italian constitutional law. Instead, keeping in mind that the majority of readers will be encountering the Italian Constitutional Court here for the first time in any detail, we have sought to allow the Court's own voice to emerge. For both of the first two reasons, the book includes a larger number of longer excerpts from the Court's judgments than might otherwise have been needed. These permit the reader to enter more fully into the Court's own judicial style.

In almost all cases, the translations of the Court's judgments are our own (where, exceptionally, they are official translations, it will be so noted in the text). As any good translator knows, it can be extremely difficult to render accurately both the literal meaning and a sense of the literary form of a text. This is all the more true of Italian legal language, which can be (from an Anglophone perspective) exceptionally dense and complex. Moreover, legal terms and constructs invariably contain many embedded presuppositions about the nature of law, the state, and society that can be very difficult to carry across to a different language. As a result, the translated excerpts may not always come across as the most fluid English prose but they do provide as faithful a taste of the "literary style" of Italian constitutional decisions as we have been able to convey.

Finally, this book also represents a conscious effort by all four of the coauthors to work in a systematically collaborative way. The individual chapters have not been separately authored and then collected into a single volume. Rather, all of the coauthors contributed substantially to each of the book's parts. In this we have sought to emulate some of the most successful examples of comparative legal scholarship, which so often depends on collaborative efforts to be able to bridge the gaps of understanding across legal traditions. Our labors have brought together two comparatists and two constitutionalists, three Italians and one American, two women and two men, a constitutional judge and three professors—in short, a microcosm of constitutional dialogue to contribute to the macro-dynamics of global constitutionalism.

Acknowledgments

THIS BOOK HAS been a truly cooperative effort not only of the four coauthors, but also of the many people who, at different stages and in different ways, contributed to its progress. As a consequence, each of us is indebted to numerous persons, and should acknowledge the contribution of each and all of them. In an attempt to thank most of them, we must begin with the participants in the seminar on the first draft of the book, which was held at the University of Florence, in a classroom of the Department of Legal Science, July 10–11, 2013. On that occasion, we benefited from the insights, comments, and suggestions of some of the most authoritative scholars and judges from both sides of the Atlantic: the Hon. Samuel Alito of the Supreme Court of the United States, Professor Anthony J. Bellia of Notre Dame Law School, the Hon. Guido Calabresi of the U.S. Court of Appeals for the Second Circuit, Professor Vicky Jackson of Harvard Law School, the Hon. Jeffrey Sutton of the U.S. Court of Appeals for the Sixth Circuit, Professor Cesare Pinelli of the University of Rome "La Sapienza," the Hon. Sabino Cassese of the Italian Constitutional Court, and Professor Vincenzo Varano of the University of Florence.

Professor Eric Longo, of the University of Macerata, gave valuable advice on our discussion of social rights and also served as our statistical expert. Without him, the tables in the appendices would have been, at a minimum, less clear, and probably would not have found their way into the book at all.

Professor Andrea Pin, of the University of Padova, shared with us his knowledge of fundamental rights jurisprudence, especially in the area of immigration, which has become crucial in the Italian political, social, and legal life of the last ten to fifteen years.

We are deeply indebted also to Mariangela Sullivan Crema for her extremely successful effort to put into beautiful English some decisions of the Italian Constitutional Court, written in a style that is often very difficult to translate.

Alessandra De Luca, of the University of Florence, has been a very careful reader of the various drafts. Many of her comments have been taken into account.

Last but not least, we owe our deepest thanks to a small group of doctoral and postdoctoral students of the University of Florence—Matteo Balloni, Sara Benvenuti, Luca Giacomelli, Sara Martini, Lucrezia Palandri, and Fan Yjan—who acquired a remarkable ability to move around the dozens of messy files that have been exchanged among the authors, always with high spirits and cheerfulness, as well as to Felicia Caponigri of Notre Dame Law School, who provided exceptional assistance with everything from translation and editing to organization of our Florence seminar.

I   The Constitutional Court

1   The Historical Development of Italian Constitutional Adjudication

1. Constitutional Justice prior to 1948

The emergence and development of constitutional adjudication in Italy presents a basic puzzle. Over the decades since the adoption of the Constitution of 1948, the Constitutional Court, and the system of judicial review in which it is the central player, have become strong and stable, effective, and politically legitimate. At the same time, if we look at the longer historical trajectory of the Italian legal tradition in the century prior to the Constitution, and even in the first decades of the post–World War II Republic, the preconditions for such a development seem remote. Everything from the theoretical foundations of sovereignty to the institutional weakness of the Judiciary was aligned against the probability that constitutional judicial review could take root and flourish in Italy. How, then, did such a system succeed in being grafted onto a tradition of law and politics to which it was completely alien? As we will see both in this chapter and in the rest of this book, the factors that made that possible have affected the institutional character and jurisprudence of the Constitutional Court throughout its history, up to the present. Moreover, the keys to this puzzle are of course relevant far beyond the boundaries of Italy. Many of the obstacles to creating an entirely new but effective system of constitutional justice that were present in Italy are structurally very similar to those faced in a variety of countries around the world today. Thus, the story of the conception, gestation, birth, and growth of the Constitutional Court yields valuable lessons for efforts to establish and strengthen constitutional justice elsewhere as well.

In Italy as in the rest of Europe, the great liberal revolutions of the late eighteenth century provoked strong movements toward constitutional and representative forms of government. The end of the Napoleonic empire and the "restoration" that followed the Congress of Vienna in 1815 led throughout Europe to support for constitutional charters that both protected the rights of citizens and established a separation of powers that included the creation of representative parliaments (in various forms).

Consistently with these developments, in 1848 Carlo Alberto, the King of Sardinia, promised to his subjects that he would adopt a statute to establish a representative system of government. Until then the small Kingdom of Sardinia, which would eventually become the Kingdom of Italy in 1861, was still an absolute monarchy, with all of its powers concentrated in the hands of the heir to the Savoy dynasty. Carlo Alberto was brought to this decision most immediately by the fact that in February of that year the Kingdom of Two Sicilies and the Grand Duchy of Tuscany both accepted new constitutions under the pressure of popular revolts. Carlo Alberto thereafter hurried to concede a constitution to his people because, as his minister said, "it is necessary to grant it rather than to have it imposed."[1]

After sleepless nights and innumerable meetings, on March 4, 1848, Carlo Alberto adopted a "fundamental, perpetual, and irrevocable law of the Monarchy." This Albertine Statute went on to serve as the constitutional foundation of Italy for the next one hundred years.

I.I. THE FIRST ITALIAN CONSTITUTION

The Albertine Statute consisted of 84 articles. Inspired by the French constitutional text of 1830 and that of the Kingdom of Belgium of 1831, it follows the general structure of liberal European constitutions. It is primarily devoted to establishing the rights and duties of citizens and to setting forth the powers of the respective governing institutions (the King, the Senate and Chamber of Deputies, the Ministers, and the Judiciary).

The Albertine Statute did not, however, recognize any power of judicial review of legislation, nor was there any subsequent movement toward developing such a power notwithstanding the Statute's status as "fundamental, perpetual, and irrevocable

---

[1] U. Allegretti, *Profilo di storia costituzionale italiana*, Bologna, Il Mulino, 1989, p. 368.

law". The prevailing juridical views throughout the period of the Albertine Statute regarded it as a "flexible" constitution, not a "rigid" one—that is, it was deemed capable of being modified at any time by the same means as any other law, making it therefore incapable of serving as a standard for judicial review of ordinary legislation.

The conventional reading of Italian legal history ascribes this dichotomy between *flexible* and *rigid* constitutions to the writings of two prestigious Oxford colleagues, Albert Venn Dicey and James Bryce. Dicey's *An Introduction to the Study of the Law of the Constitution* (1885)[2] and, even more, Bryce's *The American Commonwealth* (1888)[3] were very influential texts in early twentieth-century Italian legal and political thought. Nevertheless, explaining the Italian approach to the Albertine Statute requires a little more than citation to the work of those British authors. After all, Bryce was very familiar with the Constitution of the United States (he had been the English ambassador there) and with the "rigidity" introduced into the American system by Chief Justice John Marshall and *Marbury v. Madison*. On this basis he distinguished the written American Constitution with the unwritten British one, and associated flexible constitutions with unwritten ones while he considered all written constitutions to be rigid.[4] The Italian borrowing of the English theorists, therefore, was thus arguably based on a misreading of their work. More important, the work of Dicey and Bryce entered the Italian juridical scene well after the Albertine Statute had already been in effect for decades.

The English theories of flexibility had their technical and textual link to the Italian constitutional system in the absence of any established amendment procedure for the Albertine Statute:

> Our statute did not say who and by what means it could be subsequently amended. Consequently, not presuming that it could remain unchangeable for centuries, nor that the power to correct it should remain in the hands of the king, the power to amend it could only fall on the parliament, that is, on the direct representative of the sovereign body and the proper organ for issuing legal norms.[5]

---

[2] Translated into French (the official language of the Kingdom of Sardinia) as *Introduction à l'étude du droit constitutionnel,* in 1902.

[3] Bryce's volume was originally translated into Italian by Attilio Brunialti, who is considered to be among the founders of political science and constitutional law in Italy, as *La Repubblica americana*, Torino, UTET, 1913–1916.

[4] J. Bryce, *Flexible and Rigid Constitutions,* in *History and Jurisprudence*, vol. I, New York, Oxford University Press, 1901 (the original essay dates 1884).

[5] F. Racioppi, I. Brunelli, *Commento allo statuto del Regno*, Torino, Unione tipografico-editrice torinese, 1909, p. 191.

In other words, lacking an amendment clause, assuming that the Statute could not be thought of as forever unchanging, and recognizing that the King had "irrevocably" ceded his own lawmaking power, the only body capable of modifying it would be the holder of the legislative power. Parliament, in the ordinary exercise of its legislative functions, could therefore pass any laws without constraint by the Albertine Statute because the latter was itself subject wholly to the same, ordinary legislative authority of Parliament.

At the same time, other comparative experience and theory existed throughout the era of the Albertine Statute that could have allowed the emerging Italian constitutional system to develop a rigid approach to that basic document and to accept some form of constitutional judicial review. For instance, other constitutional models did exist that distinguished between ordinary laws and constitutional laws (e.g., the Constitution of Belgium), or that required a supermajority to amend the constitutional text rather than the simple majority of ordinary legislation (e.g., the Constitution of Naples of 1848). Above all, the United States Constitution already provided an example of a constitution that had been interpreted to be "rigid" without having any explicit language in it to establish judicial review.

At the least, then, we need to identify the other factors, beyond imported British ideas and the silence of the text itself, which may have pushed the Italian tradition to adopt and maintain a flexible approach toward its first written constitution. Those factors can be found in the general climate and jurisprudential orientation of Italian legal and political culture in the era of classical Liberalism, and in particular in the twin emphases on the absolute sovereignty of the Parliament as legislator and on the correspondingly subordinated authority of a Judiciary lacking independence.

1.1.1. Parliamentary Omnipotence

The absolute authority of Parliament was in fact the cornerstone of Italian legal and political thought in the Liberal era. As one author of the period put it, precisely in connection with an analysis of the power of Parliament to modify the Albertine Statute, "the Italian Parliament, like the English one, regards itself as omnipotent, and as permanently constituent."[6] As these words reveal, this "super-principle" of the Italian constitutional order of the time is clearly linked to English theories of parliamentary sovereignty that were widely cited throughout Europe. Dicey expressed the idea, which had already been established and developed before him in William

---

[6] G. Arangio-Ruiz, *Istituzioni di diritto costituzionale italiano*, Milano, Fratelli Bocca, 1913, p. 466.

Blackstone's *Commentaries on the Laws of England* (1765–1769) and John Austin's *Province of Jurisprudence Determined* (1832), by saying:

> The principle of Parliamentary sovereignty means neither more nor less than this, namely that Parliament thus defined has, under the English constitution, the right to make or unmake any law whatever: and, further, that no person or body is recognized by the law of England as having a right to override or set aside the legislation of Parliament.[7]

From this starting point, the idea of a rigid constitution that prevailed even over ordinary legislation, such as the one existing across the Atlantic in the United States, was very difficult to comprehend, let alone accept. Alexis de Tocqueville revealed the gulf between the two views in an illuminating passage describing how different judicial attitudes toward the law emerge from divergent ideas about the relationship between the constitution and society:

> The political theories of America are more simple and more rational [than in France or England]. An American constitution is not supposed to be immutable as in France; nor it is susceptible of modification by ordinary powers of society as in England. It constitutes a detached whole, which as it represents the determination of the whole people is no less binding on the legislator than on the private citizen, but which may be altered by the will of the people in predetermined cases, according to established rules. . . .
>
> It would be . . . unreasonable to invest the English judges with the right of resisting the decisions of the legislative body, since the Parliament which makes the laws also makes the constitution; . . .
>
> But . . . [i]n the United States the Constitution governs the legislator as much as the private citizen: as it is the first of laws, it cannot be modified by a law; and it is therefore just that the tribunals should obey the Constitution in preference to any law. This condition belongs to the very essence of the judicature; for to select that legal obligation by which he is most strictly bound is in some sort the natural right of every magistrate.[8]

From there, Tocqueville recalls the famous phrase of Delolme to describe the omnipotence of the English Parliament: "It is a fundamental principle with the

---

[7] A. V. Dicey, *Lectures Introductory to the Study of the Law of the Constitution*, London, MacMillan, 1885, p. 35.

[8] A. de Tocqueville, *Judicial Power in the United States, and Its Influence on Political Society*, in *Democracy in America*, vol. 1, Ch. VI, pp. 126–130.

English lawyers, that Parliament can do everything except make a woman a man, or a man a woman."

Using the same underlying conception of Parliamentary sovereignty, in Italy everyone accepted the succinct conclusion that every law that is properly issued is constitutional.

1.1.2. The Lack of an Independent Judiciary

Tocqueville's contrast among England, France, and the United States not only underscores the divergent understandings of the scope of legislative power vis-à-vis the respective constitutions in these systems, it also highlights the correlative differences in the roles of judges. In Italy, the severe lack of judicial independence was the other important element accounting for the impossibility of establishing a system of judicial review.

Ordinary judges in Italy at the time of the Albertine Statute were entirely subordinated to the other powers of the State, and especially to the Executive. Without any guarantees of independence or autonomy, "magistrates could always be removed at the pleasure of the king. In the same way, there were no criteria for the nomination of judges, because they were recruited without any guarantee of independence whatsoever. Only for the magistrates of the Senate and for the courts of appeal was it even necessary to have a law degree."[9]

The Albertine Statute itself established in Article 68 that "Justice emanates from the King, and is administered in his Name by the Judges that He appoints." In contrast, it also provided in Article 73 that "The interpretation of the laws, in an obligatory way for all, is the exclusive task of the legislative power."

In short, "the Italian Judiciary, for various reasons, was not capable of opposing the omnipotence of the [Parliament] in such a way as to give life to an Italian power of judicial review."[10]

1.2. TWO EXCEPTIONS TO THE ABSENCE OF JUDICIAL REVIEW

Notwithstanding the solid uniformity of the prevailing views outlined above regarding the impossibility of constitutional review of legislation in Italy under the Albertine Statute, two very specific exceptions nevertheless can be found to the rule against judicial scrutiny of the validity of laws prior to 1948.

The first exception was in circumstances where a legislative act might be impugned for procedural reasons. In order to apply any law, the judge first had to verify that

---

[9] P. Marovelli, *L'indipendenza e l'autonomia della magistratura italiana dal 1848 al 1923*, Milano, Giuffré, 1967, p. 18.

[10] M. Bignami, *Costituzione flessibile, Costituzione rigida e controllo di costituzionalità in Italia (1848–1956)*, Milano, Giuffré, 1997, p. 19.

it was valid and in force, and this implied the need to exercise a preliminary check of the "formal requisites of law"—for instance, whether the text approved by the Chamber of Deputies was the same as that of the Senate, that the text had been published in the Official Gazette as required, that any necessary time lag between promulgation and taking effect had expired, etc. In such cases, although they were rare (one single example: *Cassazione Roma,* June 20, 1886), both the courts and scholars agreed that the judge should not apply any act lacking such formal and procedural validity. The second exception had a more significant scope of application, and its history is revealing of the challenge of trying to establish any form of judicial review in Italy prior to the Second World War.

Starting in the first half of the 1920s, many jurists began to oppose the practice of the government of the King, on the basis of the Albertine Statute, of issuing decrees having the force of law (so-called "Royal Decree-Laws"). Article 6 of the Albertine Statute stated: "The King issues decrees and regulations necessary for the execution of the laws, without suspending their application or eliminating them." In other words, the King could not by decree or regulation modify the primary source of law itself, the Parliamentary statute. Nevertheless, from the very beginning of the period of the Albertine Statute in 1848, the government and King used Royal Decrees to suspend or modify statutes, especially in order to declare "states of siege" in situations of threats to public order (such as rebellions or popular revolts) or natural disasters (such as the earthquake of Messina in 1908).

The Government, and some jurists, justified this practice at first on the basis of necessity. In addition, as a partial check on this extensive government power, starting in 1859 the decrees contained a clause requiring the presentation of the decree to Parliament for its "conversion" into ordinary legislation (although no time period for doing so was specified).

This practice grew disproportionately during the First World War, when more than one decree-law was issued on average per day. The arrival of the Fascist regime in 1922 made the problem even worse.

In contrast to the reluctance to consider a substantive judicial control over Parliamentary laws, the reaction of the scholarly community was strongly opposed to the expanding uses of decree-laws. Vittorio Emanuele Orlando, for example, although he otherwise excluded the possibility of judicial review of legislation, wrote that decree-laws "are in form irremediably unconstitutional—all of them! And even if the Judiciary cannot attribute to itself a parliamentary competence of 'annulling' the norms issued by the executive branch, nevertheless it can rightfully refuse to apply them in a concrete case."[11]

---

[11] *Id.,* p. 57.

Thanks in significant degree to Ludovico Mortara, a prominent law professor-turned-judge and then President of the Court of Cassation, there also began to appear judicial decisions affirming the possibility of a form of judicial review of decree-laws. In particular, decisions authored by Mortara held that decree-laws not containing the clause mandating their conversion by Parliament into ordinary law were illegitimate (*Cassazione Roma*, January 24, 1922), and also that judges may refuse to apply decree-laws when there is no urgency necessitating this exceptional form of lawmaking (*Cassazione Sezioni Unite*, November 16, 1922). Moreover, courts began to require that conversion by Parliament, which otherwise could take years, occur within very short time periods. Similarly, on the basis of this case law the use of decree-laws in criminal law was altogether prohibited.

The experiment was destined not to last long, however. By 1923, the "inconvenient" Judge Mortara had already been forced into an early retirement. By 1925, Fascism openly began to show its true authoritarian nature. Typically the explicit revelation of Mussolini's dictatorial intentions is associated with his famous speech to Parliament on January 3, 1925, where he openly spoke of a coup d'état and defended the barbaric assassination of the opposition figure Giacomo Matteotti by Fascist squadrons. Just two days later was the formal opening of the judicial term for that year, a solemn occasion in which the Judiciary formally expresses its evaluation of the questions most important for the administration of justice in the nation. On that occasion, the *Procuratore generale* (Attorney General) of the Court of Cassation expressly and publicly requested that "in Italy the same power be conferred on the highest judges that is conferred on them in America by the rules of the most free of peoples, that of the United States"—that is, the power of judicial review.[12]

The response of the Fascist regime was swift and decisive. Soon after the speech of the *Procuratore generale*, the Government obtained from Parliament a Law (no. 100 of 1926) on the powers of the Executive, which, without formally abrogating the Albertine Statute, was in open conflict with it. The law not only gave the Executive explicit authority to issue decree-laws, but also specified "the judgment of the necessity and urgency [of the decree-laws] is not subject to any control other than the political control of the Parliament." In this way, judges were excluded from reviewing decree-laws essentially by defining them as "political questions," and the brief foray into judicial control of constitutional legitimacy was suppressed.

---

[12] R. De Felice, *Mussolini il fascista*, Torino, Einaudi, 1968, pp. 40–41.

2. American-Style Constitutional Review during the Postwar Transition

With the fall of Fascism in July 1943 and the collapse of the regime's institutions, Italy entered into a transitional period. When the war finally ended in the Spring of 1945 with the liberation of all Italian territory, the antifascist parties and the King agreed on a pact: on the one hand, the King did not abdicate, but instead agreed to withdraw to a strictly private life and to name his son as the caretaker, or *Luogotenente*, of the Kingdom (literally, the "Lieutenant," thus not giving him the title of King); on the other hand, the Italian people would be given an opportunity, by referendum, to choose between a monarchy and a republic, and to elect a Constituent Assembly to draw up a new constitutional document.

The decree-law establishing this compromise (D.L.Lt. June 25, 1944, n. 151) provided that "until such time as the new Parliament is established, acts having the force of law shall be issued by the Council of Ministers through legislative decrees approved by the *Luogotenente* of the Kingdom." In this way, in the absence of an elected Parliament, the Executive formally acquired legislative power.

Moreover, even more interesting for the purposes of understanding the development of a system of constitutional justice in Italy, after the election of the new Constituent Assembly a new Legislative Decree of the *Luogotenente* (D.Lgs. Lgt. March 16, 1946, n. 9) established that "during the period of the Constituent Assembly and until the convocation of the first Parliament in accordance with the new Constitution, legislative power remains delegated to the executive, except in constitutional matters."

The phrase "except in constitutional matters" in fact had significant implications. It meant that legislative power (then in the hands of the Executive) could not intrude upon the substance of the constitutional order. It thus affirms directly the "rigidity" of constitutional matters by establishing that they could not be modified or derogated by "ordinary" legislation. This opened the door to a new form of judicial review, one as diffuse as the American model first created by *Marbury v. Madison*. As a result of this distinction, during all of the nearly two years of sessions of the Constituent Assembly (from June 2, 1946 to May 8, 1948), ordinary Italian judges were empowered to exercise a constitutional control of legislation, and in this way they began to experiment with an American-style, diffuse system of judicial review.

This is even more remarkable given that, until the new Constitution would come into effect on January 1, 1948, Italy had no written constitutional text at all, except for perhaps the Albertine Statute. In fact, an intense debate took place over just this point: What constitutional norms should judges apply? The answer was found in a few general principles of constitutional law, such as separation of powers, or equality. On this basis, the Court of Cassation issued its first judgment of uncon-stitutionality in 1947 (*Cassazione Sezioni Unite*, July 28, 1947), refusing to apply the legislation at issue to the parties in the case (but not nullifying the law through a judgment of general effect).

This experiment with the American model of diffuse review represented a signifi-cant period for the development of Italian constitutional adjudication. Although the Constitution itself came into force on January 1, 1948, for a series of reasons (which will be discussed further in the following sections) the Constitutional Court did not become operative until January 1956. In the interim, Transitional Provision VII of the Constitution provided that "Until such time as the Constitutional Court begins its functions, the decision on controversies indicated in Article 134 [i.e., questions of con-stitutionality] shall be conducted in the forms and within the limits of the provisions already in existence before the implementation of the Constitution." Thus, the practice of constitutional judicial review by ordinary courts in fact lasted almost a full decade.

During that period, judges in courts at all different levels of the judicial system issued about 70 decisions regarding the constitutionality of laws. These cases had several of the typical hallmarks of constitutional decisions within diffuse systems of judicial review. They did not limit themselves to the formal or procedural validity of legislative acts, but instead used the new Constitution as a parameter for making substantive and material judgments about constitutionality. Moreover, these cases not only examined legislation enacted by the new Parliament after the entry into force of the 1948 Constitution, they also reviewed laws preceding the new constitutional order. And finally, the decisions regarding constitutionality were limited to the concrete case before the court and did not have a general effect on the validity of the law as such.

3. A Complex Conception: Designing the Constitutional Court

The Constituent Assembly that was elected on June 2, 1946 (by universal suffrage, for the first time in Italian history) had the task of drafting a new Constitution, in place of the Albertine Statute, for an Italian State that was reborn out of the ashes of Fascism after the Second World War. By referendum, the Italian people chose to establish a republic rather than a monarchy (by 54.3 percent to 45.7 percent). The "founding fathers" of the Constituent Assembly were left with virtually all of the other fundamental decisions that needed to be made. Would the form of govern-ment be a presidential system or a parliamentary one? Was it to be a unitary or a fed-eral State? What individual rights would be recognized and guaranteed? And, most relevant to our discussion here: Would the constitutive document also establish a system of constitutional adjudication, and if so, according to what model?

The Assembly was formally in session from June 25, 1946, until December 22, 1947, when the Constitution was approved. However, it remained in extended working sessions up until January 31, 1948, because of the need to approve various "constitutional statutes,"[13] including, as we will see in further detail below, one regarding the Constitutional Court.

3.1. THE CONSTITUENT ASSEMBLY DEBATE

The Constituent Assembly was composed of 556 delegates. The two strongest political groups, which together comprised almost 80 percent of the total Assembly, were the Christian Democrats on the one hand (with 207 seats), and on the other the Italian Communist Party and the Proletarian Unity Socialist Party (with 219 seats combined). The remaining 130 seats were distributed among various parties, most of which represented a generally secular, liberal-democratic ideology. The three political groupings entered the debate with divergent views on the issue of constitutional adjudication.

One group, associated principally with the Christian Democrats, favored having a system of constitutional adjudication. Even before the fall of the Fascist regime, their leaders had been issuing statements—similar to those of other Christian political parties in France and Germany—in support of a high court with the power to guarantee the constitutional order. In a 1943 pamphlet, Alcide de Gasperi, the Italian statesman and founder of the Christian Democratic Party (writing under the pseudonym "Demofilo"), advocated a supreme court that "would protect the spirit and the letter of the Constitution, defending it against every abuse by public powers and every threat from the [political] Parties."[14] De Gasperi and others called for a court not only as a guarantee of constitutional rigidity, but also to protect what they regarded as the supreme value of the human person and the basic social principles that the Constitution should embody.

Some liberal-democratic parties, such as the Republicans and the Action Party, were allied with the Christian Democratic position, although for somewhat different reasons. The Liberal Party, which represented the pre-fascist political class, was substantially divided between a conservative wing more wedded to an older conception of Parliamentary sovereignty (and thus reluctant to accept limits on legislative

---

[13] In the Italian Constitution, in addition to the text of the Constitution itself, there are other legal sources called "constitutional statutes" (or "constitutional laws") endowed with the same legal value as the Constitution. They are approved by the Parliament through a special procedure—provided by Art. 138—that is the same as that requested to amend the Constitution.

[14] Demofilo (pseudonym of Alcide De Gasperi), *Le idee ricostruttive della Democrazia Cristiana*, in *Atti e documenti della Democrazia Cristiana*, Roma, Edizione Cinque Lune, 1959, pp. 12–15.

power) and a more progressive wing in favor of establishing a system of constitutional adjudication. The latter included Luigi Einaudi, who later became the first President of the Republic of Italy, and who in the Constituent Assembly was the only person who spoke in favor of the American model of judicial review.

The political Left, and in particular the Communist Party, was instead strongly opposed to the creation of a Constitutional Court, for various reasons. A theoretical objection derived from the communist conception of the State. As Palmiro Togliatti, the leader of the Communist Party, expressed it:

> Only the national assembly can pronounce upon the constitutionality of law, as the Parliament cannot accept any control other than that of the people. The proposed Court may be composed of the most illustrious men, the most prepared in the subject of constitutional law, but as they are not elected by the people they do not have the right to judge acts of Parliament.[15]

They also had a strong practical suspicion of the proposed court, based on the notoriety of the American experience of the United States Supreme Court placing strong obstacles in the path of Franklin Delano Roosevelt's New Deal social policies. Togliatti, again, stated the objection succinctly in the Constituent Assembly. He described the Constitutional Court as "something bizarre" that would lead to "a fear that tomorrow there may be a majority that is the direct and free expression of the working classes, who want to renew profoundly the political, economic, and social structure of the country."[16] In short, the communists saw the Court as a conservative organ destined to block the socialist reform of the State in the event that the political alliance of the leftist parties succeeded in winning the future elections.

This same line of pragmatic reasoning, however, eventually led the communists to change their course as the debate continued. What if the parties of the Left did not win the elections? What if they found themselves in the opposition? At that point their interests would be reversed. In the words of Piero Calamandrei (one of the Assembly's rapporteurs on the question of the Constitutional Court, an expert in constitutional law, and ultimately the key figure in determining the design of the Court), "in preparing a democratic constitution it is more opportune and more prudent to start from the point of view of the minority" rather than the majority.[17]

This led the parties of the Left to shift and to accept in principle a constitutional court, but on condition that it would be composed exclusively of judges appointed

---

[15] *Atti Assemblea Costituente* (Working papers of the Constituent Assembly), p. 92.

[16] *Atti Assemblea Costituente* (Working papers of the Constituent Assembly), p. 121.

[17] *Atti Assemblea Costituente* (Working papers of the Constituent Assembly), p. 127.

by Parliament (thus bringing the court back into the dynamics of "political" decision-making). With that reversal, the Constituent Assembly as a whole arrived fairly quickly at the conclusion that there needed to be a system of constitutional control on legislation.

As soon as the discussion moved on to the means of realizing that end, however, it was clear that the members of the Constituent Assembly had very vague and divergent ideas among them. On the one hand, very few of them had sufficient technical expertise to grapple with the complex questions posed by the different models of constitutional adjudication. On the other hand, they were dealing with a problem that was absolutely novel: Italian constitutionalism. As the Constitutional Court said of itself some years later in Judgment 13/1960, such an organ was "unprecedented within the Italian legal order." Whereas for organs such as the Parliament, the Judiciary, the Executive, and even the President (within a Parliamentary system), previous experience could serve as a reference point, even if only to criticize and modify prior practices, no such precedents or comparative examples existed within the Italian experience for a mechanism of constitutional control. As we have already seen, throughout the century of the Albertine Statute, Parliamentary omnipotence reigned supreme, alongside an exceptionally weak and subordinated Judiciary. Fascism had completely erased any real possibility of judicial review of legislative decisions. And even if the transitional period did witness a de facto form of diffuse review, it was entirely a judicially created practice inspired generically by the example of the United States, with no systematic structure or regulation to it. In sum, there were no sufficient Italian models upon which to rely.

As a result, foreign models of constitutional adjudication provided the only available reference points. Two in particular were known to some degree to members of the Assembly: that of the United States, and that of the Austrian Constitution of 1920. Both were born in particular historical, cultural, and political contexts quite different from the Italian one, so there was no suggestion that either could simply be transplanted directly into the new Italian constitutional order (with the exception of Einaudi's plea to wholly adopt the U.S. model). The Assembly's task would be one of elaborating a new institution proper and appropriate to the emerging Italian constitutional environment by mixing elements of the other models and generating a new hybrid form of judicial review.

The United States, on one side, offered a model in which the review of legislation is clearly judicial—that is, it is conducted by regular courts within the judicial branch, in the exercise of their ordinary jurisdictional functions—and it is diffuse among any judge who is called to apply the impugned law. It is also what in Italy would be referred to as "incidental"—that is, the exercise of constitutional review arises from within an actual case or controversy, which then also makes it concrete.

The judgment in the end is thus, strictly speaking, only applicable *inter partes* in the case at hand (although the subsequent applicability of the decision as a judicial precedent in future cases can give it much broader effect).

On the other side, the Austrian model of 1920, deeply influenced by the thought of Hans Kelsen, represented a system of constitutional control that was centralized in a single, specialized tribunal. Conceived of as a "negative legislator," the Court is in an important sense not understood to be part of the Judiciary at all, and is therefore composed of special judges all named by the Parliament. Certain designated institutional actors may raise questions of constitutionality directly in the Court on an abstract basis—that is, independently of the application of the law in question to a concrete case—and consequently a judgment of unconstitutionality has an *erga omnes* effect by nullifying the offending legislation and rendering it generally inapplicable.

Of the three initial proposals for the new Italian Constitutional Court presented and discussed in the Constituent Assembly, none reproduced in a "pure" form either of these two foreign models. Instead, all the proposals offered certain elements of the American form of review alloyed with aspects of the Austrian one.

Almost all of the parties started with a default preference for the Kelsenian model of centralized control in a specialized body, although the delegates were divided as to whether it should be considered a fundamentally judicial organ in its nature and composition, or instead a political one. In certain ways, this debate never did get resolved in the Assembly.

The American model was not really taken into consideration because of a number of difficulties stemming from the continental constitutional tradition. Certainly, a more rigid conception of the separation of powers and the absence of stare decisis were obstacles to the transplant of the diffuse model in Europe. However, more relevant is the fact that—as Mauro Cappelletti pointed out:

> [c]ontinental judges usually are "career judges" who enter the judiciary at a very early age and are promoted to the higher courts largely on the basis of seniority. Their professional training develops skills in technical rather than policy-oriented application of statutes. The exercise of judicial review, however is rather different from the usual judicial function of applying the law[18].

Such an innovative and delicate function was, therefore, attributed to a special and specialized institution, the composition of which would radically differ from that of any other court.

---

[18] M. Cappelletti, *The Judicial Process in Comparative Perspective*, Oxford, Clarendon Press, 1989, pp. 136–146.

The second point of debate had to do with the means of access to the Constitutional Court. On this question the draft proposed by Calamandrei, which proved to be the one that the Constituent Assembly as a whole used as its framework, argued for a two-track approach to access. First, Calamandrei suggested a diffuse and incidental, American-style, mode of access: in the context of the proceedings in any court, the judge could decide a constitutional question, with effect *inter partes*. That decision could then be appealed to the First Section (i.e., a panel or chamber of the plenary court) of the Supreme Constitutional Court. Second, Calamandrei included an Austrian-style direct access, by which a constitutional challenge to a law could be brought to the plenary Court within three years of the law's adoption, by certain named institutional parties (the Attorney General, or five members of either house of the legislature, or the First Section of the Constitutional Court ruling on a matter through the incidental method of access). In this latter instance, if the Court were to find the law unconstitutional, it would not have the direct power to annul the law or suspend its application. Rather, Parliament would be called to effect the abrogation itself—a system somewhat reminiscent of that in the United Kingdom today under the 1998 Human Rights Act—or eventually to "convert" the ordinary statute into a constitutional statute.

One can see various sources of inspiration in Calamandrei's very complicated and cumbersome draft. Kelsen's thought is evident, particularly in the way that any substantive constitutional defect in an ordinary statute could be "cured" merely by using a constitutional amendment procedure to reapprove the same law. At the same time, the introduction of a diffuse system of review and an incidental means of access not only reflects the American influence but also the contemporaneous practice of the Italian courts that the delegates were experiencing during that transitional postwar period. The mixed sources of the proposal affected subsequent developments as well.

Another important innovation presaged in the Calamandrei proposal was to entrust the Court with jurisdiction over various other types of cases beyond the constitutionality of Parliamentary acts, including conflicts of authority between the State and the Regions, or between different organs of the State, and impeachment proceedings against the President or members of the Executive.

3.2. THE INCOMPLETE COURT

In addition to the confusing and complex debates over the more technical aspects of the Court's design, time constraints also worked against the Constituent Assembly's ability to settle the details of the Constitutional Court. For the most part, the articles of the Constitution dealing with the Constitutional Court (Arts. 134–137) were the last ones to be discussed (they are in fact included at the end of the constitutional text). By that time, the rest of the essential structure of the constitutional order was settled, and little time remained—the debate on the Constitutional Court had begun in November 1947, and the entire work was to be finished by early December, in time for a final vote of approval on December 22 so that the Constitution could take effect on January 1, 1948.

[handwritten margin note: potential area of correspondence]

Pressed for time, and having heard the pros and cons of the different foreign models of constitutional adjudication, the delegates decided at a certain point to limit themselves to fixing in the Constitution only a few basic principles regarding the composition and function of the Court.

In Article 134, the Constitution provides:

The Constitutional Court shall pass judgment on:

- controversies on the constitutional legitimacy of laws and enactments having force of law issued by the State and Regions;
- conflicts over allocation of the powers of the State, and between those powers allocated to the State and Regions or between Regions;
- charges brought against the President of the Republic, according to the provisions of the Constitution.

Article 135, instead, establishes:

The Constitutional Court shall be composed of fifteen judges, a third nominated by the President of the Republic, a third by Parliament in joint session and a third by the ordinary and administrative supreme Courts.
The judges of the Constitutional Courts shall be chosen from among judges, including those retired, of the ordinary and administrative higher Courts, university professors of law and lawyers with at least twenty years practice.
Judges of the Constitutional Court shall be appointed for twelve years. . . .[19]

Finally, with considerable ambiguity, Article 136 specifies that "When the Court declares the constitutional illegitimacy of a law or enactment having force of law, the law ceases to have effect on the day following the publication of the decision."

All other decisions regarding "the conditions, forms, terms for proposing judgments on constitutional legitimacy, and guarantees on the independence of constitutional judges" are remanded by Article 137 to a separate constitutional statute to be adopted later, while leaving to subsequent ordinary laws "the other provisions

---

[19] This term was later reduced to nine years.

necessary for the constitution and the functioning of the Court." In other words, the Constitution establishes some important general parameters for the Constitutional Court, but leaves much of its definition essentially incomplete.

The novelty of the Constitutional Court within the Italian legal order at this point was still only on paper, with the potential to be realized only with the adoption of further constitutional and ordinary statutes. The Constituent Assembly, even after the approval of the Constitution on December 22, 1947, continued to work on an extended basis, in part precisely in order to avoid either leaving the Court incomplete or entrusting to the future Parliament the task of deciding on the missing structural features of the Court. On January 28, 1948, therefore, in the Constituent Assembly's final action, it adopted Constitutional Law No. 1 of 1948, entitled "Norms regarding judgments of constitutional legitimacy and on the guarantee of the independence of the Constitutional Court."

The law contained just three articles, two of which regulate access to the Court. The first specifies the incidental method: "a question of the constitutional legitimacy of a law of the Republic or of an act having the force of law, raised *ex officio* or raised by one of the parties in the course of a proceeding and not considered manifestly unfounded, shall be submitted to the Constitutional Court for its decision." The second concerns the direct method of review:

> When a Region claims that a law of the Republic, or an act having the force of law, intrudes upon the sphere of competence assigned to it by the Constitution, it may (. . .) bring forward a claim of constitutional legitimacy to the Court. (. . .) It also provides for the possibility of one Region to impugn the laws of another Region.

With this law, the possibility of a direct action by an individual citizen for the protection of his rights, which had been discussed in the Constituent Assembly and contained in some of the draft models, disappeared.

The law's third article is limited to establishing a series of guarantees of immunity for the judges of the Court.

Even after this constitutional statute, half the work of making the Constitutional Court functional still remained to be done. The ordinary law needed to define the procedural and technical requirements to activate the supervisory power of the Constitutional Court had yet to be adopted.

4. A Long Gestation: The Activation of the Court

The first Parliament of the Republic of Italy took office on May 8, 1948, and immediately found itself with the task of completing the design of the Constitutional

Court. The members of that body employed almost the entirety of their first term in office—nearly five years—to regulate concretely the functioning of the new Court. They did so, in the end, through both an ordinary law (No. 87 of March 11, 1953) and also another Constitutional Law (No. 1 of 1953), known as "Norms integrating the Constitution concerning the Constitutional Court."

The drafting of these two laws was extremely complex, notwithstanding the fact that the Executive had quickly introduced proposed bills during the first Parliamentary session in 1948. The text of the ordinary law went back and forth between the House of Representatives and the Senate no fewer than five times before definitively being debated. The Constitutional Law, requiring the application for the first time of the constitutional amendment procedure established in Article 138 of the Constitution, needed to be approved twice by each house of the legislature, each time by a two-thirds majority, and with the two votes occurring at least three months apart.

In the end both acts received very large supermajorities of votes (over 90 percent in the case of the ordinary law), a truly remarkable fact considering the otherwise intense polarization of Italian politics at the time between the governing Center-Right and the opposition on the Left. Notwithstanding those deep political divisions, Parliament found broad consensus on the laws activating the Court in recognition of their fundamental importance.

Still, the five-year delay in constructing this consensus was significant, and today has provoked divergent interpretations among constitutional scholars. An earlier conventional narrative characterized the first term of the new republican legislature as a period of "majority obstructionism" and of a paradoxical reversal of position by the political parties relative to those they held in the Constituent Assembly. According to this reading of history, the majority (consisting of the Christian Democrats, the Republican Party, and the Liberal Party), having gained initial control of both the Legislative and Executive Branches, was no longer interested in activating that same Constitutional Court that they were so committed to supporting earlier. The socialist-communist opposition, in the meantime, although quite contrary to the idea of a Constitutional Court in the Constituent Assembly (at least at the beginning of the debate), now regarded it as a fundamental instrument for protecting the Constitution against the power of majorities.

More recent studies have shown that there is more to the story, however. Other factors also contributed to the delay, including important technical and institutional complexities. The vagueness of the Constitutional provisions left much still to be defined, including a series of very fundamental design decisions (detailed further in the following section). The absence of any well-developed constitutional theory or prior experience left the legislators with few resources to draw on when considering this "unprecedented" organ, and led to the presentation and discussion of a very wide range of divergent, and even irreconcilable, ideas and institutional models. All this took place in the context of having to work out the details of a new constitutional system more generally. For instance, the first Parliament did not even have established procedures for the approval of constitutional statutes (another innovation in the Italian legal system).

For all these reasons, despite the five-year delay, the approval of the laws activating the Constitutional Court during the first term of the Parliament was extremely significant. Livio Paladin, one of the most noted scholars of Italian constitutional history, regarded it as the most important constitutional development in at least the first 20 years of the Republic.[20]

4.1. FUNDAMENTAL CHOICES

The legislative completion of the Constitutional Court's design required difficult choices, among significantly differentiated proposals, regarding a set of questions that would be fundamental to the future character of the Court. Five of them stand out, in particular.

First, the parliamentarians realized that their task was not merely to provide for the regulatory implementation of constitutional norms that had already been established, but rather to complete the missing pieces of the constitutional design itself. The choice was to integrate the Court fully into the overall constitutional design and structure.

This was the reason behind their decision to adopt another Constitutional Law—that is, another law having the same constitutional status as Constitutional Law No. 1 of 1948, which had been adopted by the Constituent Assembly. In fact, Article 1 of the 1953 law provides that "The Constitutional Court exercises its functions within the forms, limits, and conditions of the Constitution, the Constitutional Law of February 9, 1948, and the ordinary law issued with regard to the first activation of the preceding constitutional norms." In this way, the prior Constitutional Law of 1948 was confirmed (against the position of some who had doubts about its legitimacy, given that it was adopted by the Constituent Assembly rather than the new Parliament), and at the same time the new ordinary law activating the Court was given a privileged status to ease the concerns of those who were afraid that the new legislative norms in some ways exceeded the authority of a "normal" ordinary law.

---

[20] L. Paladin, *Per una storia costituzionale dell'Italia repubblicana*, Bologna, Il Mulino, 2004, p. 130.

The second fundamental choice was to create an entirely new power in the Court: the jurisdiction to review the admissibility of popular referenda (as will be described further in Chapter 2).

Third, the Parliament had to define more clearly just how "strong" the Constitutional Court's judgments of unconstitutionality would be. As mentioned earlier, Article 136 of the Constitution was somewhat ambiguous about the effect of the Court's judgments, merely providing that a law found to be unconstitutional "ceases to have effect on the day following the publication of the decision." Combined with the method of incidental review, this language could have been interpreted to mean that the Court's decision was only prospective in effect, and that paradoxically therefore it would not affect the application of the law to the specific case in which the question arose. The law activating the Court made the answer more certain: "Norms declared unconstitutional cannot be applied as of the day following the publication of the decision. Whenever a final criminal conviction has been pronounced on the basis of a law that has been declared to be unconstitutional, its execution and all its penal effects shall cease." In other words, starting on the day after the Court's judgment, the unconstitutional norm decision cannot be used by anyone—judges included—and thus the decision of unconstitutionality has a retroactive effect. This is a point that was completely misunderstood by ordinary Italian judges in the early years of the Constitutional Court's jurisprudence, as we will see below.

A fourth critical choice Parliament made in its initial legislation regarding the Court has particularly interesting comparative implications. In the Parliamentary debate, that quintessentially American form of public disagreement among judges was introduced: the idea of allowing the Justices of the Constitutional Court to write dissenting opinions. The consensus among the legislators, however, was decidedly against the practice of allowing individual Justices to issue separate opinions (whether dissenting or concurrent). As the parliamentarian who served as the reporter for the constitutional bill put it, separate opinions would have facilitated "a kind of control over the activities of the judges by organized political forces." In short, the decision not to allow separate opinions was seen as another means of insulating the Justices from the vicissitudes and pressures of politics.

Fifth and finally, the precise manner in which the Justices of the Court would be appointed constituted a highly contentious question that needed to be resolved. The Constitution itself was limited to specifying that five Justices of the Constitutional Court would be appointed by "the ordinary and administrative Supreme Courts," five by the Parliament in a joint session, and five by the President. The further specification of these provisions was relatively easy with regard to the Constitutional Justices to be appointed from the magistracy: three would be appointed by the

Court of Cassation, and one each would come from the Council of State and from the Court of Accounts. For the Justices appointed by Parliament and the President, however, the debates proved to be thornier. They divided along one basic question: Should the appointment of the Justices of the Constitutional Court reflect the will of the majority in the government, or should it remain more independent of the current political constellation in any given time? A strong faction of Parliament favored a more "American" approach in which the appointment of Constitutional Court judges would represent the preferences of the Executive Branch. Thus, they proposed that the appointment of Justices appointed in a joint session of the Parliament should be by a simple majority vote (the majority being representative of the Executive, given the Parliamentary system), and that the President's power to appoint should be understood to apply only to candidates who were proposed to the President by the Prime Minister and his cabinet.

After a long debate, in the end the opposite position prevailed. The parliamentary vote necessary to appoint a Constitutional Court Justice is a qualified majority (a two-thirds majority, which becomes a three-fifths majority after the third unsuccessful ballot) that ordinarily would require Parliament to name persons who obtain at least a portion of the opposition's support as well as the majority's vote. After the President of the Republic threatened to resign over the issue, his power to appoint Justices was completely freed from the constraints of the parliamentary majority.

4.2. THE DELAY IN THE PARLIAMENTARY ELECTION OF JUSTICES

After five years' delay, the implementing legislation of 1953 was meant to clear away the remaining obstacles to the activation of the Court, and in fact the transitional provisions of the implementing legislation provided that the Court was to convene its first session within two months. With the resolution of the critical issues regarding the appointment of the Constitutional Court judges out of the way, both the Judiciary and the President accordingly proceeded very quickly to name their ten Justices to the Constitutional Court. Parliament, however, found itself in a political deadlock notwithstanding the agreement just reached on the details of its five appointments, which delayed the full composition and activation of the Court by another two years.

The causes of the deadlock and delay have been amply debated, especially among political scientists. It is safe to say that, at the very least, there was a structural misalignment between the supermajority voting requirements and the actual composition of Parliament in that period. In its second legislative term (1953–1958), approximately 45 percent of the members of Parliament belonged to the centrist governing coalition, while about 40 percent voted with the opposition Leftist parties, and a collection of other parties (mostly on the political Right) constituted the remaining 15 percent.[21] The opposition therefore had sufficient votes to block any action, and chose to prevent any vote from succeeding unless there was a judge connected to the principal parties of the Left. The Center-Right parties were unwilling to cede on this point, and thus for two years Parliament was deadlocked.

Finally, in November 1955 the political parties reached a compromise on a slate of Justices that included two named by the Christian Democrats and one each by the Liberal Party, the Communist Party, and the Socialist Party. This effectively constituted a defeat for the Christian Democrats in spite of their plurality share of Parliament. However, the appointments of the President of the Republic, then Giovanni Gronchi (who succeeded Einaudi in 1955) were aimed at maintaining a certain ideological balance among the judges of the Court, in addition to bringing high levels of technical juridical ability. As Gronchi put it, the "magic formula" for his appointments was "one pre-fascist Liberal, one [politically] independent Catholic, one Christian Democratic representative, one technician with monarchist sympathies, and one republican jurist."[22]

5. The Birth of a New System of Constitutional Adjudication

The first 15 Justices of the Constitutional Court finally took their oath of office almost exactly eight full years after the approval of the new Constitution. The President of the Republic convened them to begin their first judicial term in January 1956, and the Court held its first public hearing three months later, on April 23, 1956. A number of the key decisions made in the first year of the Court's work imprinted it with a certain initial institutional character that had an enduring impact on the Court in subsequent years.

5.1. A CONTEXT OF UNCERTAINTY

When the Court finally took its first deep breaths, after a long and difficult birth, the air was saturated with uncertainty about the legal nature of the Constitution, the powers of the Constitutional Court, and the Court's proper role in the new Constitutional order as a whole.

Some of the initial uncertainties facing the Court were of a jurisprudential nature, arising in particular from the general judicial culture in which it immediately found

---

[21] F. Bonini, *Storia della Corte costituzionale*, Roma, NIS, 1996, p. 95.
[22] *Id.*

itself. While the Parliament was engaged in protracted legislative draftsmanship and in battles over the procedures for appointing Justices to the Constitutional Court, ordinary judges in were already operating within the framework of the new 1948 Constitution. As mentioned earlier, the Constitution included a transitional provision providing that "Until such time as the Constitutional Court begins its functions, the decision on controversies indicated in Article 134 [i.e., questions of constitutionality] shall be conducted in the forms and within the limits of the provisions already in existence before the implementation of the Constitution." This invited judges to continue, after the effective date of the Constitution and prior to the activation of the Constitutional Court, to engage in that diffuse constitutional review begun during the transition period. After the adoption of the 1948 Constitution, however, instead of doing so merely on the basis of vague and unwritten general principles of constitutional law, they had the written text of the new Constitution to apply.

This reality posed a real challenge to the prevailing judicial culture as a whole. How would the Judiciary apply the new Constitution? How would the judges interpret the constitutional text? What legal effect would they attribute to the new constitutional dispositions?

A majority of the judges on the bench in the 1950s, and especially the older ones who had reached the higher courts, had studied and been formed during the Fascist period or even earlier, during the ascendancy of "parliamentary omnipotence" and a flexible constitution. It was not easy, therefore, for them to understand clearly the challenges that arose from having norms of different hierarchical rank within the legal system. To be sure, even before the 1948 Constitution, they had dealt with the relationship between statutes and regulations, especially in the area of administrative law, but undoubtedly that problem had characteristics different from those relating to a legal norm that is hierarchically superior to Parliamentary acts. One difference stems from the way in which a constitution is written: it tends to be much less detailed than a statute, and the Italian one in particular contains many broad principles of a very general nature. In addition, the Italian Constitution (as will be evident in more detail later in this book) contains a number of programmatic norms—that is, norms that establish objectives to be realized in the future rather than strict rules of action, limitation, or organization.

In the face of these new problems of constitutional interpretation, Italian judges (especially and most important, those of the Court of Cassation) generally adopted two jurisprudential positions. Both of them were very conservative in nature; that is, they were largely inspired by a sort of cultural inertia to resist the novelty of the new constitutional system.

First of all, in the period prior to the activation of the Constitutional Court, ordinary judges introduced a distinction between legislation adopted prior to the 1948 Constitution and the norms that came into effect with the new Constitution itself. Applying the basic principle of temporal succession, the courts held that, where the Constitution provided a norm that conflicted with preceding legislation—for instance, Fascist laws violating basic liberties—then the Constitution should be applied "insofar as it abrogated the preceding norm," in the same way as would ordinarily occur when one legislative act succeeds a contrary one. Judges in this way avoided the recognition of the Constitution as a "higher" law, and instead limited themselves to using the customary interpretive canons developed to deal with parliamentary legislation.

This approach produced several dilemmas. Above all, it put in doubt what the effect of the Constitution would be on laws adopted by the new Parliament after January 1, 1948. Second, it implicitly substantially diminished the scope of authority of the Constitutional Court: if the Constitution were to be treated, with respect to pre-1948 laws, merely as if it were a subsequent parliamentary act, then the adjudication of the compatibility of those prior statutes with the Constitution would fall within the authority of the ordinary Judiciary rather than the new Constitutional Court. And finally, at the most general level, the doctrines being developed by ordinary judges presupposed that in assessing a conflict between a statute and the Constitution, the judges were facing a conflict of rules rather than a conflict between a constitutional principle and a legislative rule. Through this general characterization of the legal problem one can see a judicial culture that was much less advanced in understanding the nature of a rigid and written constitution than, for example, the more sophisticated legal culture that prevailed in the contemporaneous Parliamentary debates.

The second notable jurisprudential approach characteristic of the prevailing judicial culture prior to the activation of the Constitutional Court had to do with the Constitution's "programmatic" provisions. As already noted, many of the articles of the 1948 Constitution are formulated as very general and abstract norms (e.g., Arts. 1, 3, 4, 8, 9, 11, etc.). Others, however, are not merely broad and general but truly programmatic insofar as they articulate objectives or goals to be attained (e.g., Arts. 24(3), 31, 32(1), 34(3–4), 35(2), etc.). Ordinary judges asked to apply these latter provisions affirmed that they necessarily needed implementing legislation from Parliament in order to become justiciable, and without which they could not be applied in any way by the Courts. As long as no such legislation had been adopted, those constitutional dispositions remained essentially ineffective.

This jurisprudential position, which regarded large parts of the Constitution as programmatic in nature and in need of legislative implementation, had immediate practical implications. In particular, it resulted in the continued validity of a wide range of Fascist legislation. While the judges waited for the new legislation necessary to affect the general principles of the new Constitution, many of them did not regard themselves as being able to address challenges to the constitutionality of prior legislation.

Both of these lines of jurisprudence cast a shadow of legal uncertainty over the normative effectiveness of the 1948 Constitution, just as the new Constitutional Court finally came into being.

Other critical questions also arose, with regard to the institutional powers of the new Constitutional Court as the "adjudicator of constitutionality." The confused and complicated debate over models of constitutional adjudication in the Constituent Assembly, and the extended period of legislative incompleteness of the system, led many scholars to entertain doubts about how to understand the scope of the institutional authority of the new Constitutional Court as a "supreme" or "sovereign" organ in general within the topography of the Constitutional system.[23]

A third area of uncertainty had to do with the Constitutional Court's powers to regulate its own internal structures and procedures and its own personnel. The lack of clarity about the Court's juridical nature as an unprecedented constitutional actor also resulted in the absence of any legislatively prescribed norms regarding the internal organization of the Court.

On the one hand, this generated an administrative and organizational challenge. Speaking to journalists later that year, the first President of the Constitutional Court, Enrico De Nicola, described the situation clearly and realistically: "We were installed here on April 23 of this year. When we arrived we didn't even have chairs or a single staff member and had to go get even a glass of water for ourselves. Our work therefore had to first begin from an administrative point of view."[24]

Even more significantly, the situation constituted a structural and procedural problem as well. The legislative norms activating the Court barely specified the form of the proceedings before the Constitutional Court, instead merely incorporating by reference the rules of procedure of the Council of State. This was an omission even more notable and consequential in a judicial system of the civil law tradition, where the inherent self-regulatory powers of the courts tend not to be as developed and explicit as in systems of the common law tradition.

---

[23] P. Barile, *La Corte costituzionale come organo sovrano: implicazioni pratiche*, in *Giurisprudenza costituzionale*, 1957, p. 907 ff.

[24] A. Simoncini, *L'avvio della Corte costituzionale e gli strumenti per la definizione del suo ruolo: un problema storico aperto*, in *Giurisprudenza costituzionale*, 2004, p. 3082.

Against this backdrop, the Justices of the Constitutional Court were clear and decisive in confronting the climate of uncertainty. Within the first three months between the installation of the Justices and the first hearing of the Court, and even more in the first period of activity after that, the Court already demonstrated an assertiveness quite contrary to the prevailing inertia fostered by the political and legal culture surrounding it. The Constitutional Court showed itself to be acutely and clearly self-aware of its proper constitutional identity.

The Court's assertion of its institutional weight was evident in a variety of ways, starting even with the symbolic elements. For example, in the so-called "Battle of the Thrones" the first two Presidents of the Constitutional Court refused to participate in any official ceremonies of the Republic until the official State protocol was amended to provide for the seat of the President of the Constitutional Court to come prior to that of the Prime Minister, which they eventually succeeded in obtaining.

5.2. THE COURT'S RULES OF PROCEDURE

Beyond mere symbolism and protocol, however, the Court's self-conscious constitutional identity became especially evident in its invocation of its own inherent powers of self-regulation to fill the lacunae of its rules of procedure.

As already mentioned, the 1953 legislative provisions that activated the Constitutional Court only addressed its rules of procedure by referring to the rules of the Council of State, the highest tribunal for administrative law matters. The same statutory scheme also provided that the Court could adopt its own rules (known as Integrative Norms) "to regulate the exercise of its functions." At the time and even long afterward, it was generally agreed that this additional authorization was only intended to give the Constitutional Court a secondary and derivative authority aimed at regulating its internal administrative and organizational matters. These internal rules, adopted purely as a result of the internal deliberations and decisions of the Constitutional Court itself, were meant to be added to the legislatively adopted rules of procedure of the Council of State, to cover circumstances on which the latter were silent. Almost immediately (by mid-March 1956), however, the Constitutional Court adopted its "Integrative Norms Regarding Proceedings Before the Constitutional Court" that went far beyond the letter and spirit of the original legislative authorization, as many commentators immediately perceived. Here the Constitutional Court effectively reversed, relative to that intended by the implementing legislation, the order of applicable norms regulating the procedural aspects of its judicial activities: the rules of procedure of the Council of State basically became subsidiary to those adopted by the Constitutional Court on its own initiative, exactly the opposite of the priority established in Article 22 of Constitutional Law 87/1953.

This reversal had two important implications for the identity and independence of the Constitutional Court. First, it made the Court the master of its own proceedings in a way that ordinary and administrative courts in Italy were, and still not are. The procedural rules of the Council of State, like those of courts in typical civil law systems generally, are approved by the legislature in statutory form, implying a certain hierarchy of institutional authority from which the Constitutional Court implicitly asserted its independence.

Second, the Constitutional Court in this way implicitly contested and rejected the legislative assimilation of its proceedings to those of an administrative law tribunal such as the Council of State. Instituting certain significant and distinctive procedural dimensions, the Constitutional Court underscored its novelty and constitutional identity. Two illustrative examples suffice: the regulation of the internal deliberations and decisions of the Constitutional Court, and the rules regarding the publicity of its decisions.

The Court's President, De Nicola, in the same briefing to journalists already cited, noted explicitly that:

> among the rules of procedure, there are some extraordinary innovations. For example, there is the fundamental innovation (which unfortunately requires of us and will require of us enormous effort) that the Court will not only approve the disposition of the case but also the reasoning, that is, the texts of the decisions. Therefore, it has double the work.[25]

The Court thus distanced itself from the general practice of other collegial judicial bodies in Italy (and often elsewhere in the civil law tradition), which would ordinarily have only voted to approve the final disposition of the decision and not the reasoned basis for it.

In close relationship with this choice, the Court also established the requirement that the publication of its decisions in the Official Gazette would apply not only to judgments of unconstitutionality but also to all of its other types of decisions, including those rejecting a constitutional challenge. Although this step may not appear to be either unusual or surprising today, especially to those accustomed to common law judicial practices, at the time and in the context of Italy it was a significant move away from the practices of other tribunals such as the Council of State. It also revealed a gulf between the Constitutional Court's own understanding of the

---

[25] *Id.*, p. 3074.

importance of publicizing its decisions (including the reasoning behind them) and the Legislature's views on the same question at that time. The Court, by its own initiative in its rules, established a reporting system by which all of its decisions would be officially published; the 1953 implementing legislation, in contrast, provided for the publication only of the dispositive orders of judgments of unconstitutionality, and nothing more. Even before the Constitutional Court decided a single case, the Justices already had a very clear vision of the public value of the constitutional reasoning in its decisions.

5.3. THE "ITALIAN *MARBURY V. MADISON*": JUDGMENT 1/1956

Perhaps the strongest and most serious challenge to the normative force both of the new Constitution and of the new Constitutional Court in its initial phase came from judicial positions, described earlier, which interpreted the Constitution essentially as if it were merely a piece of subsequent legislation rather than a hierarchically superior norm, and finding many of the Constitution's provisions to be merely programmatic and non-justiciable in the absence of implementing legislation.

Once again, the Court responded to these generalized doubts quickly and firmly, symbolically and significantly using the very first decision in its history to do so. Judgment 1/56 decisively put to rest any interpretive uncertainties regarding the hierarchical legal force of the Constitution and the authority of the Court. In this sense, it is not unreasonable to regard it as a sort of "Italian *Marbury v. Madison.*"

The case presented the Court with a constitutional challenge to the 1931 Law on Public Security, a prototypically authoritarian Fascist-era piece of legislation. Article 113 of the law provided that anyone who wished to use posters or flyers to disseminate his or her views was required to obtain the prior authorization of the proper police authority. Article 21 of the 1948 Constitution, however, explicitly guaranteed that "Everyone has the right to freely express their thoughts in speech, writing, or any other form of communication." The several lower court cases joined together before the Constitutional Court involved 30 criminal proceedings involving defendants charged with violating Article 113 and sentenced to prison under the associated provisions of the Penal Code. In addition, the Court of Cassation (having reviewed the issue according to its understanding that questions of the constitutional validity of pre-1948 legislation are within the province of the ordinary Judiciary) had already deemed Article 113 of the Law on Public Security to be valid.

The argument presented by the Attorney General (in this context, the functional analog in Constitutional Court proceedings to the Solicitor General of the United

States) perfectly synthesized the systemic challenge that the case posed to the legal strength of the Constitution itself:

> The Attorney General argued that laws enacted prior to the Constitution are not subject to constitutional scrutiny by this Court, because prescriptive norms contained in the Constitution abrogate conflicting prior laws, but the determination of the existence of such a conflict is the exclusive province of the ordinary Judiciary. Further, the Attorney General argued that constitutional norms that are programmatic do not have any effect whatsoever on the validity of laws enacted prior to the Constitution. (Judgment 1/1956)

The Constitutional Court responded to these doubts very directly, affirming clearly both its own authority and the normative value of the Constitution itself. In view of the fundamental importance of this landmark first judgment, an extended excerpt is warranted:

> With regard to the competence of this Court, challenged by the Attorney General, we must first note that it is the exclusive competence of the Constitutional Court to decide controversies regarding the constitutional legitimacy of laws, or other acts having the force of law. This cannot be put into question, and is established in Art. 134 of the Constitution. In fact, a declaration of unconstitutionality cannot be made but by the Constitutional Court, as required by the Constitution in Art. 136.
>
> The assumption that the new juridical institute of "unconstitutionality" is only applicable to laws enacted after the Constitution, and inapplicable to those enacted before it, cannot be accepted. From a textual standpoint both Article 134 of the Constitution and Art. 1 of Constitutional Law no. 1 of February 9, 1948, speak of constitutional legitimacy without making any distinction between laws enacted before or after the Constitution. This textual reading is logical. Indeed, the relation between ordinary and constitutional laws, and the place they take up in the hierarchy of sources of law, does not depend on, and is unaltered by, whether they are enacted before or after the Constitution. . . .
>
> The two juridical institutes of abrogation and the unconstitutionality of laws are not identical and function on different levels; their effects and their reach are not the same. The field of abrogation is narrower than that of unconstitutionality, and in the case of abrogation through general principles of law the requirements set forth are still more stringent. . . .
>
> The well-known distinction between prescriptive norms and norms that have programmatic characteristics may be indeed dispositive in deciding

the abrogation of a law. But it is not dispositive in constitutional judgments, because, in some cases, the unconstitutionality of a law may derive from programmatic norms. Such norms have varying content. Some limit themselves to tracing future programs that are generic and difficult to enforce because they are contingent upon the verification of certain conditions. Other programmatic norms are more concrete, and are binding on the legislator, and influence the interpretation of prior legislation that remains in place. Still others establish fundamental principles that also reverberate upon all legislation.

In order to ascertain whether there is a conflict between the concrete norms of Art. 21 of the Constitution and Art. 113 of the Law on Public Security, it is necessary to look at their content and their relation.

Some have argued that there is no contrast between the two on the basis that speaking one's mind, which must be free, is not the same as disseminating those thoughts, but this distinction is not embodied in any constitutional norm.

However, norms that ascribe a right generally do not preclude the regulation of the exercise of that right.

To discipline the modality of the exercise of a right, in order to ensure that one individual's pursuit of his ends is reconcilable with that of others, is neither a violation nor a negation of the right. Even if such discipline imposes an indirect limit on the right itself, it should be remembered that the notion of a limit is intrinsic to the notion of right. In the context of a systematic legal order, all spheres necessarily limit each other in order to ensure an orderly civil co-existence.

The enunciation of the right of freedom to express one's thoughts, of course, does not mean the Constitution permits activities that would disturb the public peace, or remove the police from their role in preventing crimes.

Under this analysis, the constitutional legitimacy of Art. 113 would not be in doubt if its conferral of power on the public authority were strictly linked to the end of preventing actions that could become crimes, or actions which would, in all reasonableness, lead to crimes.

No such finding can be made in the article under review. By requiring an authorization (in order to exercise the right to freedom of expression), Art. 113 makes the right conferred to all by Art. 21 of the Constitution almost seem dependent on a concession by the public authorities' unlimited discretion. In fact, the discretion granted in Art. 113 is such that, independently of any concern for the public peace and the prevention of crimes, the public authorities are able to grant or deny authorizations in order to permit or prevent any given expression of thought on a case by case basis.

It is true that this wide scope of discretion has been subsequently reduced by Legislative Decree No. 1382 of November 8, 1947. That decree allows recourse against actions by the public security authorities to the *Procuratore della Repubblica*, in cases where an authorization is denied. The decision of the *Procuratore della Repubblica* is then dispositive of the grant or denial of an authorization.

Despite this provision, the original indeterminacy (of the grant of discretion) remains. The sphere wherein police action and power should be enclosed is not in any way delineated. Therefore, both the public authorities, and the *Procuratore* who takes over after recourse is made, are invested with an extension of too much discretionary power.

The Constitutional Court must therefore declare the unconstitutionality of Art. 113 of the Law on Public Security, with the exception of clause five, requiring that "advertisements cannot appear outside of places not designated by the relevant authorities." This requirement is not in conflict with any constitutional norm, and is therefore valid to all effects.

The other provisions of the article are not implied by the declaration of unconstitutionality. This however, does not mean they cannot be replaced by more adequate provisions that regulate the exercise of free speech in order to avoid abuses, and to not offend the right to freedom of speech enunciated in Art. 21 of the Constitution. . . . It is desirable that such a delicate matter be soon regulated satisfactorily, with a new discipline that is well suited to the new norms of Constitution. . . .

It is without a doubt clear that the provisions of Art. 663 of the Penal Code, referring to Art. 113, become inoperative, and will also be overtaken by the declaration of unconstitutionality. . . .

In just these few short pages, the Constitutional Court breaks sharply from the juridical and political characteristics of the Italian legal tradition that would have been hostile to the creation of a true system of constitutional adjudication. At the same time, it sets down a series of basic building blocks for the consolidation of the new constitutional order of the Italian Republic, and of its own place within it.

First and most directly, the Constitutional Court in Judgment 1/1956 affirms that the Constitution is composed of true and proper legal norms that are not merely aspirational or programmatic in a very broad and loose sense; they are instead immediately binding on all exercises of public authority. Likewise, the Court establishes the Constitution as a comprehensive higher law, in the sense that every other law or legal act must respect all of the norms of the Constitution in their entirety.

Second, the Court asserts forcefully its own exclusive competence over questions of constitutionality, and thus its distinctive institutional identity within the new constitutional order.

Third, the Constitutional Court exhibits a new and unprecedented kind of adjudicative style, insofar as it engages in an elaborated, public, reasoned discussion about the normative constitutional order. This would have been almost unthinkable at the time in the traditional self-conception of the French-influenced Italian Judiciary, historically subordinated to the legislative branch. The mode of discourse of the Constitutional Court reinforces its different character from an ordinary court within the Italian tradition, and highlights its novel, highly public, role in a democratic constitutional space.

Fourth, even while asserting its supreme and exclusive authority to judge the constitutionality of laws, the Court also defers to Parliament by inviting it to regulate the matter further, and by recognizing that some of the programmatic norms of the Constitution will indeed require legislative action in order to become fully effective. In this way, the Constitutional Court simultaneously accomplishes two distinct ends. On the one hand, the Court takes its place as an equal interlocutor among the institutional organs of the constitutional order, while on the other hand it emphasizes that its role is differentiated from Parliament and is not that of a judicial legislator. The consequent dialogic relationship between the Constitutional Court and Parliament will thereafter be an interesting and important feature of the Constitutional Court's jurisprudence and a key factor in its long-term dynamism and success, as we shall see in more detail in subsequent chapters.

Fifth and finally, it is significant that the Constitutional Court asserted its authority and constitutional identity, and the normative force of the Constitution generally, in the context of a dispute over the validity of a Fascist law that restricted basic liberties deemed to be essential in a democratic order. The Court immediately establishes its credentials as part of a new, democratic, constitutional order that is protective of human dignity and freedom, and distances itself from the nation's authoritarian past.

6. Taking a Deep Breath: The Court's Relationship to the Body Politic

In sum, the emergence of the Italian Constitutional Court as the centerpiece of a viable, new system of constitutional adjudication represented the complete reversal of an Italian legal tradition that had been inhospitable for over a century to any idea of constitutional judicial review. A few overarching features stand out if we step back from the details to take a more panoramic view of the Court's role in achieving this transformation.

The first group of Justices of the Constitutional Court, notwithstanding their differences in age, backgrounds, and personalities, seemed particularly united in what might be called a "realist" vision that focused steadily on those factors that would make the Court effective in practice as a constitutional actor. That is, they fully understood that the role of this totally new actor would depend more on the concrete acceptance of it by all the other constitutional actors than by its formal legal force within the Constitution. In addition, they shared a common awareness of the need to recover, after the betrayals of the Fascist regime, a deeper osmosis between society and State.

Thus, the Justices' self-consciousness of the new Court's irreducible constitutional identity was coupled with the perceived need to have this constitutional identity metabolized by the body politic, including both the institutional system of the new constitutional order and the broader society. To do this the Court sought legitimacy by appealing to two basic reference points to support its actions: acceptance in public opinion, and acceptance among the other constitutional actors of the Republic.

With respect to the former, we have already seen the Court's insistence from the beginning on the importance of extensively giving public reasons for its decisions, and its early practice of meeting periodically with journalists to provide fuller explanations of the Court's work during each term. The Court's constant preoccupation with public perceptions went far beyond that, however. On the occasion of a celebration of the first 12 years of the Constitutional Court, Aldo Sandulli, a Justice named to the Court in 1957 and who served as its President in 1968–1969, gave eloquent and vivid witness to this reality:

> Today the Court . . . is deeply felt by the Italian people. One valid confirmation of this is the increasing attention that the press—the most immediate expression of public opinion—dedicates to the activities of the Court and to the expectations that are tied to it. Just as it is true that the institutions of a political regime acquire their force not only and not principally from what is written in their statutes, but from the roots that they sink into the body of the collectivity, so no one can doubt that the Court must be considered to be solidly incorporated into our [constitutional] order as an essential and characteristic component of the system. . . . The support that the Court finds in the consensus of the social body—of which it feels itself to be, and is, the flesh and blood—makes its jurisprudence, in turn, a valid force in the context of the national society.

The Court's second basic reference point—acceptance among the other actors of the constitutional system—is abundantly evident in its efforts not to be excluded or marginalized from the circuit of institutions. The Justices were aware that being perceived as a stranger among the other constitutional actors would have led to the Court's practical (even if not theoretical) failure. As a result, "collaboration" with the other organs becomes the Court's basic principle of action, and every effort is made to avoid either separation or evasiveness from engagement. Conscious of the formidable force that the form of a judicial opinion gives to its decisions, the Court tries to use them as a last resort, and prefers to commit itself, insofar as possible, to finding the means to collaborate in the realization of constitutional values. This approach consistently characterized the Court's relationship with Parliament and the Executive, as political actors within the constitutional order. In doing so, the Court asserts its own political role alongside them.

The Constitutional Court's attitude is, in part, different with respect to the Judiciary, however. Here, the Court does emphasize a certain distance, its foreignness from ordinary courts and judges. Yet, this is not with the aim of challenging the proper authority of the judicial branch. As the first President of the Constitutional Court declared, "the Court of Cassation was the supreme organ of the Judiciary and it remains such even now." Differentiation is the condition for seeking a necessary collaboration in the complementary functions of the Constitutional Court and ordinary courts. In his remarks at the Constitutional Court's inaugural session, President De Nicola focused on this point:

> in the single task which links the [Constitutional] Court to the judicial authorities [i.e., the indirect method of constitutional judicial review in concrete cases], one and the other must both look toward a single aim with unity of intent and action: the Court, as the custodian of the Constitution [i.e., the hierarchically superior law]; the Judiciary, as the custodian of the ordinary law.[26]

Adding this observation to the earlier discussion, one could say that in the period of its initial activity the Court tried to maintain a certain equilibrium between two interdependent, but sometimes competing, goals. On the one hand, it forcefully asserted its own specific constitutional identity and role; on the other, it sought a collaborative relationship with the other constitutional actors, based in mutual recognition that makes the constitutional identity of the Court a practical reality. The balance shown in Judgment 1/1956 is a paradigmatic example of this dual aim.

---

[26] *Id.*, p. 3082.

Overall, the development of the Constitutional Court, from its conception through its gestation, birth, and first breaths, is aptly summarized by a later Justice of the Court, Enzo Cheli:

> The current structure of our system of constitutional adjudication was not born as the product of a model fully defined in all of its aspects from the beginning. Rather, it was the result of a complex process of historic layering that started from the work of the constituent phase, became more precise in the activating laws of 1948 and 1953, and then reached the point of consolidation—especially in the first decade of the Court's life—through its jurisprudential practice, through the fine-tuning of its procedural instruments, and through the definition of the relationship of the Court with the political instruments of the State as well as with the organs of the judicial power.[27]

7. The "Eras" of the Constitutional Court

Given the principle of collegiality and the rules governing the appointment of the President of the Court—both of which shall be described in Chapter 2—the history of the Italian Constitutional Court cannot be easily divided into distinct eras identified by the name of the Chief Justice as is generally the case, for instance, with the Supreme Court of the United States. Nevertheless, at least four periods of the Constitutional Court can be singled out, taking into consideration the role of the Court within the constitutional order, its relation with the other branches of government, and the different ways in which judicial review has been exercised.

The first period of the Court runs from 1956, when the Court held its first session, to the early 1970s. In these decades the Court played a central role in the modernization and democratization of the legal system, as well as in the affirmation of the values entrenched in the new Constitution. In its process of systematic reform, the Court in a certain way substituted for Parliament, which was slow and timid in modifying statutes inherited from earlier periods. After the landmark first decision of 1956, the Court—thanks also to the stimulus provided by progressive judges who raised numerous constitutional challenges to the laws enacted before the Constitution entered into force—was able to purge the legal system of many unconstitutional norms dating back to the nineteenth century and, above all, from the Fascist era.

---

[27] G. D'Orazio, *La genesi della Corte costituzionale*, Milano, Giuffré, 1981, p. 111.

In the second period, from the mid-1970s to the mid-1980s, the Court was no longer devoted to controlling the constitutional validity of statutes that were adopted before the Constitution but, for the first time, reviewed (and often struck down) recent laws that had been drafted and approved by the republican Parliament. For this reason the Court began to play a more politicized role characterized by balancing techniques, essentially in the search for equilibrium and mediation among the various interests and values involved in constitutional questions. Nevertheless, due to the length of the constitutional process and delays in constitutional adjudication, the statutes that the Court reviewed in these years were generally not enacted by the contemporary Parliament; rather, the Court considered the constitutional validity of statutes enacted by a post-Constitution Parliament but not yet the Parliament sitting at the time when the decision was rendered.

Almost paradoxically, the Court's success during the first stages of its life turned out to be one of the reasons the Italian system of constitutional adjudication is quite inefficient. By the beginning of the 1980s the great number of constitutional questions the Court had to decide made it rather difficult to issue opinions at an acceptable pace. Given the fact that all of the Court's jurisdiction is mandatory, and that the Court does not have any possibility of screening cases, there is a significant backlog. The third period of the Court was therefore devoted to reducing the length of the proceedings and consequently reducing the number of pending cases. During the three years from 1987 to 1989, the Court regained efficiency through the elimination of the backlog and the reduction of the time needed for a decision to be rendered. Since the end of the 1980s the Court has been able to decide the constitutional questions referred by the judges *a quo* within six to nine months; before that, the referring judges had to wait three to four years before having an answer from the Court to their constitutional questions. The main procedural devices through which the goal of efficiency was reached was a massive use of summary declarations of inadmissibility (*ordinanze di manifesta inammissibilità* and *manifesta infondatezza*).[28] Having substantially reduced the time of the proceedings, the Court for the first time was able to decide questions regarding the constitutional validity of statutes just enacted, even while the issues are still being debated in the political arena, instead of years later. At the same time, the Court's rapid turnaround and the fact that it began to issue decisions on newly adopted laws meant that the Court began to rule on the constitutionality of laws even before they had yet received a consolidated judicial interpretation in the ordinary courts, and therefore that the Constitutional Court began to perform a task that traditionally belonged to ordinary judges.

---

[28] For further details, see Chapter 2.

8. The Present and Future of the Court: Constitutional Justice in Global Context

Three principal developments have shaped the fourth, and current, stage of Italian constitutional adjudication. First, in 2001 a major constitutional reform[29] reconfigured the relationship between the central State and the Regions, creating an unexpected increase in the number of direct complaints from the State against Regions' legislation and vice versa, and, consequently, a loss of centrality of the incidental system of judicial review.[30] Second, since the beginning of the new century, the Constitutional Court has increasingly discouraged ordinary judges from referring as many questions to the Court as they had done previously. Instead, ordinary judges are being encouraged to apply the Constitution directly themselves, utilizing their interpretive power. Third, two new actors are gaining importance on the constitutional scene: the European Court of Human Rights and the European Court of Justice.

The broader constitutional landscape of Europe has dramatically changed during the last decades as well. The growing significance of international and supranational organizations aiming at the protection of human rights (such as the Council of Europe) or at the creation of an integrated economic-political space (such as the European Union), has been coupled with the increasingly prominent constitutional roles of national higher courts through, for instance, expanding powers of judicial review.

In this context, the Italian Constitutional Court in the present era is ever more connected to other European courts, and its future depends greatly on how these relationships will be concretely built. As we will see in detail in the final portions of this book, today "national" constitutional adjudication happens "in the European space," and "constitutional justice" can no longer be considered a national monopoly.

---

[29] *See* Chapter 6.
[30] *See*, again, Chapter 2.

2 The Constitutional Court: Rules and Model

1. The System of Constitutional Justice Designed by the Constituent Assembly

During the Constituent Assembly, described in Chapter 1, an unclear and imprecise debate took place over the nature of the system of constitutional justice and the role of the new Constitutional Court. Moreover, the Assembly held this debate during its very last weeks. As a result, only a few articles in the last chapter of the constitutional text (Title VI, Articles 134–137) are devoted to the Court. The details of its jurisdiction and its effective functioning were left to future constitutional and ordinary statutes.

Piero Calamandrei, one of the Framers, has described it as a "paradox" that Parliament has the task of regulating the Court, considering that one of the Court's powers is to ascertain the constitutional validity of ordinary legislation.[1] Similarly, Laurence Tribe talks about the "paradox" of Article III of the U.S. Constitution, which invests Congress not only with the power to establish new federal courts

---

[1] P. Calamandrei, *La Costituzione e la legge per attuarla*, in *Dieci anni dopo* (1945–1955), Bari, Laterza, 1955.

inferior to the Supreme Court but also with the power to regulate the jurisdiction of those very same courts that have the power of judicial review.[2] In constitutional terms, both sides of the Atlantic thus seem to consider it paradoxical to grant legislatures the power to regulate their very own watchdogs, the courts.

The system of constitutional justice that arises from Articles 134–137 of the Constitution and from Constitutional Law 1/1948, Constitutional Law 1/1953, and Law 87/1953 is, as are many other European systems, rather complex. The power of the Court to ascertain the constitutional validity of legislative acts, even if very important, is only part of its jurisdiction.

Indeed, the Italian system of constitutional justice has been defined as ambiguous and as a "hybrid."

The ambiguous nature of the Italian Constitutional Court derives primarily from the inherent ambiguity attached to any system of constitutional adjudication: the Court determines the validity of statutes, an act that is traditionally political, but it does so on the basis of rules and principles that are typical of judicial proceedings. This ambiguity reflects a classic and partly unresolved question that deeply affected the debate among the Framers: whether the nature of the Constitutional Court is political or jurisdictional.

From a more technical point of view, the Italian system, like other European systems, is a hybrid: it combines elements typical of the American model of judicial review with elements typical of the Austrian model. It is well known that the former is diffuse and concrete. Since *Marbury v. Madison*, every judge resolves issues of constitutionality while in the course of deciding a real case or controversy. Following Chief Justice Marshall's reasoning, whenever a law conflicts with the Constitution and both the law and the Constitution apply to the case, the judge must disregard the first and apply the second: "This is the very essence of judicial duty."[3] The power of the judge to set aside a law was a surprise for Tocqueville who, from the standpoint of a nineteenth-century European, considered it perhaps the greatest peculiarity of the American legal system and "the more difficult to understand for a foreigner."[4] It is also well known, on the other hand, that the Austrian model is centralized and abstract: constitutional questions can be decided only by a specialized body, the Constitutional Court, itself conceived as a jurisdictional organ distinct from the ordinary Judiciary. In the original version of the system, shaped by Hans Kelsen for the 1920 Austrian Constitution, only certain given actors had access to the Constitutional Court. Moreover, its review was abstract because it only

---

[2] L. Tribe, *American Constitutional Law*, vol. I, New York, Foundation Press, 3rd ed., 2000, p. 267.

[3] *Marbury v. Madison*, 5 U.S. 137, 178 (1803).

[4] A. de Tocqueville, *Democracy in America*, New York, Washington Square Press, 1961, p. 47.

necessitated a theoretical contrast between the statute and the constitution, rather than a concrete case or controversy to which the challenged statute had been or should have been applied.

Within the spectrum of these two prototypical models, the Italian system of judicial review lies in the middle. While the Constitutional Court exclusively decides a constitutional question, the question still reaches the Court through ordinary judges in specific cases. When a constitutional issue arises during an ordinary proceeding, the judge must refer it to the Constitutional Court for its consideration. Thus the Italian system of judicial review is centralized, following the Austrian prototype, but the initiative is diffuse throughout the Judiciary, following the American style. Moreover, judicial review in the Italian system has "concreteness" insofar as the constitutional issue that must be decided by the Court is strictly linked to the real case from which it has been referred.

The following paragraphs describe the Italian system of constitutional review in greater detail, giving particular emphasis to those rules through which we may understand the model and its evolution.

2. Composition

Article 135 of the Constitution outlines the essential characteristics of the composition of the Court, which adjudicates as a unitary body rather than in panels.

The Court's composition reflects a need to ensure a combination of excellence in legal skills with an attitude appropriate to the legal discussion of policy-oriented issues. This explains why, according to Article 135, paragraph 1, of the fifteen Justices attached to the Court, five are appointed by the President of the Republic, five by Parliament in joint session, and five by the highest ordinary and administrative courts. Although the President of the Republic is not technically part of the Executive Branch, the way in which Justices of the Constitutional Court are recruited reflects how Montesquieu's traditional division of powers is used to reach a sort of equilibrium within the Court. It also reflects the above-mentioned ambiguous nature of the Court: it is a partly judicial and partly political body.

Taking its composition into account, the Italian system can be considered an intermediate model between, for example, the German one, where the *Bundesverfassungsgerichtshof* is entirely elected by Parliament, and the American one, where the Justices of the U.S. Supreme Court are nominated by the President of the United States and confirmed by the Senate. Another important difference between the American process of nomination and the Italian process of appointment is the former's openness to the public and its consequent media coverage. In contrast, the latter is closed within the technical political sphere, and public opinion is completely divorced from the process.

Parliamentary appointments to the Italian Constitutional Court are made by secret ballot and require a two-thirds majority, which becomes a three-fifths majority after the third unsuccessful ballot. If one compares this system with the quorums needed for the election of the President of the Republic, the conclusion could be reached that it requires a broader consensus to become a Constitutional Court judge than the Head of State. By convention, the Justices elected by Parliament are distributed along various political parties according to their relative political influence. The special majorities required for the election ensure that the appointment has the consent of various political forces represented in Parliament. The same kind of convention applies to appointments made by the President of the Republic, who informally seeks the advice of the sitting Justices. As to the Justices to be appointed by the Supreme Courts, the implementing statutes provide that three of them are appointed by the Supreme Court for civil and criminal cases (the Court of Cassation, *Corte di Cassazione*), and one each by the Supreme Court for administrative law cases (the Council of State, *Consiglio di Stato*) and the Court of Accounts (*Corte dei Conti*).

The clear political character of the appointments by the President of the Republic and Parliament is balanced by the professional qualifications required by Article 135, paragraph 2 of the Constitution. Constitutional judges are selected from among judges of the highest courts (even if retired), and law professors and attorneys of at least twenty years' experience. By and large, it can be said that constitutional judges have always fulfilled these expectations and that only on a few occasions have certain appointments been sharply criticized.

The independence of the Court and its Justices is assured in several ways. First of all, the Court has the full authority to verify the formal prerequisites for the appointments of its Justices. Second, the Court has full organizational and financial autonomy, which entails among other things the power to make its own rules of procedure, and jurisdiction over its employees. Considering that in Italy, as in most civil law countries, the courts (even those at the top of the judicial hierarchies) are not vested with any rule-making power, and that generally every step of the ordinary civil and criminal procedure must be regulated by statute, recognition of such a power in the Constitutional Court is of considerable importance and shows its peculiar role in the Italian system of government. In fact, in order to justify the nature of the Court's power, these norms are qualified as "rules of a supreme body," and therefore ranked as primary sources of law, given the position of the Court as a "constitutional organ" independent from all other state organs.[5]

---

[5] *See also* Chapter 1, section 5.2.

The independence of individual Justices is pursued through a nonrenewable, nine-year term of office. The term of office is the same as many other European Constitutional Courts such as those operating in Spain, Portugal, Hungary, and Poland. It is similar to that of the German *Bundesverfassungsgerichtshof* (twelve years) and is rather long considering other institutional positions: the President of the Republic is elected for seven years; and each Justice holds his or her office for a term almost double that of ordinary members of Parliament, elected for five years. Moreover, a nine-year term is long enough to guarantee a consistent and coherent case law, but does not "freeze" it, as may happen when life tenure is provided (as is the case not only in the United States but also, in practice, in Switzerland, Belgium, Austria, and Ireland).

Only the Court itself may remove Justices of the Constitutional Court (but note that no Justice has ever been removed). Justices are immune from legal responsibility for acts done and opinions expressed in the course of their office, and have a relatively high salary preestablished by law. The Constitution and other statutes also provide for the incompatibility of the office of Justice with many other duties and activities, both public and private. Nothing, on the other hand, is established concerning the incompatibilities after the end of the term of office, and it can be considered unsatisfactory from the point of view of the independence and impartiality of the Court and its members that the latter frequently take other important offices soon after stepping down from the constitutional bench.

Considering both the particular role of the Constitutional Court within the institutional system and its dual nature (political and judicial), it is understandable that the Framers believed it inappropriate to staff the Court with ordinary judges. In Italy, as in every civil law country, ordinary judges are career judges: that is, they are state officials who enter the Judiciary immediately after law school, after taking a highly selective public exam, who are provided with life tenure, and whose independence is guaranteed by a special body, the High Council of the Judiciary (*Consiglio Superiore della Magistratura*). Constitutional Court Justices are, on the contrary, appointed through a completely different system, have a different tenure, and have a different background from that of ordinary judges, with the exception of those members elected by the Supreme Courts who are "ordinary judges" in the sense that they come from the ordinary Judiciary and therefore bring the expertise of the bench to the Court.

As to the social background of the Justices, it may be noted that no seats on the Court are reserved for ethnic or religious minorities and that the first woman, Fernanda Contri, was appointed only in 1996. Since then, four other women have served on the constitutional bench.

The Justices of the Court elect the President of the Court from among their members, for a renewable term of three years. The President tends to be elected based only on his or her seniority, and sometimes for only a few months before his nine-year term expires. It may be interesting to note that only four presidents of the Court have completed a full term of office as president—Ambrosini (1966), Elia (1984), Saja (1990), and Granata (1999), the first three of whom were also reelected. On the other hand, prevailing practice has allowed the appointment of one president for a mere 45 days. For all these reasons, it is not easy to single out the eras of the Italian Constitutional Court with reference to its presidents as is possible, for instance, with the U.S. Supreme Court, using the Warren Court, the Burger Court, and the Rehnquist Court as recent examples.[6]

Even though the general principle of collegiality applies to the Court (as detailed further below), the President is vested with important powers. He represents the Court publicly and before the other political organs of the State, and gives the annual address on the state of the Court. The President chooses the reporting Justice for a case, who is in charge of writing the final opinion, a critical responsibility given that this final opinion is always the opinion of the Court and that concurring and dissenting opinions are not permitted. The President convenes the Court in *Camera di Consiglio* (behind closed doors) when the parties to the case have not filed an appearance and when a case is manifestly inadmissible or unfounded. Eleven Justices are required to decide a case, but in case of parity, the vote of the President prevails.

2.1 THE PRINCIPLE OF COLLEGIALITY

A strict principle of collegiality distinguishes the Italian Constitutional Court not only from the supreme courts of common law countries but also from some of its European counterparts, including the German *Bundesverfassungsgerichtshof* and the Spanish *Tribunal Constitucional*. In fact, both Germany and Spain permit constitutional judges to write separate opinions, notwithstanding the civil law tradition in which decisions of appellate and supreme courts are considered to come from the entire body and to represent a unique will and therefore preclude the identification of individual personalities within the judicial body. Following the common law style to some extent by allowing constitutional judges to publish concurring and dissenting opinions, Germany and Spain have evidently taken advantage of the migration of constitutional ideas. This is not yet the case in Italy. After an intense debate that considered both the strengths and the weaknesses of separate opinions,

---

[6] *See also* Chapter 1, section 7.

as well as the historical, cultural, and institutional reasons that explain the differ-ence between common law and civil law judicial style, the principle of collegiality (and the related principle of secrecy of deliberation) still prevails.

The debate has gone on, since the beginning of the Court's operation, not only among scholars but also among the Justices. It culminated recently in a seminar organized in 2002 by the Constitutional Court, during which many positive effects of separate opinions were underlined: separate opinions favor courts' accountabil-ity and the transparency and sharpness of their reasoning; a plurality of opinions candidly shows the complexity of constitutional interpretation; moreover, the dissenting opinion of today can become the majority of tomorrow and therefore separate opinions can contribute to the dynamism of case law. On the other hand, the principle of collegiality is a way of protecting the Court from the pressures and interferences of politics: allowing Justices the opportunity to express their views freely, without having to justify their position outside the Court. This is particu-larly important in a system where Justices have no life tenure but a fixed term of nine years. In addition, the prohibition on disclosing individual opinions favors judicial modesty and is thought to discourage judges from excessive emphasis on the judge's person as an individual rather than in the institutional role of the judge. Most important, the necessity of crafting the Court's decisions through compro-mise, which unfortunately does in some cases contribute to cryptic and opaque reasoning, corresponds to the nature of the Constitution itself, which represents a very complex compromise among many fundamental principles that all need to be balanced. In the end, the continued existence of the principle of collegiality is a function of the necessity of finding equilibrium between law and politics.

The Italian Constitutional Court reaches its decisions as follows. First, the President assigns the case to the Reporting Justice. The Reporting Justice is assisted by judicial clerks in the preparation of the file of the case, which is circulated among the Justices' individual chambers a few weeks before the discussion. The file of the case consists of precedents, statutes, and regulations, *doctrine* (that is, scholarly com-mentary and analysis), and foreign references. It is worth noting that judicial clerks, in contrast to the American experience with the Supreme Court, are experienced professionals selected from among ordinary judges and law school professors.

The case may be discussed in a public hearing (*udienza pubblica*) or behind closed doors. A public hearing is for cases involving conflicts between the State and Regions and conflicts between powers of the State that reach the Court through the direct method of judicial review, and also for issues that reach the Court through the incidental method of judicial review when the parties appear before the Court. Cases are instead debated behind closed doors when they reach the Court through the incidental method but the parties do not appear, or when a preliminary decision on the admissibility of a conflict between powers of the State must be taken. Cases regarding the admissibility of referenda are debated behind closed doors if the parties do not appear.[7]

After the public hearing, the Reporting Justice presents the case to the rest of Court in closed session and suggests a tentative solution. This is the time for each Justice to give a speech starting from the most junior one; the Chief Justice has the last word. After the reply of the Reporting Justice, the Court votes by a show of hands. Once the decision is taken by the Court, the Reporting Justice writes the opinion accordingly. When the draft opinion is ready, it is read to the whole Court in a special session devoted to the reading of opinions. At this point the Justices may suggest changes and corrections to the opinion of the Reporting Justice. Finally, after a last formal check by the Chief Justice's office, the final version of the decision is published in the *Gazzetta ufficiale*, the official journal of the Italian Republic.

Bearing in mind that comparison of the United States system with the Italian system entails a comparison of one system in which constitutional issues are decided by ordinary judges (and in the last instance by the Supreme Court) to another system in which constitutional issues are decided only by a special body through a special procedure, another important difference between common law and civil law courts is the former's discretion to decide which cases to hear. Case selection, effected in the United States primarily through the *certiorari* procedure, is extremely important not only because it dramatically reduces the number of cases to be decided but also because it allows the Court to select what to decide and when. The Italian Constitutional Court only has mandatory jurisdiction and therefore lacks this power. It must decide all the cases properly set forth before it. Nevertheless, in order to keep up with its caseload and gain efficiency, the Italian Constitutional Court uses procedural devices (such as decisions of *manifesta infondatezza* (manifestly unfounded claims) and *manifesta inammissibilità* (manifestly inadmissible claims, that are rendered *per curiam*) in order to efficiently resolve some cases. The Court, as has been described in Chapter 1, used this kind of decision abundantly from 1987 until 1989. Although it was successful in substantially reducing the Court's backlog of cases, the Court's use of these tools has also been sharply criticized as representing a "strategic" use of procedural decision in order to avoid mandatory jurisdiction.

More recently, as will be discussed in section 6 below, fewer cases reach the Court via the incidental method of judicial review, which is, as we shall see shortly, one of the two avenues through which a question regarding the constitutional validity of a

---

[7] The avenues through which cases reach the Constitutional Court here mentioned, that is, the jurisdiction of the Court, are discussed *infra*, section 3.

law can reach the Court. The reduction in the number of questions can be explained on two different grounds. On one hand, the abundant use by the Court of the procedural decisions of *manifesta infondatezza* (manifestly unfounded claims) and *manifesta inammissibilità* (manifestly inadmissible claims) mentioned above discourages ordinary judges from referring constitutional issues. On the other hand, since the mid-1990s, ordinary judges, following the case law of the Constitutional Court, have adopted the so-called *interpretazione conforme a Costituzione* (interpretation in accordance with the Constitution): that is, they themselves construct meanings of statutes that are compatible with the Constitution and do not violate it. Judges sometimes force the literal meaning of the text in order to save the statute and therefore do not refer it to the Constitutional Court. Ordinary judges' use of *interpretazione conforme a Costituzione* is contributing to a changing of the Italian model of judicial review, as we shall see in section 6.

3. Jurisdiction

European constitutional courts are generally assigned broad jurisdiction: they not only review the constitutionality of statutes but also, for instance, solve conflicts between the central government and subnational states, as happens in Germany, or between the State and the Regions. This last is the Italian case. Moreover, there are systems, such as the Spanish or German ones and many of the new systems of constitutional justice of Central-Eastern Europe, that allow direct recourse to the Court in cases of infringement of citizens' fundamental rights and liberties. Comparing the Italian Constitutional Court with many of its European counterparts, the adjudicatory authority of the former is not very broad.

Looking at Article 134 of the Constitution, and Article 2 of the Constitutional Law of March 11, 1953, n. 1, we may single out four main areas of jurisdiction.

3.1 CONFLICTS OF ATTRIBUTIONS

The Italian Constitution, based on the idea of a strong institutional pluralism, establishes complex relationships between the branches of government. Due to this complexity, the Constitutional Court settles "conflicts of attributions" which may arise among the different powers of the State.

The "conflicts of attributions," that is to say disputes regarding which body is entitled to exercise a certain power, find their way to the Constitutional Court when they are not resolved through political mediation. These conflicts may derive from the horizontal allocation of state powers among the constitutional organs of the

State (*conflitti interorganici*), and from the vertical allocation of powers between State and Regions and among Regions (*conflitti intersoggettivi*).

In the first case, the Court has jurisdiction over conflicts "arising between organs entitled to take final decisions for the branch of government to which they belong and to establish the amount of their power as provided by the Constitution" (Art. 37, § 1, Law No. 87/1953). The word "organs" has been given a broad interpretation and includes, for example, Parliament, the Chamber of Deputies, the Senate, the President of the Republic, the Prime Minister, and, according to a relatively recent case, even a single member of the Council of Ministers.[8] Other State institutions may also be included, such as the *Consiglio Superiore della Magistratura* and the Court of Accounts. In the case of conflicts of attributions between constitutional organs, the Court must determine the sphere of competence conferred upon the State powers by constitutional provisions, and it must declare to which organ the challenged power belongs. When the Court concludes an act to have been adopted by a body that was not competent to do so under its constitutional allocation of powers, the Court must annul that act.

As to conflicts between State and Regions or among Regions, it must be remembered that the Constitution provides for a strong decentralization of many functions from the State to the Regions, and that the Constitution has been recently and notably amended to strengthen that decentralization even further. If the State invades the sphere of autonomy attributed to the Regions or if a Region exceeds its own sphere, the Constitutional Court has original jurisdiction over the conflict. Obviously, the parties to the controversy are the State and the Regions that stand before the Court respectively in the persons of the Prime Minister and the President of the Regional Government (*Giunta regionale*).

3.2 CHARGES AGAINST THE PRESIDENT OF THE REPUBLIC

The Constitutional Court also has jurisdiction over charges against the President of the Republic. The President of the Republic is not responsible for acts performed in his executive role, and can be prosecuted only for high treason or offenses against the Constitution. In such cases he shall be impeached by an absolute majority of the members of Parliament sitting in joint session, and then tried by the Constitutional Court. When judging a Presidential impeachment, 16 lay judges enlarge the

---

[8] In 1995 the Senate cast a vote of no confidence against the Minister of Justice. The Minister had filed an action based on a conflict of attribution between himself and the Senate, and the case was decided by the Constitutional Court in 1996. *See* Judgment 7/1996.

composition of the Court. It must be noted here that until the reform adopted with Constitutional Law 1/1989, which amended Article 134 of the Constitution, the Court also had jurisdiction in cases of impeachment of Ministers who now are prosecuted, subject to the consent of Parliament, by ordinary courts. In the Court's history, no President has ever been impeached and, as for Ministers, in only one case, the 1979 *Lockheed* case, has this occurred.

3.3 ADMISSIBILITY OF REFERENDA

According to Article 75 of the Constitution, a popular referendum can be held, when 500,000 electors or five Regional Councils request it, in order to totally or partially repeal a statute. The Constitutional Court is given the authority to decide on the admissibility of a referendum, based on the fact that, following Article 75 of the Constitution, tax or budgetary laws, laws for amnesty or general pardon, or laws authorizing the ratification of international treaties cannot be subject to referendum. Whereas in the several categories of jurisdiction mentioned above, and of course in the case of legislative review, the Constitutional Court plays a quintessentially judicial role, in the referendum process its role is different. Here, there is no actual case or controversy, and the Court performs its duties *ex officio*, due to its position as a constitutional body *super partes*. Nevertheless, because the Court has to decide whether a statute falls within one of the "prohibited" categories of Article 75, the judgment over the admissibility of a referendum can also be difficult. Indeed, the decision is not at all mechanical: the Court has given itself broad interpretative power and has decided not only that the kinds of laws mentioned in Article 75 cannot be subject to referendum but also that constitutional laws and laws *costituzionalmente vincolate* (constitutionally mandated), that is laws needed for the correct working of constitutional bodies, are outside the scope of referenda. In a recent case, for instance, the Court had to decide whether to allow a referendum aimed at the abrogation of parts of the electoral law, which can be considered in its entirety a law *costituzionalmente vincolata*. Even in the event that the referendum would have been successful, the abrogation of parts of the law would have not resulted in a situation that left the country with no electoral law, but only with an altered law, therefore in the end the Court considered the referendum to be admissible. Eventually the referendum was held but did not reach the required quorum. At the very beginning of 2014, with a tremendously important and criticized decision, the Constitutional Court itself invalidated part of the electoral law, with an opinion making ample references to foreign electoral systems (see Judgment 1/2014).

3.4 JUDICIAL REVIEW OF STATUTES

Finally, there remains the power of the Court to review the constitutional validity of statutes. Indeed, the power of judicial review used to be by far the most important power of the Court, but, since the constitutional amendments of Articles 123 and 127 of the Constitution implemented through two important constitutional laws of 1999 and 2001, the conflicts of attribution between the State and the Regions have gained more importance. In fact, because the constitutional reform reassessed the balance between the central State and the Regions' respective legislative powers, the Court has increasingly been called upon to resolve issues of the allocation of power and authority (division of competences) among different levels of government, rather than to guarantee fundamental rights through the exercise of judicial review. The process of transformation of the docket of the Court has been questionably labeled as "*dalla corte dei diritti alla corte dei conflitti*": "from the Court of rights to the Court of conflicts."[9]

4. The System of Judicial Review

The Constitutional Court exercises its power of judicial review of legislation through the direct method and the incidental method. The former has essentially an abstract character because standing is given to public bodies and the statute is challenged per se and not as applied. In the latter method, when an ordinary judge has doubts about the constitutional legitimacy of a statute that must be applied to a real case or controversy, she must suspend the proceeding and refer the question to the Constitutional Court. Broadly speaking, the direct method is a means of guaranteeing the allocation of power between the State and the Regions, while the incidental one acts as a means of guaranteeing individual rights and freedoms. In both cases, the ultimate scope of judicial review is the protection of the constitutional order.

As previously mentioned, access to the Constitutional Court in Italy is more limited than in other countries. For example, the Italian system does not allow, as is the case in Germany (*Verfassungsbeschwerde*) or Spain (*amparo*), that any person may bring a constitutional complaint before the Court alleging the State's direct infringement upon one of their basic rights. Nor does the Court grant a parliamentary minority the right to raise a constitutional question, a power typical of the French system (*saisine parlamentaire*) but also known in Spain, Austria, Germany, and Portugal. Indeed, it has been proposed several times in Italy, most recently by

---

[9] The expression has been used by many scholars and also by judges. *See* the *Annual Conference* of Justice Annibale Marini, President of the Constitutional Court, on Feb. 9, 2006.

the *Commissione Bicamerale*[10] in 1997, that the jurisdiction of the Constitutional Court be widened by introducing these other avenues of access: individual direct complaints for the protection of fundamental rights, and direct access by a parliamentary minority. Although viewed positively insofar as they would have enlarged the scope of constitutional protection, these proposals were criticized and in the end were rejected, following the failure of the *Bicamerale* as a whole. This was due, first, to the fact that discretionary power of case selection is unknown in the Italian tradition; thus, a serious consequence of the enlargement of the Court's jurisdiction would be a potential flood of cases before the Court. Second, there was a widespread concern that these changes would increase the Court's involvement in the political process.

4.1 THE DIRECT METHOD OF JUDICIAL REVIEW

From a purely statistical point of view, the direct method of judicial review has played an increasingly important role in the Court's activity, relative to the incidental method. This is especially true following the recent reform of Title V of the Constitution, mentioned above.[11]

Article 123 of the Constitution deals with the Regional Charters, which establish the form of government of the individual Region and the fundamental principles of its organization and functions. The second paragraph of the same article (as enforced by Article 9, paragraph 1 of Law 131/2003) allows the central government to challenge the constitutionality of a Regional Charter within 30 days of its publication.

Article 127, paragraph 1, authorizes the central government to bring a direct action before the Constitutional Court and challenge the constitutionality of a regional statute, within 60 days from its publication, when the latter is deemed to exceed the powers of the Region.

Article 127, paragraph 2, as implemented by Article 9, paragraphs 2 and 3 of Law 131/2003, provides in turn that a Region can raise a constitutional challenge directly before the Constitutional Court, against national legislation or statutes of other Regions when it deems its authority invaded by either. The action must be brought within 60 days from the publication of the challenged statute.

Among other things, Article 9 of Law 131/2003 further provides that in the context of a direct action challenging a piece of State or regional legislation, the

---

[10] The *Commissione bicamerale per le riforme istituzionali* is a body composed of members of both Houses of Parliament and created by constitutional statute (Constitutional Law No. 2 of 1997). A comprehensive project of constitutional reform was submitted by the *Commissione bicamerale* to Parliament in November 1997, but had no consequences.

[11] *See* statistical tables in Appendix III.

Constitutional Court can, on its own motion, temporarily suspend the implementation of the legislation in question on the grounds that it would cause irreparable prejudice to the rights of the citizens.

4.2 THE INCIDENTAL METHOD OF JUDICIAL REVIEW

Until the recent constitutional reform reassessed the allocation of legislative power between the State and the Regions, the incidental method of judicial review not only was the most important and frequent way of raising questions of constitutionality of legislation before the Court but also occupied a great part of its docket. After the reforms described in the previous section, the incidental method has lost part of its quantitative importance. Moreover, the evolving use of the incidental method has also in some respects changed the nature of the Italian Constitutional system of judicial review more generally. This is particularly evident when we examine the relationship between the Constitutional Court and ordinary judges. In fact, the Italian system is becoming more "diffuse," in light of the new role of ordinary judges who to some extent apply the Constitution directly in their own adjudication.

The incidental method of judicial review is expressly provided for by Article 1 of Constitutional Law 1/1948, which establishes:

> A question concerning the constitutional legitimacy of a statute or of an act with the same force, raised by the judge on his own motion or upon request of one of the parties in the course of a judicial proceeding, and considered by the judge to be not manifestly unfounded, must be referred to the Constitutional Court for its consideration.

The incidental method of access to the Constitutional Court, regulated in detail by Law 87/1953, establishes a procedure that can be considered concrete because the laws whose constitutionality is in doubt are considered in their concrete application to an actual controversy and not per se.

4.2.1 A Judge in the Course of a Judicial Proceeding Must Raise a Question

In the incidental method of judicial review, the ordinary judge has the power, and to some extent the duty, to raise issues of constitutionality before the Constitutional Court so as to obtain a binding decision from that body. Thus, the judge has the right to invoke the jurisdiction of the Court, provided that the law whose constitutionality is in doubt is relevant to the decision of the concrete case before her. The proceeding is then suspended until the Court decides the preliminary issue of constitutionality. Considering the various models of constitutional justice operating in the world, the Italian system's hybrid nature lies precisely in this method: the decision about the constitutional validity of the statute is reserved solely for the Constitutional Court, but the initiative is spread throughout the entire Judiciary. Since the ordinary judge is entitled to refer the question to the Constitutional Court for judicial review, the judge has the keys to the Constitutional Court. He is—in the famous words of Piero Calamandrei—its gatekeeper.[12]

Since the judge is the gatekeeper of the Constitutional Court, in order to understand who has access to the Court it is essential to look at the laws and the Court's decisions defining the notion of "judge." Who are the entitled "judges" who may refer a question of constitutionality to the Constitutional Court (known as the judge *a quo*)? Are they all only the ordinary civil, criminal, and administrative judges? Can the question be referred to the Court by other adjudicatory authorities such as the *Consiglio Superiore della Magistratura* (again, the governing body of the Judiciary) or the Court of Accounts? And what about independent authorities and arbitrators?

According to the various sources regulating the incidental method of judicial review, the constitutional question must be referred to the Court "in the course of a judicial proceeding" by a "judge" (Art. 1, Constitutional Law 1/1948); "in the course of a judgment before a judicial authority" (Art. 23, Law 87/1953); or by the "judge in front of whom the case is pending" (Art. 1, *Norme integrative per i giudizi davanti alla Corte costituzionale*, "Integrative Norms").

Given the dual nature of the Italian system—both abstract and concrete—the opinions of the Court that interpret the relevant statutes have not always been consistent. On some occasions the opinions, by broadly reading the notion of "judge," favored wider access to the Court, and consequently the abstract and general interest in the legitimacy of the legal order prevailed; on other occasions, the word "judge" was defined more strictly, thereby reducing access to the Court.

Notwithstanding some uncertainties, we can identify two different periods in the Court's case law. During the first period (1956–1971), in order to declare a great number of Fascist laws unconstitutional and to implement the new Constitution's values, the Court favored expansive access by interpreting the notion of "judge" in a broad sense. The only condition required was that the constitutional question be referred by a permanent part of the Judiciary, capable of rendering a final decision on the case (Judgments 129/1957 and 83/1966). As a consequence of this line of opinions, the Court concluded that the following bodies have standing to

---

[12] P. Calamandrei, *Il procedimento per la dichiarazione di illegittimità costituzionale*, in *Opere giuridiche*, vol. III, Napoli, Morano, 1965, p. 372.

refer constitutional questions: the disciplinary division of the *Consiglio Superiore della Magistratura* (Judgments 12/1971 and 284/1986), the disciplinary division of the National Bar Association (Judgment 114/1970), the Patent and Trademark Commission (Judgments 37/1957, 158/1995, 236/1996), and the Tax Court (Judgments 287/1974 and 215/1976). Moreover, since 1957 the Court has allowed constitutional questions to be referred from noncontentious proceedings (*procedimenti di volontaria giurisdizione*).[13] Last, but not least, the Court has recognized its own power to raise questions of constitutionality; this means that the Court, when deciding cases, is capable of dealing with questions, however strictly related, that are different from the original one (Judgments 13/1969, 56/1968, 125/1977).

Although in the first two decades of activity the Constitutional Court interpreted the notion of "judge" quite broadly, it nevertheless did not recognize, for example, either public prosecutors or examining judges in a civil proceeding (where the final decision requires the entire panel of the tribunal) as having standing to refer constitutional questions to the Court (Judgments 40, 41, 42/1963, 52/1976, 415/1995 and Judgments 109/1962, 295/1996).

Since the early 1970s, the Constitutional Court has given the term "judge" a narrower meaning, requiring not only that the referring authority be part of the Judiciary and capable of rendering a final decision on the case but also that it exercises a judicial and not an administrative function (Judgments 103/1984, 33/1991, 429/1991, 335/1995). It seems the Court now looks for two different requisites for a legal recognition of standing: a subjective one, regarding the nature of the referring body; and an objective one, regarding the specific function the body is performing.

The reason for the change in case law lies in the position that the Court has gained within the institutional system. The Constitutional Court is no longer a new and unprecedented body in search of authority. The Court is a cornerstone of the Italian system of government, and therefore can afford to regulate and limit its jurisdiction. The constitutional values introduced in 1948 are now widely shared among judges. Judges no longer need encouragement to refer constitutional questions. Moreover, especially since the mid-1990s, ordinary judges collaborate with the Court: they do not refer questions if it is possible (even at times forcing the plain meaning of the constitutional text) to construct the challenged statute in a way that does not violate the Constitution (*interpretazione conforme a Costituzione*).

---

[13] Judgments 129/1957 and 24/1958. In the *volontaria giurisdizione* proceedings, the judge's powers are close to that of an administrative officer and generally his adjudicatory authority is needed to ascertain a personal status: for example, the consensual separation of spouses (the initial step of the divorce procedure) or the adoption of an adult person both need the "decree" of a "judge."

The situation can be analogized to that of the U.S. Supreme Court, which, in the face of an increasing caseload in the past decided an ever greater number of cases, reaching an average of 180 full opinions in the 1980s. Since then, however, the number of full decisions has decreased, and now the yearly caseload averages just 70. It is likely the American Court no longer needs to decide a great number of cases given the fact, among other things, that its authority is no longer in dispute. Moreover, the U.S. Supreme Court uses its discretion to select cases that address the most important issues, while also avoiding harder cases by for instance, using its broad spectrum of passive virtues.[14]

Notwithstanding the more recent attitude of the Italian Constitutional Court, a special position has always been given to the Court of Accounts, which has standing to refer questions when ruling on Government acts (Judgments 226/1976 and 348/1991). In fact, it is only through this method of referral that the Constitutional Court may review budgetary laws. Standing has also been assigned to the Court of Accounts in its capacity to audit the administration of the State budget according to Article 100 of the Constitution (Judgment 244/1995).

Finally, there are two additional problematic situations regarding the Court's recognition of "standing to refer": arbitrators and independent authorities. In the former case, standing is generally denied. The latter's standing has never been decided by the Constitutional Court, but many scholars favor a positive solution, especially with regard to the Antitrust Authority.

4.2.2 The Question of Constitutional Legitimacy Must Be Relevant and Not Manifestly Unfounded

A judge, before referring a question to the Constitutional Court, and suspending the case pending before her, must verify that the question is relevant and not manifestly unfounded. In the referring order to the Court the judge *a quo* must explicitly state the relevance and plausibility of the question, the statute challenged, and the constitutional provision(s) that it allegedly violates. In the end, two important requirements must be met for a constitutional issue to find its way to the Court: its resolution must be essential to the decision of the case, and the issue must have a *prima facie* foundation on the merits.

The first requirement reveals the objective connection between the original proceeding (*giudizio a quo*) and the process in the Constitutional Court. In this

---

[14] A. M. Bickel, *The Least Dangerous Branch. The Supreme Court at the Bar of Politics*, New Haven and London, Yale University Press, 1962, p. 111 ff.

connection lies the concrete nature of the incidental method of judicial review. In fact, the question of constitutionality can be referred to the Court only when its solution is necessary to decide the actual controversy pending before the judge who needs the answer to her constitutional doubts. In other words, the statute, the constitutional validity of which is contested, must be applicable to the case.

The constitutional issue can reach the Court only if it originates from a "case or controversy." Consequently, the Court will not decide merely theoretical or hypothetical questions. The court will not, using words more familiar to common lawyers and international lawyers, issue advisory opinions. Similarly, the constitutional question must be ripe and not moot. Thus the Italian system examines the general, or abstract, legality of the constitutional order through the vindication of the individual concrete right.

The judge *a quo* must also verify that the constitutional question is not manifestly unfounded. This means that the "gatekeeper" of the Court must perform her role in an effective manner. In a system in which the idea of case selection is not accepted, at least formally, the referring judge in effect "screens" cases. However, this screening should be broad and loose, because the judge should refer all the questions that are *prima facie* meritorious, that is, every question in which there is even a reasonable doubt of constitutionality.

Nevertheless, in the last two decades the Court has constrained the allegedly excessive willingness of ordinary judges to find a *prima facie* constitutional question to refer to the Constitutional Court. The Court has increasingly used summary decisions of *manifesta inammissibilità* and *manifesta infondatezza* to suggest that judges have misused or abused their referring powers. As has been already noted, given that the jurisdiction of the Constitutional Court is entirely mandatory and that the Court is constantly overworked, these summary decisions seem to be used by the Court as a hidden means of case selection. Does the Court thus seem, especially in certain periods, headed toward the functional equivalent of *certiorari* policy?

In part as a reaction to this extensive use of summary decisions, in part because constitutional values have finally percolated through the culture of the ordinary judiciary, and in part following suggestions in the Constitutional Court's case law, ordinary judges no longer refer as many cases to the Court as they did prior to the early 1990s. As previously mentioned, ordinary judges attempt to directly apply the Constitution via the "*interpretazione conforme a Costituzione.*" The rationale for this doctrine lies in the notion that statutes are to be quashed only if their contrast with the Constitution is clear beyond any reasonable doubt and there is no other way to resolve it. A similar doctrine is not unknown to the U.S. Supreme Court's case law: "Where a statute is susceptible of two constructions, by one of which grave and doubtful constitutional questions arose and by the other such questions can be avoided, [a court's] duty is to adopt the latter."[15]

In the end, the relationship between the proceeding *a quo* and the constitutional process is somehow problematic, and the case law is not always consistent. Such a lack of clarity reveals a strategic use of procedural decisions by the Court. It seems that a policy-oriented use of the doctrines of justiciability and, more generally, of the passive virtues, is not unknown to the Italian Constitutional Court. Moreover, the passive virtues, similarly to their use in the United States, serve not only as a method of coping with caseloads but also to balance the Court's agenda and the Court itself with other branches of government.

4.2.3 The Question Can Be Raised by the Parties or by the Judge on His Own Motion

There is no doubt that the constitutional question must be referred to the Court by a judge. However, the parties and the public prosecutor, or the judge *ex officio*, may all raise the issue of a statute's constitutional validity in the course of an ordinary proceeding. Here again, the duality of the Italian system, both concrete and abstract, is evident: when the initiative comes from the parties, a private rights model of litigation prevails; when the initiative is by the judge, a public law model of litigation emerges. In both situations however, the constitutional legitimacy of the legal order is realized through a real case or controversy.

When a judge raises a constitutional question on her own motion, she must still ascertain the existence of the two previously mentioned fundamental conditions. Therefore, she must justify the following in her referral decree (*ordinanza di remissione*): the determinative character of the issue, the impossibility of a valid construction of the contested statute, and the reasons for considering the statute unconstitutional. She must also include a precise indication of the provisions of the statute considered unconstitutional, as well as the norms of the Constitution or of the constitutional laws that the statute seemingly violates.

The parties may also raise constitutional questions. In this case, the judge *a quo* will analyze the question of constitutionality by considering the same requisites and conditions, but the question alleged by the parties or by the public prosecutor can be rejected in a reasoned decision, when the judge considers that it has no relevance to the case or no due foundation. However, rejection does not prevent the parties from raising the same question at any further stage of the proceedings.

[raised by public but still through a judge]

---

[15] *Jones v. US*, 526 U.S. 227, 239 (1999), quoting *Attorney General v. Delaware & Hudson Co.*, 213 U.S. 366, 408 (1909).

The parties are expressly granted the opportunity to raise constitutional questions by Article 1 of Constitutional Law 1/1948 and by Article 23 of Law 87/1953: any party to the original proceeding, following the preliminary decision of the judge *a quo*, has access to the Constitutional Court. That is to say, all parties in the proceeding have standing to raise constitutional questions in order to vindicate their private rights: the plaintiff, the defendant, the appellant, the respondent, the intervenor, and the party joined in the action. Therefore, access to courts and access to constitutional justice are strictly related, and the extent of individual access to the Constitutional Court is directly proportional to the reading of Article 24 of the Constitution, the first section of which establishes that "[e]veryone may bring cases before a court of law in order to protect their rights under civil and administrative law." Anyone who has the right of action in the ordinary court has, as a consequence, access to the Constitutional Court. But the contrary is also true, and rights that are not protected by ordinary courts do not find their way to the Constitutional Court.

Although a great number of procedural guarantees contained in the Italian Constitution are effectively protected—such as equality before the law and before the courts; judicial independence; right of action; right of defense; right to a reasoned judgment; and right to a last resort recourse before the Court of Cassation—access to the courts is still problematic. It is well known, for example, that the judicial protection of diffuse or collective interests is inadequate. Given the close relationship between a judge *a quo* and the Constitutional Court, this inadequacy is reflected at the level of constitutional justice.

5. Acts that Are Subject to Judicial Review

According to Article 134 of the Constitution and Article 1 of Constitutional Law 1/1948, the Constitutional Court decides on the validity of "laws and enactments having force of law issued by the State and Regions" and on "a law or an act with the same force." These provisions limit substantially the scope of judicial review and show the partly ambiguous nature of the Constitutional Court, which was born principally as an instrument for the protection of the legal order and only indirectly as an institution for the vindication of fundamental rights.

While it is relatively easy to understand that the Court has jurisdiction over the statutes of the State and the Regions—to which the Charters of the independent Provinces of Trento and Bolzano, the Charters of the ordinary Regions, and the decrees implementing the Charters of the Special Independent Regions (Sicily, Sardinia, Trentino-Alto Adige, Friuli-Venezia Giulia, Val D'Aosta) can be compared—it is more difficult to define other cases of "acts with the same force."

First of all, the Court has established its adjudicatory authority over "delegated legislation." In the Italian system, Parliament can issue a *legge delega* (delegating law), which gives the Executive the power to legislate over a specific subject matter within a specific time (Art. 76 of the Constitution); the *legge delega* is thus a frame within which the Executive can legislate. The act with the force of law that the Administration adopts following the *legge delega* is called a *decreto legislativo*. Both the *legge delega* and the *decreto legislativo* have been recognized as subject to judicial review; the benchmark for the former is the Constitution, but for the latter the benchmark is both the Constitution and the *legge delega* itself, which must be respected by the *decreto legislativo* in order to be constitutionally valid. Another problematic case has been that of the *decreto-legge* issued by the Executive "in extraordinary cases of necessity and urgency" under Article 77 of the Constitution. The *decreto-legge* must be converted into an ordinary statute by Parliament within 60 days of its publication. Due to the very brief life of the *decreto-legge*, it proved to be impossible for the Court to judge its validity, that is to check whether the *decreto-legge* was issued in genuinely "extraordinary" cases. Once the *decreto-legge* was converted in law, it was said that all its possible defects were cured. In order to sanction the abuse of the *decreto-legge*, the Constitutional Court eventually rejected this line of reasoning and subjected to judicial review the statute that converted the *decreto-legge* for the purpose of verifying whether the original *decreto* was issued in compliance with the strict provisions of Article 77. The Court also subjected to judicial review a "reiterated" *decreto-legge*—instances when the Executive was not politically capable of getting Parliament to convert the *decreto-legge* into an ordinary statute within 60 days, and would therefore often enact a new *decreto-legge* with the identical content. ~~spread in politics reading on 'parliament' that this became illegal in 1990s.~~

Overall, the power of judicial review is limited to what, in the civil law tradition, is thought of as "primary legislation." On the other hand, the Court has no power to review "secondary legislation" such as administrative acts and regulations, or the internal rules of other governmental bodies (such as those of the Chambers of Parliament). One of the reasons for this limitation can be found in the Kelsenian theory of the sources of law on which the original Austrian/centralized model of judicial review was based. Obviously, also administrative acts and judicial decisions—which, following the *"principio di legalità,"* are subordinated to primary legislation—must not be in contrast with the Constitution, but in order to check their validity the Constitutional Court is not called into account. The limitation of the reviewing power of the Constitutional Court to primary legislation is justified by the *"principio di legalità"* that lies at the bottom of the validity of all acts adopted by the Executive and Judicial Branches of Government. Acts of the Executive and Judicial Branches can be in conflict with the Constitution, but their validity is

[handwritten marginalia: referring to administrative acts being illegale / illegale acts]

always mediated by the law on which they are based. Therefore, when administrative acts, regulations, or judicial decisions are unconstitutional there are two possibilities: (1) if they are issued in conformity with the law on which they rely—that is, with primary legislation—then the underlying statute itself will be unconstitutional; or (2) if they are in conflict with the statute, and the statute does not violate the Constitution, then the problem is not one of unconstitutionality, but simply of illegality (*illegittimità*). In the first case, it is for the Constitutional Court to declare the statute unconstitutional, and consequently, the administrative or judicial act on which it is based will automatically collapse. In the second case, the administrative act in contrast to primary legislation will be annulled by the competent administrative tribunal, and the judicial act will be subject to ordinary judicial remedies. The problem with this theory is that the scenario of the sources of law has changed deeply in recent decades, resulting in a more complex and pluralistic system where there are acts of the Executive that can be considered "autonomous," that is, disconnected from primary legislation and therefore not subject to any kind of review.

Within this context, it is important to consider Article 138 of the Constitution, which establishes the procedure to adopt "laws amending the Constitution and other constitutional laws." Are constitutional amendments and constitutional laws subject to judicial review? In other words, is it possible to have an "unconstitutional constitutional law"? The Court, with Judgment 1146/1988, answered this question affirmatively, holding that constitutional legislation cannot violate the "supreme principles of the constitutional order."[16] From a formal perspective this means that constitutional amendments and constitutional laws must be adopted only following the extremely difficult procedure established by Article 138. The Court's holding also has a substantive component, however. There are parts of the Constitution that cannot be subject to modification. In the case of Article 139, the constitutional text itself provides that the republican form of government cannot be changed. In other cases, the Court has declared that some constitutional principles are untouchable, such as the "inviolable rights" of Article 2.[17]

Since Judgment 14/1964, acts of the European Union are not considered to be part of the Italian legal system and therefore are not reviewable by the Constitutional Court. Even though EU regulations are directly applicable in all Member States and EU directives can also have "direct effect" in the national legal system, they are considered formally to belong exclusively to the European Union legal order. The consequence of this approach is that EU law and Italian law are two separate but coordinated systems. Following the decisions of the European Court of Justice,

---

[16] Excerpts of the judgment are reported in Chapter 4.
[17] *See* Chapter 4, section 2.1.

especially the *Simmenthal* case of 1978, the principle that governs the relationship between the two systems is the "primacy" of EU law over Italian law. As a result of the principles of "separation" and "primacy," in case of conflict between EU law and domestic law, ordinary judges have the responsibility to apply the former and to disregard the latter. In the words of the Constitutional Court: "[European Union] rules with direct effect prevent ordinary judges from applying conflicting domestic rules, when there is no doubt about the conflict" (Judgment 170/1984). In the end, the Constitutional Court has no power of judicial review over EU acts "because Article 134 of the Constitution refers only to statutes and acts with the same force of the State and the Regions, while [EU] regulations and directives do not belong to the State legal order" (Judgment 232/1975). Nevertheless, the Italian legal order has an untouchable core that can hold back the expansion of EU law. The already mentioned "supreme principles of the constitutional order" can operate as "counter-limits" to EU law. If an EU act infringes these "supreme principles," the primacy of EU law makes way for the primacy of domestic law. In the words of the Court: "domestic law remains applicable when the limits of the fundamental principles of the constitutional order and of the inviolable rights of the person come into account—limits that can be vindicated only by the Constitutional Court" (Judgment 284/2007).[18]

6. The Italian Model of Judicial Review: "Cooperative" and "Networked"

Throughout this chapter we have described the Italian system of constitutional justice as a hybrid, combining some main features of two prototypical models, the American and the Austrian. This original Italian model has also evolved through the working rules of the Constitutional Court, its exercise of jurisdiction, and the style and nuances of its decisions. Especially when considering the incidental method of judicial review, we can see on the one hand that the relationship between ordinary judges and the Court has changed over the last two decades; and on the other hand that the centrality of the incidental system has given the way to the direct method of review through which conflicts between State and Regions are adjudicated.

As for the relationship between ordinary judges and the Court, the original "American" features of the system are acquiring more force today. The Italian model of judicial review is becoming more diffuse and more concrete. Today, ordinary judges are playing a more important role: they not only have the power to refer

---

[18] The relation between the Constitutional Court and the European Union is discussed in detail in Chapter 7.

(or to refrain from referring) issues of constitutionality but are also called to apply the Constitution directly by means of the *interpretazione conforme a Costituzione*, as described earlier.

Why does the Constitutional Court encourage lower judges to assume such a broad and anti-formalistic approach to interpretation, an approach that apparently strips the Court of a portion of its power? The answer to this question lies partly in cultural reasons and partly in pragmatic ones. The Court favors the penetration of constitutional values into everyday life: the more an interpretation conforming to the Constitution progresses, the more constitutional values percolate through social life and become part of public discourse. On the pragmatic side, as previously mentioned, the judge's obligation to explore a statutory construction in conformity with the Constitution before referring the question to the Court can be considered one way of screening cases and controlling the Court's caseload.

The increasingly diffuse character of the Italian system of judicial review, and the concomitant loss of centrality of the Constitutional Court, can also be seen from a general European perspective. In fact, new powerful actors have become part of the institutional scene: namely, the two European Courts (the European Court of Human Rights and the Court of Justice of the European Union), both of which participate in the judicial review of national legislation, especially concerning individual rights.

Following the decisions of the European Court of Justice, especially the *Simmenthal* case of 1978 (see Chapter 7), ordinary judges in charge of specific disputes are empowered to disregard any domestic statute that contradicts the law of the European Union, without referring the question to the Constitutional Court. The Constitutional Court itself in 1984 confirmed this power of judicial review by ordinary Italian judges, within the scope of application of the law of the European Union.

As for the European Court of Human Rights, an important turning point was the adoption of Protocol n. 11 in 1998, which introduced the direct individual complaint. Since then, the European Court of Human Rights in Strasbourg, France, has become a seat of final review for many national cases involving human rights issues, a sort of European Supreme Court. Not surprisingly, since the introduction of the individual complaint, the number of cases pending before the Court has increased enormously; presently its docket is overloaded. Given this situation, many Contracting States have encouraged, in recent years, national judges, even at the lower level, to decide cases in light of the European Convention on Human Rights and in light of the case law of the European Court of Human Rights. The hope is that the more domestic judges take the case law of the European Court of Human Rights into account, the fewer cases will be brought to Strasbourg, thereby reducing the risks of condemnation for the Contracting States. As interpreters and guardians of the European Convention on Human Rights, ordinary judges and the European Court of Human Rights—not the Constitutional Court—are now becoming the leading actors on some of the most difficult and controversial cases on human rights, for example, abortion and euthanasia, same-sex marriage, artificial procreation, and freedom of religion and conscience. More precisely, with Judgments 348 and 349/2007, the Constitutional Court expressly established that the European Convention on Human Rights and the European Court of Human Rights' interpretations of it are "intermediate norms" (*norme interposte*), falling between statutory law and the Constitution, and that they can therefore be used as benchmarks in reviewing the constitutionality of a national statute.

In addition to becoming increasingly diffuse, the Italian system of judicial review is becoming more concrete. Since the early 1990s, the Constitutional Court has required ordinary judges to be extremely precise in their referral orders. Judges must describe the constitutional issue exactly, identify the contested statute and the allegedly violated constitutional norms, show that it is not possible to construct the statute in a way that makes it constitutionally valid, give exhaustive reasons about the merits of the question, and explain that the question is relevant to the decision of the case at hand. If the referral order does not satisfy these requirements, the issue is summarily dismissed through the *ordinanza di manifesta inammissibilità*. These details of the referral order strictly link the proceeding before the Constitutional Court to the case from which the constitutional issue originated. The Court thereby emphasizes the importance of the real case or controversy from which the question derives, and the result is a more concrete form of judicial review.

In the recent development of the Italian model of judicial review, the Constitutional Court is no longer a lonely actor in the institutional scenario, but also the incidental method has lost part of its importance—even though in the last few years a very new trend seems to be emerging, giving renewed importance to the incidental method. Two reasons can explain the previous decline in importance of the incidental method of judicial review.

First of all, as has been shown, the Constitutional Court discourages ordinary judges from referring many questions: they are instead encouraged to directly apply the Constitution themselves, although they are not allowed to set aside the piece of legislation that conflicts with the constitutional provisions. Second, constitutional reform reassessing the relationship between the central State and the Regions in 2001 created an unexpected increase in the number of direct complaints. As a result of the reform, the number of decisions rendered as a consequence of a direct method of judicial review rose from 2 percent in 2002 to 26.61 percent in 2011. For some years (between 2003 and 2006) most of the activity of the Court was devoted to solving problems of divisions of competences between different levels of government, more than to the guarantee of fundamental rights.[19]

Considering these trends and developments, how can we categorize the Italian system of judicial review today? Stressing the relationship between the Constitutional Court and ordinary judges, we could describe the model as rooted in a loyal cooperation: both the Justices and the judges play specific and important parts necessary for the smooth and correct functioning of the whole system of constitutional adjudication. If we also take into account the position of the Italian Constitutional Court with respect to the European Courts, we could moreover classify the Italian model as a composite system of judicial review, especially when it comes to the protection of fundamental rights.

---

[19] *See* statistical tables in Appendix III.

3 Forms and Methods of Judicial Reasoning

1. A Concurrent Plurality of Methods of Interpretation

While originalism, the idea of a "living" Constitution, and the use of foreign law in constitutional interpretation are hotly debated political matters in the United States, they are less controversial in Europe. Generally speaking, issues regarding the forms and methods of constitutional interpretation are less divisive in Italy than in the United States.

[handwritten: makes sense considering US political polarization]

Because the question of method is not an ideologically polarized one, it is common to find an originalist approach in the opinions of both progressive and conservative Justices of the Italian Constitutional Court. The same can be said about the use of transnational law, or the dynamic interpretation of the Constitution.

If a distinctive mark of the Italian Constitutional Court must be identified, it is that it tends to a "syncretistic" or "integrated" reasoning, using a combination of different approaches to constitutional interpretation. The text matters, but the Court does not stick strictly to a literal interpretation. The original intent can be important, but historical analysis alone has never been used as a conclusive argument to resolve a constitutional issue. Foreign law is often taken into account but does not control the decisions of the Court. Changes in the public opinion and the

[handwritten: foreign law > historical context is diff. from US.]

67

(margin handwritten note: diff from US which a [?]cular on specific clause)

legal interpretation adopted by lower courts (the so-called *diritto vivente*, that is "living law") do affect the Court's reasoning, but the Constitutional Court always maintains the last word rather than mechanically following the evolution of popular understanding. The Court does not disdain teleological interpretation, when necessary, nor does it consider the coherence with its own precedents irrelevant. Moreover, and more to the essential point, the Court interprets the Constitution as a whole, as an integrated system, avoiding the fragmented interpretation of a single provision detached from the context and the relationship with other principles, rules, and rights inscribed in the Constitution.

For example, in Judgment 200/2006—which deals with the pardon power of the President of the Republic (and that is discussed in detail in Chapter 5 because it gave rise to an important conflict between the President and the Executive)—history and custom are part of the reasoning, but the Constitutional Court's own precedents and the evolution of the purpose of the pardon power are also taken into consideration. The Court begins with an historical account of the issue:

> The power to grant pardons, formerly a personal prerogative of absolute sovereigns, essentially retained that character even after the advent of the Constitutional Monarchy, which attributed particular authority and prestige to the figure of the Monarch, since the ability to pardon punishment is the greatest sign of power. It was in this historical context that, in Italy, the power of the King to "grant pardon and commute sentences" was recognized, first in Art. 5 of the February 8, 1848 Decree (the act by which Carlo Alberto announced the promulgation of the Statute) and, later, in Art. 8 of the Statute itself. The prerogative was evidently understood as strictly connected to the features of "inviolability" and "sacredness" attributed to the person of the Monarch.
>
> Considering this, it was not by chance that the first Code of Criminal Procedure of the Kingdom of Italy (that of 1865) provided in Art. 826 that the "petitions for pardons of sentences" be "directed to the King and presented to the Minister of Grace and Justice". Thus the Code set a norm that, while it did not resolve the question of the nature of pardons (or who had the right to give them), nevertheless designated a place for dealing with the question that was outside the judicial sphere.

Then the Court surveys the debate of the Framers, following a sort of originalist approach:

> 5.2 Considering the transition from Monarchy to Republic and the concomitant shift in the institutional framework, it is important to recall the

salient point of the debate that took place during the Constituent Assembly, which led to the confirmation (in the text of the 1948 Constitution) that the Head of the State was entitled to power intimately connected (at least from a historical perspective) with the figure of the Monarch. Art. 87, eleventh paragraph of the Constitution, a provision virtually identical to Art. 8 of the Albertine Statute, provided that the President of the Republic could "grant pardons and commute sentences". The Constituent Assembly discussed the implications of this choice, laying particular emphasis on how the institution had evolved in the application of the Statute over time. In particular, the Assembly on the October 22, 1947 session, emphasized that the power to grant pardons, originally one of the "attributes . . . still personal in nature, leftover from among the rights proper to monarchs, without any involvement from other constitutional bodies", had progressively shifted even under the power of the Monarchy. From the principle that "the King pardons as an individual, and not as a representative of the State" we progressively passed to the recognition that "the Head of the State under the Monarchy, according to the Albertine Statute, has no personal power; all his powers are exercised to the extent that he is a representative of the State, and all are subject to the general principle of ministerial responsibility". Not by chance, the same 1948 constitutional framework reiterated the requirement that all acts of the President of the Republic must, on pain of invalidity, be countersigned by "proponent" Ministers (a term indistinguishable from "competent" Ministers, according to later interpretation). This led the Constituent Assembly to reject a proposal, advanced during the same October 22, 1947 session, to exclude presidential acts adopted "by prerogative" from the requirement of countersignature. . . .

The Court proceeds with a systematic or integrated interpretation of the Constitution, one that connects the presidential power of pardon with other provisions of the Constitution concerning the function of punishment, fundamental rights, and so forth:

In conclusion, the role of pardon is to implement constitutional values enshrined in the third paragraph of Art. 27 of the Constitution, above all granting that sense of "humanity" by which all sentences must be inspired (and which also assures full respect for the principle enshrined in Art. 2), without overlooking the "rehabilitative" element of punishment. This particular function of the pardon power appears to be consistent with constitutional jurisprudence. This Court, analyzing the institution of the "conditional" pardon, has observed that it performs a task "logically parallel to the personalization of punishment found in Art. 133 of the Criminal Code," and tends "to temper the rigor of the pure and simple application of criminal law through an act that is not mere clemency, but which, in harmony with the constitutional order, and in particular with Art. 27 of the Constitution, in some way favors correction of the criminal and his reintegration into the fabric of society" (Judgment 134/1976)......

Finally, the Court finds a place in its reasoning also for paying attention to the evolution of political and juridical practice with respect to the issue, over the history of the Republic:

6.2. A close examination of the practice of granting pardons after the adoption of the Constitutional Republic reveals, through government statistical data, that the institution—or, more precisely, the function it accomplishes—has continued to evolve.

If, indeed, frequent recourse was made to pardons until the 1980s, so much so that the idea of potentially applying it to prison policy was legitimized by 1986—coinciding, not by accident, with the enactment of Statute n. 663 of October 10, 1986 (Amendments to the law governing incarceration and the implementation of measures that deprive or restrict personal freedom)—then a significant transformation of its usage has occurred since. A telling comparison can be made, for example, between the 1,003 pardons granted in 1966 and the mere 104 granted in 1987, and this number has continued to decline, dwindling to a few dozen.

This change may be ascribed, as we noted above, to the introduction of legislation governing prison conditions and the implementation of custodial sentences based on the conviction that the need to routinely adjust criminal sentences to account for peculiarities of individual cases—a need satisfied until that time almost exclusively through the use of pardon power—should be met using the tools provided by the criminal, criminal procedure, and penitentiary provisions of the law (e.g. parole, house arrest, community service, etc.), which are also more appropriate in that they restore the issue to the judicial purview.

As a result, pardon power has been restored to its role as an exceptional tool intended to remedy situations of extraordinary humanitarian need, correcting the practice that had cropped up as a result of certain missteps in the early decades of applying the constitutional provision of Art. 87, eleventh paragraph....

If Judgment 200/2006 represents a case in which the Court referred extensively—but not exclusively—to history, custom, and the evolution of the purpose of pardons, Judgment 1/2013 instead provides a very good example of the "integrated" interpretive approach of the Court, an approach that explicitly goes beyond textualism and seeks to take into account the coherence of the legal order as a whole. The case deals with the problem of the accidental recording of phone conversations between the President of the Republic and a Senator who was being investigated for possible involvement with organized crime. The facts of the case, which gave rise to a serious conflict between the President and the Judiciary, are again well described in Chapter 5. Here the Court begins with a textual analysis of the specific provisions at issue but moves beyond it, aiming more broadly at an interpretation in conformity with the Constitution as a whole:

> A mere textual exegesis of constitutional and state provisions is insufficient to resolve the present conflict of allocation of powers; instead it is necessary to consider the totality of constitutional principles which give rise to the position and role of President of the Republic within the Italian constitutional system.
>
> We note that all legal provisions must be interpreted in light of the Constitution, and not vice versa, in every jurisdiction (not only the Constitutional Court). Our fundamental Charter contains principles and rules, which not only apply to other sources of law and, therefore, condition state legislation, rendering it illegitimate in cases of conflict, but which also contribute to shaping that legislation through judges' need to attribute to all regulations the meaning that most closely adheres to constitutional parameters and to raise the question of legitimacy before this Court only when insurmountable textual barriers make it impossible to identify a conforming interpretation (Judgment 356/1996). Naturally, this Court, as judge over the laws, must be animated by the same principle.
>
> A judicial interpretation's conformity with the Constitution cannot be limited to a merely textual or literal comparison between the legislative regulation under interpretation and the applicable constitutional norm.

Therefore, the Court requires an integrated interpretation that considers the Constitution as a whole:

> The Constitution consists, most importantly, of principles that are tightly interconnected and balanced among themselves, and any evaluation of constitutional compliance must be carried out in light of the whole complex, rather

than individual clauses considered in isolation. A fragmented interpretation of a provision, whether constitutional or legislative, runs the risk of creating paradoxical outcomes in many cases, with the result that it would contradict its own protective purpose.

In this broad and integrated interpretive approach, the Constitutional Court also takes into consideration the European Convention on Human Rights (ECHR), as interpreted by the European Court of Human Rights (ECtHR) in Strasbourg (and as incorporated into the Italian legal system via Article 117 of the Constitution), in order to reach a comprehensive and balanced protection of fundamental rights. A good example of this approach can be found in Judgment 170/2013. In this case, the Bankruptcy Court of Florence challenged part of a 2011 statute, which had some negative retroactive effects on private parties, as a violation of Articles 3 and 117 of the Italian Constitution and of Article 6 of the ECHR.

What the referring judge has found unconstitutional must be examined holistically, such that Art. 6 of the European Convention on Human Rights, as applied by the European Court of Human Rights, be read in connection with the other constitutional provisions, in this case Art. 3, in keeping with constitutional jurisprudence when dealing with the efficacy of ECHR rules under Judgments 348 and 349 of 2007. Indeed, this Court has held that "the ECHR provision, as soon as it satisfies the conditions of Art. 117 of the Constitution, as a *norma interposta*, becomes subject to the balancing function regularly applied by this Court in all judgments within its jurisdiction" in order to achieve the necessary "integration of protections" (Judgment 264/2012), which it is this Court's unique responsibility to ensure. Therefore, even when ECHR provisions implicate Art. 117, first paragraph of the Constitution, evaluating their constitutionality "must be carried out in light of the whole complex, and not individual clauses considered in isolation", since "a fragmented interpretation of a provision . . . runs the risk of creating paradoxical outcomes in many cases, with the result that it would contradict its own protective purpose" (Judgment 1/2013). In other words, this Court performs a "systematic and not fragmented" evaluation of the rights implicated by the provision under scrutiny, and effects the balance necessary to assure the "maximum expansion of protection" of all relevant rights and principles, constitutional and transnational, considered as a whole and always in a relationship of reciprocal integration (Judgments 85/2013 and 264/2012).

This methodology leads the Constitutional Court to focus on the ECtHR case law on retroactive legislation.[1]

4.3 Turning to the case at bar, the principles described above reveal, first and foremost, that "the prohibition of retroactivity of laws (Art. 11 of the "Rules on the Law in General" [Conflicts of Laws]), albeit a fundamental feature of the rule of law, does not receive the privileged protection under the law given to Art. 25 of the Constitution," which is reserved for criminal matters. As a consequence, "the Legislature may, with respect to this provision, issue laws with effective retroactivity, even under an authentic interpretation, provided that the retroactivity finds adequate justification in the need to protect principles, rights, and goods of constitutional significance", which amount to "compelling reasons of general interest" under the ECHR (among many *see* Judgment 78/2012).

Even so, it is required that retroactivity not conflict with other constitutionally protected values and concerns (*see* Judgments 93/2011 and 41/2011). This Court has articulated a series of general limitations on the retroactive effectiveness of laws dealing with the protection of constitutional principles and other values of rule of law. These include "respect for the general principle of reasonableness, which is reflected in the prohibition of unjustified discrepancies in treatment; protection of citizens' legitimate expectations as a principle inherent to the rule of law; coherence and certainty in the legal order; [and] respect for the functions constitutionally reserved to the Judiciary" (*see* Judgments 78/2012 and 209/ 2010).

In situations comparable to the instant case, this Court has already stated that a retroactive regulation cannot betray the expectations of private individuals, especially those arising with reinforcement from significant circumstances, even if the regulation is necessary to restrain public expenditure or to address exceptional events (*see* Judgments 24/2009, 374/2002, 419/2000).

4.4. The principles concerning retroactive laws in the jurisprudence of the European Court of Human Rights, in reference to Art. 6 of the ECHR, are nearly identical, and are also applied to address conflicts of procedure, as in certain decisions of the European Court regarding Italy (*Bassani v. Italy*, December 11, 2003; *Ceteroni v. Italy*, November 15, 1996).

With specific regard to Italian retroactive laws, the European Court has repeatedly held, as a matter of principle, that the legislature is not prohibited

---

[1] In other cases, however, the two courts have reached different conclusions. On this point of convergences and divergences between the Italian Court and the European Court of Human Rights, see Chapter 7.

from generating new civil regulations with retroactive scope concerning rights derived from laws already in force, but the principle of preeminence of the law and the notion of due process set forth in Art. 6 of the ECHR prevent the legislature from interfering in the administration of justice to the point of influencing the judicial outcome of a dispute, unless for compelling reasons of general interest (*De Rosa v. Italy*, December 11, 2012; *Arras v. Italy*, February 14, 2012; *Agrati v. Italy*, June 7, 2011; *Maggio v. Italy*, May 31, 2011; *Bortesi v. Italy*, June 10, 2008; *Scordino v. Italy*, Grand Chamber, March 29, 2006). The European Court has also remarked that the circumstances cited to justify retroactive measures must be interpreted in a restrictive sense (*Arras v. Italy*, February 14, 2012) and that the State's financial interests alone do not justify retroactive intervention (*Lilly France v. France*, November 25, 2010; *Scanner de l'Ouest Lyonnais v. France*, June 21, 2007; *Chiesi S.A. v. France*, January 16, 2007; *Arnolin v. France*, January 9, 2007; *Cabourdin v. France*, April 11, 2006).

Conversely, the stage of a proceeding and extent of fact-finding, the unforseeability of the new law, and the possibility that the State is a party to the dispute are all elements the European Court considers in judging whether a retroactive law violates ECHR Art. 6: Judgment *Ogis Institut Stanislas v. France*, May 27, 2004; *Papageorgiou v. Greece*, October 26, 1997; *National & Provincial Building Society v. United Kingdom*, October 23, 1997. These decisions, even if not directly involving Italy, contain general assertions that the European Court considers applicable beyond the specific case, and that this Court considers binding on the Italian system as well.

[T]hese principles derived from case law, developed by this Court as well as the European Court, dictate a declaration of unconstitutionality.

2. Reasonableness, Proportionality, and Balancing of Values

One of the most recurring themes in the legal reasoning of the Italian Constitutional Court is the scrutiny based on reasonableness and proportionality. The concept of reasonableness was first used for the construction of the principle of equality, but it has come to have a more broad meaning. Generally speaking, the concept of reasonableness is used in a way that is ancillary to many other constitutional principles and this renders it a pervasive concept in constitutional adjudication.

In Italian case law, reasonableness and proportionality are often used as synonyms. Unlike other constitutional courts, the Italian Constitutional Court uses the words "rationality," "reasonableness," "proportionality," "adequacy," "coherence," and "congruity" interchangeably. A very clear example is offered by the following excerpt from Judgment 2/1999, a case in which the Court strikes down a provision because it is:

> Not *reasonable* and it contrasts with the principle of *proportionality*, which is the core of *rationality*, which is itself part of the principle of *equality*. [Emphasis added.]

in common law (US), proportionality = different from reasonableness

This is all the more relevant because in some other legal systems reasonableness and proportionality correspond to two different levels of scrutiny. Generally speaking, in the common law tradition, scrutiny based on reasonableness (or rationality) is very respectful of the legislature, and it simply allows courts to remove a provision that it is so manifestly unreasonable it contains no common sense. On the other hand, reasoning based on proportionality often follows a structured test, typically encompassing four steps. In the first step, the court must verify whether the legislative body has acted for a legitimate purpose, a purpose not in conflict with constitutional principles. In the second step, the court evaluates whether there is a "rational connection" between legislative means and ends. In the third step, the court must ascertain whether the legislative body has used the "least restrictive means"; that is, it must ascertain whether the legislative act pursues its goal in a way that infringes as little as possible on fundamental constitutional rights. The fourth and final step takes into account the effects of the legislative act and the court must therefore compare its costs and benefits; the last phase is extremely difficult and requires the judge to open her mind and consider the impact of the legislative act on the real world.

This well-structured proportionality test was first born in the Prussian courts and then transplanted into European law, becoming a standard used in all sorts of controversies at a global level. It can be described as a fundamental feature of the new contemporary constitutionalism. Nevertheless, when it comes to the reasoning of the Italian Constitutional Court, such a formally structured proportionality test cannot be found. The Italian Court prefers an informal interpretive approach, an approach to proportionality not articulated in a rigid sequence of progressive steps.

The Italian Constitutional Court often uses a reasoning based on reasonableness and proportionality in cases where fundamental rights must be balanced. Balancing rights is extremely important in the interpretation of a pluralist Constitution like the Italian one, in which rights are not established in absolute terms, but are all interrelated as part of a complex fabric. In the Italian Constitution, each right is limited by the others and therefore an interpretive approach that takes into account different conflicting interests is indispensable in order to reach a reasonable equilibrium between competing values.

A clear and interesting example of the Italian pluralistic approach to the protection of inviolable rights is Judgment 85/2013.[2] In this complex environmental case, the Court of Taranto, in the Apulia Region, ordered the closure of one of the most important steel mills in Europe, because it severely threatened the health not only of the workers but of the surrounding population. The clash of two different sets of rights reached the Constitutional Court. On one side were the rights to health and to a safe environment; on the other side, could be found the right to work of a great number of people and the right to free economic activity.

The rationale of the discipline in question consists of the realization of a reasonable balance between the fundamental rights protected by the Constitution, in particular [the right] to health (Art. 32 of the Constitution), from which the right to a healthy environment is derived, and [the right] to work (Art. 4 of the Constitution), from which are derived the constitutionally relevant interests to maintain employment and the need for public institutions to explain [their] every effort to do so.

All of the fundamental rights protected by the Constitution find themselves in a relationship of reciprocal integration and it is not therefore possible to pinpoint one that has an absolute dominance over the others. The protection must always be "systematic and not fragmented into a series of uncoordinated and possibly self-conflicting norms" (Judgment 264/2012). If it were not so, the unlimited expansion of one of the rights would occur, [and this right] would become "the tyrant" in comparison to other constitutionally recognized and [constitutionally] protected judicial situations, which constitute, as a whole, the expression of the dignity of the person.

For these express reasons, we cannot share the referring judge's hypothesis regarding the preliminary investigation according to which the [presence of the] adjective "fundamental" contained in Art. 32 of the Constitution, would be a tell-tale sign that the right to health has a "dominant characteristic" with respect to every other right of the person. Neither can the definition of the environment and of health as "primary values" given by this Court (Judgment 365/1993) cited by the referring judge, imply a "rigid" hierarchy between fundamental rights. The Italian Constitution, like other contemporary democratic pluralist constitutions, requires a continuous and mutual balancing between principles and fundamental rights, without a pretense of absoluteness for any of them. Therefore, the qualification of the values of the environment and of health as "primary" signifies that these same cannot be sacrificed to other interests, even if [these interests are] constitutionally protected; [it does] not [signify] that these interests are placed at the summit of an absolute hierarchical order. The point of equilibrium, for the very reason that it is dynamic and not pre-arranged ahead of time, must be evaluated—by the legislator in the adoption of the norms and by the Constitutional Court in reviewing them—according to the criteria of proportionality and reasonableness in order to not consent to a sacrifice of their essential nucleus.

From Judgment 85/2013 some important general features of the reasoning based on balancing can be drawn. First of all, no constitutional right has an absolute nature, but all rights must be balanced against each other. Second, there is no predetermined abstract hierarchy of fundamental rights, and balancing is a dynamic judgment that belongs in the first place to the legislative body and then to courts in their reviewing function. Moreover, balancing requires a judgment based on reasonableness and proportionality and cannot be limited to a pure abstract judicial syllogism. Finally, the result of balancing can never consist of the complete sacrifice of one right in favor of other constitutional rights and principles, because the essential core of each right must be preserved. In sum, the balancing of fundamental rights must tend toward the optimization of the protection of fundamental rights and principles; that is, to the "maximum expansion of protection" of every right involved.

Some of the important principles affirmed in Judgment 85/2013 were maintained again in a recent and very complex tax case. In Judgment 10/2015 the Court held that the Constitution must be interpreted in its entirety and that all rights must be reasonably balanced against each other. The Court also added a fundamental principle regarding the temporal effects of its decisions and explicitly recognized the power of limiting the retroactive impact of its judgments.[3]

7.—In declaring the challenged provisions unconstitutional, this Court must duly consider the impact that such a declaration will have on other constitutional principles, in order to assess the need for special temporal effects of the ruling on pending legal relationships.

The role entrusted to this Court as guardian of the Constitution in its entirety requires that it avoid situations where declaring a provision unconstitutional paradoxically results in "effects that are still less compatible with the Constitution" (Judgment 13/2004) than the ones that provoked the constitutional challenge. To avoid such an occurrence, the Court has a duty to modify its decisions, including their temporal impact, in such a way as to ensure that

---

[3] On the temporal effects of judgments, see *infra*, section 4.

the affirmation of one constitutional principle does not result in the sacrifice of another. [. . .]

The institutional task entrusted to this Court requires that it safeguard the Constitution as a unitary whole, so as to ensure "systematic and not fragmented" protection of all the rights and principles implicated by the decision (Judgment 264/2012). "If it were not so, the unlimited expansion of one of the rights would occur, [and this right] would become 'the tyrant' in comparison to other constitutionally recognized and [constitutionally] protected judicial situations." For this reason, the Court regularly carries out a reasonable balancing of the values implicated by the norms referred to it, given that "[t]he Italian Constitution, like other contemporary democratic pluralist constitutions, requires a continuous and mutual balancing between principles and fundamental rights, without a pretense of absoluteness for any of them" (Judgment 85/2013). [. . .]

The needs dictated by a reasonable balancing of relevant rights and principles will determine the choice of judgment technique employed by the Court: just as a ruling of unconstitutionality can be limited to only certain elements of a provision under review—as is the case, for example, with judgments of a "manipulative" nature—likewise, the modification of the Court's interventions may concern the temporal aspects of the challenged norm, limiting the effects of a ruling of unconstitutionality vis-à-vis the timing of its application. [. . .]

Considering the general principle of retroactivity found in Art. 136 of the Constitution and Art. 30 of Law n. 87 of 1953, this Court's regulation of the temporal effects of a judgment must naturally be evaluated in light of the principle of strict proportionality. Any such regulation must, therefore, be strictly conditioned upon the existence of two clear prerequisites: the urgent necessity to protect one or more constitutional principles that would be irreparably compromised by merely upholding the claim, and the limitation of retroactive effects only to what is strictly necessary to ensure due consideration of the values at stake.

3. The Use of Transnational Law and Comparative Method

Legal transplants, legal fluxes, legal grafts, the circulation of legal models, and more recently cross-fertilization, cross-pollination, and the migration of legal ideas have been common concepts for many years among comparative lawyers. The traditional vocabulary entails a legal system that "exports" and one that "imports" legal notions (e.g., judicial review, rule of law) or even entire codes or constitutions. The story of the migration of the French Code Civil or, to a lesser extent, the German Civil Code is well known. Also well known is the use of foreign constitutions as models in the process of constitution-making. One prominent historical model has been the U.S. Constitution, in particular its Bill of Rights; however, the Canadian Charter of Rights and Freedoms has, in recent years, become a leading alternative, and has influenced the drafting of the South African Bill of Rights, the Israeli Basic Law, the New Zealand Bill of Rights, and the Hong Kong Bill of Rights. As Jon Elster, commenting on the Eastern European experience with constitution building, has observed: "in constitutional debates, one invariably finds a large number of references to other constitutions" not only "as models to be imitated" but also "as disaster to be avoided, or simply as evidence for certain views about human nature."[4]

Today, instead, particularly if one considers constitutional courts and supranational courts such as the Court of Justice of the European Union and the European Court of Human Rights, a more dialogical form of relationship between different constitutional systems is emerging. The interaction among different legal systems has become less hierarchical, and judges no longer simply receive the cases of other jurisdictions and then apply or modify them for their own jurisdiction. Instead, judges around the world are building on each other's opinions in a manner that fosters mutual respect. Comparative law, the comparative method, is becoming today an increasingly common tool for interpreting domestic constitutional law.

This is nothing new. In 1989 Peter Häberle wrote about the "open dimension" of fundamental rights, noting that this open dimension favored the growth of a community of interpreters of fundamental international rights that was using the comparative method as a fifth method of interpretation, adding a new one to the four traditional methods evidenced long ago by Friedrich Carl von Savigny.[5] Häberle helped us to connect the dialogic and open attitude of courts with fundamental and human rights. In fact, judges tend to look outside their own legal order when they have to decide hard cases, when they have to decide, in the words of a former Justice of the Italian Constitutional Court, Gustavo Zagrebelsky, "fundamental aspects of fundamental rights" such as the death penalty, gay rights, affirmative action, reproductive freedom, and end-of-life choices.[6] Nevertheless, when rights are highly controversial—as in these cases—the Italian Constitutional Court is also oriented in verifying if there is a general "consensus" rather than looking to other particular

---

[4] J. Elster, *Constitutionalism in Eastern Europe: An Introduction*, 58 U. Chi. L. Rev. 447, 476 (1991).

[5] P. Häberle, *Grundrechtsgeltung und Grundrechtsinterpretation in Verfassungsstaat*, in *Juristen Zeitung*, 1989, p. 913 ff.

[6] G. Zagrebelsky, *La legge e la sua giustizia*, Bologna, Il Mulino, 2008, p. 403.

experiences. If a clear consensus is not yet formed, courts such as the Italian one are sometimes jealous of the peculiarities of their own constitutional system.

National courts talk with each other, but obviously there are courts more open to dialogue than others. Among the former, the Supreme Court of Canada and the Constitutional Tribunal of South Africa are well known: different historical and institutional reasons can explain the particular attitude of the two countries. Not equally well known is, for example, the openness of the constitutional courts of Hungary and Taiwan. The Delhi High Court and the Supreme Court of Israel also offer important examples of transjudicial dialogue.

In the United States, a singular and bitter debate is currently taking place involving both scholars and judges, between those who favor using comparative law in constitutional interpretation and those who completely reject doing so.

In Europe the scenario, as already noted, is not as ideologically divisive as in the United States and can vary from France, where the style of the decisions of the *Cour de Cassation* does not leave much room for reasoning of any sort, to Germany or England (especially after the enactment of the Human Rights Act) where the comparative method is often used.

It can also be said that in Europe transjudicial constitutional dialogue often concerns methodological issues and legal reasoning more than the merits of the case. A clear example of judicial fertilization is the principle of proportionality discussed above. Another clear example in recent years in Europe is the use of preliminary ruling.[7] Whereas for a long time the constitutional courts have been very reluctant to interact with the Court of Justice of the European Union by means of preliminary ruling, in the last few years, almost all of them (Austrian, Belgian, Italian, Spanish, French, German) have engaged a direct conversation with the Luxembourg Court.

As for Italy, the highest ordinary court, the Court of Cassation, usually does not look explicitly at foreign case law, although there is a relatively recent opinion where the comparative method was extensively used in an end-of-life case.[8] The Constitutional Court, on the other hand, often prepares its decisions taking into account foreign law. It has even organized a special unit of the Court's "study and research office" specially devoted to comparative study. However, in the texts of its judgments it typically gives only very minor importance to comparative argument among the many methods of interpretation that it uses in its syncretic approach to the Constitution.

For example, the Court was recently called to verify the constitutionality of a statute that made illegal immigration a criminal offence, punishable with a fine and

---

[7] Art. 267, TFUE.

[8] Corte di Cassazione, sez. I civile, 16 ottobre 2007, n. 21748. The case is discussed in Chapter 4, section 5.

with expulsion from the country. The documents prepared in order to reach the decision included a thorough examination of foreign law (German, British, French, Spanish, Greek, Danish, Finnish, Portuguese, American), but Judgment 250/2010 made only a cursory mention of this research, in spite of the influence it probably had on the decision.

A recent and important decision in which the Italian Constitutional Court made more significant reference to foreign jurisprudence, most notably to the German *Bundesverfassungsgericht hof,* is Judgment 1/2014. In this complex case, the Court of Cassation challenged parts of the electoral law—primarily those providing a "majority bonus" (*premio di maggioranza*)—which were eventually struck down.[9]

Because the mechanism for attributing the majority bonus provided for in the challenged provisions, which are part of the proportional election system introduced by Law 270/2005, is not accompanied by a reasonable minimum threshold of votes needed to compete for the bonus, it is, therefore, able to interfere with the democratic process as outlined in our Constitution and based on the fundamental principle of vote equality (Art. 48, second paragraph, Const.). While not binding the legislator to a particular choice of system, the principle of vote equality requires that each vote be a potential contributor, and with equal weight, to the formation of the elective bodies (Judgment 43/1961) and assumes different implications, depending on the electoral system that has been selected. In constitutional systems analogous to the Italian one, which subscribe to the aforementioned principle and do not have a constitutionalized electoral formula, constitutional judges have long expressly recognized that when a legislature adopts the proportional system, even partially, this creates a legitimate expectation in the voter that there will be no resulting imbalance in the effect of the votes—that is, an unequal evaluation of the "weight" of the resulting vote, for the purpose of assigning parliamentary seats, unless it is necessary to avoid parliamentary malfunctions (*Bundesverfassungsgericht hof,* Judgment 3/11 of July 25, 2012; but see also Judgment 197 of May 22, 1979, and Judgment 1 of April 5, 1952).

In order to properly appreciate the influence of other legal systems on the Italian Constitutional Court, a further element should be taken into account. Because of the European mandate entrenched in the Italian Constitution (Arts. 11 and 117, first paragraph), the legal reasoning of the Court often borrows rules and principles from European legislation and from the case law of the European Courts, including the Court of Justice of the European Union and the European Court of Human Rights. Moreover, the Court considers and mentions those European legal materials even when the rationale of its decision is not, strictly speaking, grounded

---

[9] This case will be extensively discussed in the next section.

on them. European judgments are often quoted for the sake of argument, and in a great number of opinions the Italian Constitutional Court offers an overview of the European principles related to the subject at stake. This implies that the Constitutional Court is wide open to the *direct* influence of European law, and, by means of it, to the *indirect* influence of other foreign legislation. In fact, supranational European legal principles often assemble and distill the experiences of all of the Member States of the European Union or the Council of Europe. In a word, an intense circulation of legal values is active in Europe, not only through horizontal contacts among different countries but also through the mediation of supranational European institutions.

4. The Decisions of the Constitutional Court and Their Effects

The characteristic and distinctive forms of judicial reasoning employed in the Constitutional Court do not only result from the methods and tools of constitutional interpretation but also from the range of different—and to jurists of other systems sometimes unusual—kinds of decisions that it is capable of issuing. Understanding the jurisprudence of the Court in any substantive area requires having a basic grasp of the variety of forms and effects of its decisions in general.

The Court can issue orders (*ordinanze*) or judgments (*sentenze*). Generally speaking, orders are only briefly reasoned and are similar to *per curiam* opinions, whereas judgments are fully reasoned. As already stated, no separate opinions are allowed: the decision always appears on its face as the decision of the whole Court.

If, in a case raised through the incidental method (see Chapter 2), the Court considers the question to be clearly irrelevant to the disposition of the case from which it is referred, or in case of other procedural and formal defects, it will issue an order of inadmissibility (*ordinanza di inammissibilità*). If the Court considers the question manifestly unfounded, once again it will issue an order (*ordinanza di manifesta infondatezza*). In both instances, the Court will send the question back to the judge *a quo*.

When the Court proceeds to examine the merits of the question, its judgment will either reject the constitutional challenge (*sentenza di rigetto*) or sustain it (*sentenza di accoglimento*).

When the decision of the Court rejects the constitutional challenge, the referring judge must apply the contested law to the case at hand, but the decision rejecting the challenge does not prevent it from being raised again, even at a different stage of the same proceeding. This kind of judgment is not, therefore, universally binding as it is only effective between the parties (*inter partes*).

On the contrary, a decision sustaining the challenge of constitutionality has *erga omnes* effects. In other words, the law is invalidated for everyone and always, just as if a subsequent statute had abrogated it. In fact (and as already discussed in Chapter 1), according to Article 136 of the Constitution, a law declared unconstitutional through a *sentenza di accoglimento* "ceases to have effect on the day following the publication of the decision." Nevertheless, the decision ends up having retroactive effects because it is applied to the case that originated the question, and to all other pending cases (although the need for certainty and stability protects so-called "consolidated effects"—such as that of *res judicata*). In the more specific context of criminal cases, Law 87/1953 provides that:

> When an irrevocable conviction is handed down under a law that is declared unconstitutional, its execution and all its penal effects cease.

Even when a judgment upholds the constitutional challenge and therefore the statute is declared unconstitutional, in cases arising from the incidental method of review, the Constitutional Court decides the issue of constitutionality but not the case itself. The fact that the Court decides only the issue and not the case, explains why the Italian system, even though a hybrid model as described in the previous chapter, still cannot be considered as "concrete" as, for instance, the American one.

Opinions that either reject or sustain a constitutional challenge have a fairly defined, standard structure, which is divided into three parts. In the first part (known as *in fatto*), the question of constitutionality is summed up as presented by the referring judge and the statements of the parties are briefly reported. In the second part (known as *in diritto*), the Court explains its position regarding the issue of relevance and, generally, the merits of the case. In the third and final part (known as *dispositivo*), the Court summarizes the content of its decision, that is, its judgment; if the decision sustains the challenge, the final part will declare the constitutional invalidity of the contested statute; if the decision rejects the challenge, the final part will explain the reasons why the doubts of the referring judge are unfounded.

Within this relatively straightforward framework, the Court has developed in its case law several other types of decisions due to the need to consider the impact of its decisions on the legal system as a whole and on the other branches of Government, especially Parliament and the Judiciary.

The development of a very nuanced typology of decisions was made possible by the theoretical distinction between *disposizione* and *norma*, that is, legal "text" and "norm." A text represents a linguistic expression that mirrors the will of the body that produces a specific legal act. A "norm," on the other hand, is the result of a process of interpretation of the text. By the use of hermeneutic techniques, one can derive multiple norms from a single text or a single norm from multiple texts. The distinction between text and norm is particularly important in that it permits the separation of the norm from the literal meaning of the text, severing in a way the link that joined them when the text was first approved. Moreover, the distinction allows the system to evolve, facilitating the interpreter's creativity and helping to reduce the "destructive" and "negative" effects of the Court's decisions, with its consequent gaps in the legal system, and giving it the ability to operate in a more subtle way. The sophisticated theory behind the distinction between *disposizione* and *norma* also helps explain why the discourse on constitutional interpretation in Italy is so different from the one in the United States.

The most important decisions in which the Constitutional Court distinguishes between text and norm are the *sentenze interpretative* (interpretive judgments). There are two kinds of *sentenze interpretative: interpretative di rigetto* and *interpretative di accoglimento.*

With the *sentenze interpretative di rigetto*, the Court shows the referring judge an alternative interpretation (norm) in accord with the Constitution and thus rejects the constitutional challenge. The Court in the last two decades has increasingly demanded a similar legal effort from the same ordinary judges: to seek constructions that save challenged statutes from unconstitutionality. A good example of *sentenza interpretativa di rigetto* is Judgment 308/2008. In this case, the Court of Appeal of Bologna and the Trial Courts of Firenze and Ragusa challenged the constitutionality of Article 155-*quarter* of the Civil Code as amended by Statute 54/2006, which modified the rules regulating the relationship between parents and children in divorce cases.

The contested article established that when the parent who is given the custody of the children is also accorded the right to live in the family home, such right is automatically withdrawn if the parent lives with another partner *more uxorio* (i.e., as a conjugal partner but without getting married) or if the parent remarries. The fact that the judge could not take into consideration the best interests of the child but "automatically" had to revoke the assignment of the family home, was considered by the referring judges to be a violation of the principle of equality and of Articles 29 and 30 of the Constitution. The Court preserved Article 155-*quarter* by giving it an interpretation consistent with the Constitution.

> In a constitutional analysis, declaring a norm invalid is justified where no possible interpretation conforms to the Constitution, not where there is a mere possibility of attributing to it a meaning which contradicts constitutional parameters. . . .

In this legal and jurisprudential context, we note that not only the assignment of the family home, but also its revocation has always (even where the law is silent) been subject to an evaluation on the part of the judge that takes into account the best interests of the offspring.

It follows that Art. 155 of the Civil Code, when interpreted literally to mean that the remarriage or cohabitation *more uxorio* of the recipient of the house are sufficient criteria, in and of themselves, for revoking the assignment of the house, is not consistent with the aim of protecting the offspring, for whom the institution exists.

The coherence of the regulation and its constitutionality may be restored if it is interpreted to mean not that the assignment of the conjugal home is revoked as a matter of law upon proof of the specified events (the establishment of a cohabitation in fact, a new marriage), but that the revocation is subject to a judgment which conforms to the interests of the minor children.

Such a reading only serves to highlight a principle already present in the law and allows for a meaning which conforms to constitutional parameters, as various lower court judges and prevalent scholars have already held.

For these reasons

The Constitutional Court

Declares unfounded, *within the limits described in this opinion*, the question of the constitutionality of Art. 155, first paragraph, of the Civil Code, introduced by Art. 1, second paragraph, of Statute n. 54 of February 8, 2006 (texts dealing with separation of parents and shared custody of children), even if read in conjunction with Article 4 of the same Statute, which was raised, in reference to Art. 2, 3, 29 and 30 of the Constitution, by the Court of Appeal of Bologna, by the Trial Court of Florence, and by the Trial Court of Ragusa, with the orders cited in the epigraph. [Emphasis added.]

On the other hand, with the *sentenze interpretative di accoglimento*, the Court considers the interpretation given by the referring judge to be in conflict with the Constitution and therefore strikes down the norm deriving from that specific interpretation, but not the text of the law itself. Whereas the *sentenze interpretative di rigetto* are often used, the *sentenze interpretative di accoglimento* are rarely used at present, although the Court used them more commonly in the past.

It must be specified here that when the case law of ordinary courts, and especially that of the Supreme Court of Cassation, uniformly adopts a given interpretation of a statute, the Constitutional Court accepts that interpretation as "living law" (*diritto vivente*). Consequently, the Constitutional Court decides the question, taking for granted that the interpretation at issue is the correct one and thus when the Court finds it unconstitutional declares the statute null and void on its face rather than simply declaring unconstitutional the norm deriving from that particular interpretation.

Even though the Constitutional Court generally does not impose its own interpretation over that of the Court of Cassation in order to avoid the so-called "war of the courts," the interpretive decisions have been questioned in general because they do impose on ordinary judges certain readings of the law—a function that is conventionally regarded as being within the proper competence of ordinary courts, not the Constitutional Court.

Certain other types of decisions have raised even greater questions regarding the scope of the Constitutional Court's competence. Cases in which the Court declares the unconstitutionality of a statute insofar as (1) it does not cover something for which it should provide, and thus the Court adds to the statute (*sentenze additive*); (2) it does cover something that it should not provide for, thus the Court removes something from the statute (*sentenze ablative*); or (3) it covers one thing rather than something else, and thus the Court substitutes something in the statute (*sentenze sostitutive*). These types of decisions arguably encroach on the sovereignty of Parliament, even if they have been developed in order to fill gaps or reconcile contradictions in the legal system without resorting to the blunt and disruptive remedy of nullifying altogether an entire law.

The *sentenze additive* are frequently used. A good example is Judgment 203/2013 in which the Court decided the constitutionality of Article 45, fifth paragraph, of Decree Law 151/2001 regulating measures in favor of parenthood. That article provided that a severely disabled person's cohabiting partner, parents, children, or siblings are entitled to a leave of absence from work in order to care for that person. The Administrative Tribunal of the Calabria Region challenged Article 45 as in conflict with various articles of the Constitution because it did not provide the leave for a nephew who wanted to take care of an uncle with whom he lived. The Constitutional Court declared the statute invalid, in light of its legislative history and its scope, insofar as it failed to consider other persons (including a nephew) entitled to leave from work.

> The validity of the question before the Court concerning the constitutional legitimacy of a portion of Art. 2, fifth paragraph, of Decree Law 151/2001 derives from the normative and jurisprudential evolution that has taken place up to the present day, the legislative *ratio* that has emerged from it, and, above all, the constitutional principles that are implicated by extraordinary leave. In particular, the part describing the category of persons legally entitled to exercise the leave described does not include third-degree relatives by marriage

(or, for obvious reasons of coherence and reasonableness, other close relatives and relatives by marriage within three degrees of relation) who live with and can care for the individual in circumstances of grave disability, in the case of the absence, death, or debilitation of the persons indicated by the law according to an order of priority, in violation of Art. 2, 3, 29, 32, and 118, fourth paragraph, of the Constitution.

The limits presently established for the persons entitled to take care of the disabled person, in fact, compromise the assistance available to people with grave disabilities in the family environment, since none of the listed persons may be available or in a suitable condition to act as caregiver. The declaration of unconstitutionality is designed to allow that, in the case of the absence, death, or debilitation of the other persons mentioned in the challenged text, and respecting the rigorous order of priority established therein, a relative by blood or by marriage, within three degrees, living with the disabled person, may provide for his or her needs, suspending work activities for a determinate period of time and benefitting from sufficient economic stability.

For these reasons

The Constitutional Court

Declares Art. 42, fifth paragraph, of Decree Law n. 151 of March 25, 2001 (the only portion of the legislative text that deals with protection and support of maternity and paternity, as established by Art. 15 of Statute n. 53 of March 8, 2000) *to be unconstitutional where it fails to include*, in the category of persons legally entitled to avail themselves of the provided-for leave and conditions, third-degree relatives by blood or marriage living with and able to take care of a person in circumstances of grave disability, in case of the absence, death, or debilitation of other persons mentioned in the challenged text. . . . [Emphasis added.]

In some cases (although very rarely by comparison to some other constitutional courts), the Italian Court may decide to start a sort of dialogue with the legislature either by deferring the effects of the declaration of unconstitutionality to a later moment and giving Parliament time to remove the unconstitutional law (*sentenze di incostituzionalità differita*), or by provisionally assenting to the constitutionality of a law, waiting for its repeal as expressly announced by the legislator itself, and postponing the declaration of unconstitutionality to a later moment in case of inaction (*sentenze di costituzionalità provvisoria*). The problem that this type of decision is designed to address, postponing the declaration to assure that the Government and Parliament have time to fill the gap created by the Court when it strikes down a statute, is not unique to the Italian legal system.[10] Comparative analysis offers several examples. The Austrian Constitutional Court can postpone the effect of a judgment nullifying a law for up to one year, thereby allowing Parliament to re-legislate the subject matter and avoid gaps. The German Federal Constitutional Court can also declare laws "incompatible" (*Unvereinbarkeit*), without declaring them null and void. This situation closely recalls the declaration of incompatibility that English judges may pronounce following Section 4 of the Human Rights Act. The German Court can also declare a law "still" constitutional. In this case the law is only temporarily constitutional while the Court retains the power to declare it permanently unconstitutional if the legislature does not modify it to conform to its judgment.[11]

Another case in which the Court decides engaging in a sort of dialogue with the legislative body is that of the *sentenza additiva di principio*. This form of judgment finds a statute unconstitutional insofar as it does not provide for something that should have been provided for and sets forth the general principle that Parliament must follow when regulating the subject matter again. In other words, the judgment establishes that Parliament has a duty to legislate and that in so doing must follow the principle laid down by the Court. Moreover, ordinary judges will also be bound by the Court's principle pending the new legislation. An interesting example of *sentenza additiva di principio* is Judgment 385/2005. In this case, the Trial Court of Sondrio challenged the constitutionality of Decree Law 151/2011, regulating measures in favor of parenthood. The contested provisions established that parental leave in the case of adoption must be granted to professional self-employed mothers but not to professional self-employed fathers, while with respect to salaried workers there was no distinction between father and mother. The Constitutional Court held these provisions unconstitutional because they did not follow the "principle" that fathers must always have the same treatment as mothers.

6. Decree Law 151/2001 has textually afforded the right to a benefit to the adoptive father or guardian who is an employee, excluding freelance professionals who, therefore, cannot avail themselves of the leave or the benefit instead of the mother.

---

[10] The issue of the temporal effects of judgments of unconstitutionality has been recently addressed by the Court in a very important and complex tax case, see Judgment 10/2015, *supra* section 2.

[11] Similarly, in the United States the Federal Court of Appeals for the Second Circuit has suggested "postponing" striking down a statute in order to give the state legislature time for a "second look." *United States v. Then*, 55 F.3d 464, 466 (2d Cir. 1995) (Calabresi, J. concurring).

This discrimination represents a violation of the principle of equal treatment between parents, and between self-employed and workers, with regard to both the protection of the family and the protection of minors. . . .

The violation of the principle of equality appears even more evident if we consider that the legislative body has granted this ability to fathers who work as employees: Not having extended an analogous ability to self employed amounts to a disparity of treatment between workers which does not appear justified by the differences between the two, even if such differences exist (differences that certainly have nothing to do with the right to participate in family life in equal measure to the mother) and does not allow these fathers/workers to benefit in equal measure with others from that protection which the law assures upon the occasion of becoming a parent, even an adoptive one.

This absence of protection appears discriminatory, since, in an identical situation, and in the event of the same occurrence, some individuals are deprived of established benefits that are accorded to others in the same circumstances.

Under the principles upheld by this Court, the task of enacting an enforceable mechanism granting adequate protection to self-employed fathers is still reserved to the legislature.

For these reasons

The Constitutional Court

Declares Art. 70 and 71 of Decree Law 151/2001 (Law regulating the protection of paternity and maternity that follows Art. 15 of Statute 3/2000) unconstitutional because it does not allow for the principle that the father is entitled to take, instead of the mother, the parental benefits that are only accorded to her.

In contrast to this rather diversified array of remedies employed by the Court in cases arising from the indirect method of judicial review, in cases involving the direct method of judicial review things have remained rather simple: either the challenged statute (State or Regional) is found unconstitutional, and therefore annulled, or the challenge is simply rejected.

Taking into consideration the various kinds of decisions created by the Court through its own case law, we may understand why the Italian Constitutional Court is no longer a "negative legislator" in the Kelsenian sense but instead also exercises an explicitly positive lawmaking function. Moreover, in some instances the Court performs a less explicit but still significant lawmaking function by "simply" declaring unconstitutional single provisions—or particular parts of single provisions—of important statutes. A very good and recent example can be found in

Judgment 1/2014. By invalidating only precise single parts of the electoral law, the Court effectively created a new electoral system. The decision was bitterly criticized, and the Court was considered excessively activist by part of the public opinion and also by some scholars. One of the problems raised by the decision concerned the legitimacy of the sitting Parliament, elected through the statute, which was declared unconstitutional. The Court seemed well aware of the problem and, more generally, of the importance and effects of the judgment. In fact, in the final part of the decision, the Court addresses the question of the impact and, more specifically, of the legitimacy of the current Parliament, referring to the "fundamental principle of the continuity of the State."

> Lastly, it is clear that the decision we are making to strike down the questioned provisions, having partly modified the law that regulates the elections of the House and the Senate, will only take effect on the occasion of a new election that will either be carried out under the portions of the law that remains in force following the present decision, or according to new electoral rules that may be adopted by the Houses.
>
> Therefore, this decision does not in any way impact the acts adopted during the time that the invalidated laws were in force, including the results of elections and the rules adopted by the elected Parliament. It is important to remember that the principle according to which the effects of this Court's *sentenze di accoglimento*—in accordance with Art. 136 of the Constitution and Art. 30 of Statute 87/1952—date back to the moment the invalidated law was enacted, a principle "that is usually referred to as the 'retroactivity' of those judgments, it is only valid for situations that are still pending, excluding those that have been completed, which, in turn, remain under the invalidated provisions" (Judgment 139/1984).
>
> The elections carried out under the unconstitutional electoral provisions are, definitively and without any doubt, concluded events, provided that the process of filling the Houses has been concluded with the proclamation of those elected.
>
> By the same token, the acts that will be adopted by the Houses prior to new elections will likewise not be impacted.
>
> The fundamental principle of the continuity of the State is relevant in this case: a principle that is not an abstraction, and that is realized concretely through the continuity of all the State's constitutional bodies, starting with the Parliament. It is therefore beyond any reasonable doubt—and hardly bears repeating—that no questions of constitutional legitimacy may be raised under the present decision, not even challenging the acts that the House will adopt

pending the period between the present decision and the new elections: The Houses are constitutionally necessary and indispensable bodies and cannot at any time cease to exist or lose the capacity to deliberate. This is so true that, for example, in order to ensure the continuity of the State, the Constitution itself provides that, following elections, the powers of the preceding Houses are extended "until such time as the new Houses meet" (Art. 61 of the Constitution), and also that "during dissolution, Parliament shall be convened within five days of such introduction" for the conversion into law of the decree-laws adopted by the Government (Art. 77, second paragraph, Const.).

II Constitutional Jurisprudence

4 Key Rights and Freedoms

1. The Rights and Duties of Citizens in the Constitution

Part I of the Italian Constitution, entitled "Rights and Duties of Citizens," contains a long bill of rights (Arts. 13–54), which is divided into four Titles: Civil Relations; Ethical and Social Relations; Economic Relations; and Political Relations.

Many of the rights set out in the first part of the Constitution, and especially in Title I (Civil Relations), are generally recognizable as the classic formulations of the Enlightenment era. These include guarantees of personal liberty, freedom of movement and residence, freedom of expression, freedom of religion, the principle of *nulla poena sine lege* (no punishment without law), and the right to judicial protection (including a right to be heard by the "natural judge" of a dispute).

The second Title, Ethical and Social Relations, primarily addresses the family, health, and education. It has no less than three articles regarding the family, marriage, the rights and duties of parents, and the obligation of the State to support family life. It also recognizes the State's obligation to protect health both as a fundamental right of the individual and as a collective interest, and to provide free care to the indigent. Various provisions not only guarantee the freedom to educate and to organize private educational institutions but also that primary education be free

95

and that the State provide support for individuals and families who do not have the means to pay for higher education.

Economic Relations, covered in Title III, address many aspects of the right to work: State responsibility to promote the training and advancement of workers and even the protection of Italian workers abroad; the right to a limitation on maximum working hours and to periods of rest; the right to compensation that is both proportionate to the quantity and quality of one's labor and adequate "to ensure them and their families a free and dignified existence"; special care for the conditions of working women, especially mothers; and the right to social security and other protection in the case of unemployment or disability. Unions and the right to strike receive special attention as well. At the same time, Title III also recognizes the freedom of private economic initiative and to private property, although subjects both to limits in order to ensure their social function and compatibility with human dignity, and explicitly allows for both the nationalization of certain industries and essential public services, as well as land redistribution programs. This section also recognizes "the social function of cooperation" in the economic sector and the right of workers to collaborate in the management of businesses. Finally, it requires the State to encourage and protect savings.

The fourth and last Title of the Rights and Duties of Citizens, Political Relations, includes the right to vote, to form political parties, and to petition Parliament. It guarantees equal opportunities to accede to public office. It also enumerates several duties of citizens: to participate in the defense of the Nation, to pay taxes (which are to be established on a progressive scale), and to abide by the Constitution and laws of the Republic.

Even this very compressed overview of Part I already begins to point to certain of the distinctive qualities of the Italian Constitution's approach to fundamental constitutional rights. First, and most important, one can immediately see that the Rights and Duties of Citizens, like the 1948 Constitution as a whole, pervasively reflects the confluence—part compromise, part synthesis—of several different and competing ideological currents.[1] As already described in more detail in Chapter 1, the three principal political groups represented in the Constituent Assembly were those of classical nineteenth-century secular liberals, socialists, and Catholics. At the same time, however, it categorizes those rights in interestingly unique ways, not following cleanly the stereotypical division often used today between "civil and political rights" and "economic, social, and cultural rights" (and sometimes adding a further "generation" of so-called "solidarity rights"), but instead bridging and combining the categories.

Similarly, the conventional association of liberal, civil, and political rights with "negative" obligations of the State, and social-economic rights with the State's

---

[1] *See* especially Art. 3, *infra* section 2.2.

"positive" obligations, does not accurately describe the Italian approach. The affirmative responsibilities of the State are present throughout; in each of the four Titles, the language of the Constitution is as likely to read that "the Republic protects . . ." as to announce that "everyone has a right . . ."

In substance, one clearly sees a strong emphasis on community, on social relations, and on civil society, and a comparatively lesser emphasis merely on the autonomous individual, relative to other constitutional bills of rights or to international human rights instruments. The names of each of the four Titles attest to this: they refer to their subject matter not as rights but as relations. Similarly, the sprinkling throughout the document of the language of duties—both the duties of the State and the duties of solidarity among citizens—speaks of a tradition of rights discourse more similar to that of Rousseau's France and Latin America (see, for instance, the 1948 American Declaration of the Rights and Duties of Man) than of the more libertarian dialect of rights typical of the Anglo-American world.

Of course, all of these initial impressions based on the mere text of the Constitution itself are only suggestive, and the real test comes in the interpretation and application of these rights and duties. An examination of the ways in which the Constitutional Court has done so with respect to a selected number of key rights and freedoms demonstrates that the distinctiveness of the Italian constitutional approach to rights does indeed carry through from the constitutional text to the constitutional jurisprudence. Before presenting some specific illustrative examples, however, we need first to account for certain Fundamental Principles that are identified at the very beginning of the Constitution, prior to Part I, and that inform the Court's understanding and approach to all of the constitutional rights and duties.

2. The Fundamental Principles of Inviolability and Equality

The Italian Constitution begins with no preamble, and instead contains twelve articles of Fundamental Principles meant to inform the whole. Two of the principles are particularly relevant to the interpretation and application of rights: the inviolability of human rights (Art. 2) and the guarantee of equality (Art. 3).

2.1 INVIOLABLE RIGHTS

The Italian constitutional text refers only once to a "fundamental" right (see Art. 32). Instead, it typically refers to rights as "inviolable." Although it is possible to consider the two expressions as equivalent in a general sense, the term "inviolability" sometimes assumes a more technical meaning in the Italian constitutional system. The proclamation of the inviolability of fundamental rights in Article 2 is not just a way of lending moral weight to the rights subsequently listed in the Constitution, but it has a precise legal and cultural significance.

Affirming that fundamental rights are inviolable is tantamount to a rejection of the public rights theory elaborated by German scholars in the nineteenth century (Gerber, Laband, Jellinek) and then followed in Italy.[2] The theory considered citizens' rights vis-à-vis the State as a consequence of the self-limitation of State powers, which the latter could always change in its favor. Affirming that fundamental rights are inviolable means, on the contrary, that they must be respected by all public authorities, including legislators and the authorities responsible for amending the Constitution. Inviolability therefore means the absolute immutability of such rights. The State has no power to annul or withdraw fundamental rights, not even through the complex procedure of constitutional amendment. This is the legal sense of the inviolability proclaimed by Article 2: fundamental rights are definitive and untouchable in their core—in their essential content.

Fundamental rights, therefore, not only restrain executive power—as in the nineteenth-century liberal State—but also constitute a limit on acts of Parliament as well as any other legal act, including constitutional laws, laws amending the Constitution, and other sources of law such as EU provisions and ECHR principles.[3]

The Constitutional Court shares this opinion, which is forcefully stated in Judgment 1146/1988.

> The Italian Constitution contains some supreme principles that cannot be subverted or modified in their essential content, either by laws amending the Constitution, or by other constitutional laws. These include both principles that are expressly considered absolute limits on the power to amend the Constitution, such as the republican form of government (Art. 139) as well as those principles that even though not expressly mentioned among those principles not subject to the procedure of constitutional amendment, belong to the essence of the supreme values upon which the Italian Constitution is founded.
>
> This Court, furthermore, has already recognized in numerous decisions how the supreme principles of the constitutional order prevail over other laws

---

[2] *See* V. E. Orlando, *Diritto pubblico generale. Scritti vari (1881–1940) coordinati in sistema*, Milano, Giuffré, 1940. *See also* M. Fioravanti, *Vittorio Emanuele Orlando: Scholar and Statesman*, in *Italian Studies in Law*, A. Pizzorusso ed., vol. I, Dordrecht/Boston/London, Martinus Nijhoff Publishers, 1992, p. 29 ff.

[3] *See* Chapter 7.

or constitutional norms, such as when the Court maintained that even the prescriptions of the Concordat, which enjoy particular "constitutional protection" under Art. 7, paragraph 2, are not excluded from scrutiny for conformity to the "supreme principles of the constitutional order" (*see* Judgments 30/1971, 12/1972, 175/1973, 1/1977, 18/1982), and also when the Court affirmed that the laws executing the EEC Treaty may be subject to the jurisdiction of this Court "in reference to the fundamental principles of our constitutional order, and to the inalienable rights of the human person" (*see* Judgments 183/1973, 170/1984).

Thus, in spite of the lack of a constitutional provision explicitly stating that fundamental rights cannot be the object of a constitutional amendment—as is the case, for instance, of Article 19, paragraph 2 of the German Constitution significantly known as the "eternity clause," or Article 53, paragraph 1 of the Spanish Constitution—the Italian Constitutional Court has clearly declared their absolute inviolability.

The Court's judgments, however, have not done away with all doubts as to the meaning and scope of such inviolability. In the first place, it is necessary to identify which human rights, or which aspects of those rights, are to be considered inviolable. Inviolability does not apply to every single expression and implication of all of the enumerated rights. The Constitutional Court instead deems that only the essential content of fundamental rights cannot be the object of constitutional amendment and must therefore be considered inviolable. The different ways of expressing these rights can, and sometimes must, be adapted to changed times by Parliament, either by means of ordinary laws or by constitutional amendment. The general constitutional provisions protecting fundamental rights can therefore be modified. What cannot be changed in any way whatsoever is the basic content of the rights. This of course then defers the question of inviolability to an assessment of the "essential" content of the right in question.

Another difficult issue is how to recognize which rights, from among all those set out in the Constitution, are to be regarded as inviolable. The Constitution itself is not clear in this respect. Inviolable rights are cited in a generic way in Article 2, and there is no reference to which of the rights subsequently mentioned in Part I can be considered as such. In the constitutional text some rights are expressly labeled as inviolable—namely personal liberty (Art. 13), freedom of domicile (Art. 14), liberty and secrecy of correspondence (Art. 15), and the right to counsel in judicial proceedings (Art. 24)—but this list is not intended to exclude other rights. Some rights, such as freedom of expression and freedom of association, are self-evidently inviolable even if not explicitly provided for in the Constitution. Given that other cases are not as clear, however, the task of identifying which rights are inviolable and of defining their essential content is largely left to the Constitutional Court.

In Judgment 366/1991 the Constitutional Court gives meaning to the "inviolability" of the liberty and secrecy of correspondence. The trial court in a criminal case in Siena referred to the Court the question of whether Article 270, paragraph 1 of the Code of Criminal Procedure violated Articles 15 and 112 of the Constitution, the former protecting the liberty and secrecy of personal communications and the latter providing for an important principle in the Italian criminal justice system, that of the absolute duty of the public prosecutor to investigate every crime of which he or she is aware (the public prosecutor has no discretionary power to prosecute or not). The first paragraph of Article 270, which was eventually held valid by the Court, provided that information from wiretaps obtained for a specific case could not be used in a different case.

Ever since Judgment 34/1973, the Court has affirmed that liberty and secrecy of correspondence and of every other mode of communication constitute an individual right that is so much a part of the supreme values of the Constitution as to be expressly qualified by Art. 15 of the Constitution as an inviolable right.

The close relationship of this right to the essential nucleus of the values of personhood—which lead to characterizing the right as a necessary part of that vital space which surrounds the person and without which that personhood could not exist and develop in harmony with the requirements of human dignity—consequentially requires a dual characterization of its inviolability. On the basis of Art. 2 of the Constitution, the right to the liberty and secrecy of personal communications is inviolable in the general sense that its essential content cannot be the object of constitutional amendment, inasmuch as it incorporates a value of personhood which is foundational to the democratic system established by the Constituent Assembly. Based on Art. 15 of the Constitution, the same right is inviolable in the sense that its basic content may not be subject to limitations or restrictions by any of the established powers except on condition that it is for the purpose of indispensably fulfilling a primary and constitutionally relevant interest, that the established limitation is strictly necessary for the protection of such interest, and that it respects a dual guarantee: the limiting measure must be provided for by a legislative act of Parliament; and the limiting measure is ordered by a reasoned act of judicial authority . . .

Based on these premises this Court (see in particular Judgment 34/1973) has strongly emphasized that the act of the judicial authority which authorizes wiretapping must be "precisely reasoned" or, to use another expression from the judgment's opinion, it must have an "adequate and specific reason". That is, its use as evidence to prove the information which has been collected through wiretaps legitimately ordered in the context of a trial must be restricted to the information strictly relevant to that same trial.

In order to directly connect these holdings to Art. 2 and 15 of the Constitution, this Court has clearly supposed that the aforementioned guarantee is an immediate consequence of the constitutional principle that wiretapping must be ordered, without exception, by an act of judicial authority . . .

From the protection of liberty of communication we therefore derive, in principle, the prohibition of the use of wiretaps validly available in the ambit of one case as evidence in a different case, for the simple fact that, if it were not so, it would frustrate the need so often affirmed by this Court that the act warranted by judicial authority for the wiretap be precisely reasoned in the sense and manner previously clarified.

Although the Constitutional Court had tried to define which rights are to be considered "inviolable" and to determine their essential content, it had also often underlined that the Constitution does not provide a hierarchy of rights. Rights, even when fundamental and inviolable, are all of the same rank so they must be balanced, especially in hard cases, one with another. Judgment 85/2013, which decides a complex environmental case, is illuminating on this point:[4]

All of the fundamental rights protected by the Constitution find themselves in a relationship of reciprocal integration and it is not therefore possible to pinpoint one that has an absolute dominance over the others. The protection must always be "systematic and not fragmented into a series of uncoordinated and possibly self-conflicting norms" (Judgment 264/2012). If it were not so, the unlimited expansion of one of the rights would occur, [and this right] would become "the tyrant" in comparison to other constitutionally recognized and [constitutionally] protected judicial situations, which constitute, as a whole, the expression of the dignity of the person.

2.2 EQUALITY

The "formal" component of the principle of equality established by the first paragraph of Article 3 of the Constitution—"All citizens have equal social dignity and are equal before the law"—is anything but new. It is an idea with ancient roots, has been widely constitutionalized since the French Revolution, and was adopted during the liberal era by all States governed by the rule of law. Since the Second World

---

[4] Judgment 85/2013 is also discussed in Chapter 3, section 2.

War, however, the principle of equality has gradually assumed new meanings and greater scope.

In the first place, in contrast to the way the principle of equality would have been understood in Italy prior to the advent of a rigid Constitution in 1948, Article 3 binds not only the Judiciary (see Art. 101) and the Public Administration (see Art. 97) but also the Legislature.

Second, the content of the principle of equality has become more complex. On the one hand, the principle is designed to prevent both arbitrary discrimination among persons similarly situated and the arbitrary assimilation of persons who are differently situated. In particular, legislation based on the "suspect" criteria mentioned by Article 3 (sex, language, race, religion, political beliefs, and personal or social conditions) is subject to strict control by the Constitutional Court. Therefore, distinctions based on these criteria very often are declared unconstitutional. On the other hand, legislative distinctions based on other grounds are subject to a less strict level of scrutiny and are examined by the Constitutional Court in light of the principle of reasonableness. In those cases, the Court judges the consistency of the distinctions or assimilations made by the legislature by comparing them with the de facto treatment used in other situations.

In addition to these formal requirements of equality, Article 3, paragraph 2, also inserts into the Constitution the principle of "substantive" equality when it states: "It is the task of the Republic to remove those obstacles of an economic or social nature which, by limiting in fact the freedom and equality of citizens, prevent the full development of the human person and the effective participation of all workers in the political, economic and social organization of the country."

Judgment 163/1993 is a good example of a decision striking down a law because it violated both the formal and the substantive components of the principle of equality. The statute of the Autonomous Province of Trento regulating the fire prevention organization applied the same minimum height requirement of 1.65 meters to both men and women to enter the firefighting service. The trial court, which had to decide whether a woman less than 1.65 meters tall had been lawfully excluded from the competition to enter the firefighting service, referred a question to the Constitutional Court. For the latter, this statutory requirement constituted an indirect discrimination based on gender because it treated in an identical way subjects who are in fact differently situated from a physical point of view.

The first clause of Art. 3 of the Constitution provides a principle that has a foundational, and therefore inviolable, value whose purpose is to guarantee the equality of all citizens under the law and to forbid that sex—like race, language, religion, political affiliations and personal and social conditions—constitute the source of any discrimination in the legal treatment of persons. The second clause of the same Art. 3 of the Constitution—apart from establishing an autonomous principle of "substantive" equality and equal opportunity among all citizens in social, economic and political life—expresses an interpretive standard that can also be seen in the breadth and effect to be given to the principle of "formal" equality inasmuch as it conditions the guarantee on effective results produced or producible in concrete relations in life, as a result of the primary constitutional imperative of removing *de facto* limits on equality (and on liberty) and of pursuing the ultimate objective of full self-determination of the person and "effective" participation in community life" . . .

The principle of equality entails that a category of persons, defined according to identical characteristics or reasonably homogeneous characteristics in relation to the ultimate objective to which the normative framework under consideration is addressed, must be ascribed a homogenous or identical judicial treatment, reasonably commensurate with the essential characteristics on the basis of which that specific category of persons was defined.

On the other hand, where the subjects considered by a particular norm, which is directed to regulating a determinate case, give rise to a class of persons having characteristics that are not homogeneous, with respect to the final objective pursued by the legal treatment given to them, that treatment will conform to the principle of equality only where it is reasonably differentiated in relation to the distinctive characteristics pertaining to the subcategories of persons which make up that class.

In brief, the principle of equality requires that the Constitutional Court verify that there does not exist a violation of any of the following criteria: (a) the accuracy of the classification used by the legislator in relation to the subjects being considered, in light of the given normative framework; (b) the provision on the part of the same legislator of a homogeneous legal treatment, reasonably commensurate with the essential characteristics of the class (or classes) of persons to whom the treatment is referred; (c) the proportionality of the expected legal treatment in relation to the classification used by the legislator, in light of the ultimate objective inherent to the normative framework in consideration: proportionality is examined in relation to the practical effects produced or producible in concrete relations in life.

The contested provision is contained in an article of a (provincial) law whose purpose is to establish particular requirements for access to management careers and technical positions in the firefighting service of the Autonomous Province of Trento. More precisely, it is specifically aimed at providing, as a selection criterion for the respective public competition, that the candidates—both of the male and female sex—have a certain minimum height (equal to 1.65 meters). The establishment of a physical requirement was not in itself contested, given that the personnel in question, even though designated to carry out managerial functions or clerical work, may nevertheless in certain circumstances be assigned to certain operational tasks—tasks that, because of the characteristics of the activity that they involve, demand that the persons executing them have a certain physical stature. That which is contested, instead, is that the provision of a minimum height that is identical for women and for men constitutes an unreasonable imposition of a uniform legal treatment on persons who are characterized, based on empirical data from median statistics, by different heights. In consequence, female candidates in the public competition mentioned previously would be penalized on the basis of their sex, having to be subjected to that which Art. 4, paragraph 2 of Statute 125/1991 defines as "indirect discrimination", as a consequence of the contested regulation.

The basis of the complaint arises from the correct application to this specific case of certain criteria of judgment, as indicated above, deriving from the principle of equality. By conditioning participation in the public competition upon the previously stated minimum height requirement, identical for men and for women, the local legislator has identified a general group of citizens as the subjects of the contested norm, without distinguishing between members of the male sex and the female sex internally to this general group. This classification evidently corresponds to a legislative judgment based on an erroneous presumption: the supposed non-existence of an average physical height difference between men and women. Or in other words, it is founded on the equally erroneous presumption that a difference of physical height existing in natural reality is irrelevant for the purposes of the requirement of uniform legal treatment.

In the first case, the violation of the principle of equality established in Art. 3, paragraph 1 of the Constitution is beyond doubt, because the legislator has classified a category of persons based upon physical characteristics that do not correspond to the natural order, bearing in mind that the ultimate objective of the legal regulation being examined is to provide access to an employment position based on criteria pertaining to physical height.

The violation of the same constitutional principle is no less evident in the second case. In fact, the latter hypothesis—which establishes an identical physical requirement for both sexes on the presumed irrelevance of height differences between men and women (consisting on average, according to anthropometric studies, in a considerable difference that is to the disadvantage to persons of the female sex) for purposes of access to employment—entails a systematic production of concrete effects proportionately more disadvantageous for candidates of the female sex, precisely because of their sex. In other words, the adoption of a uniform legal treatment—that is, the provision of a physical requirement for access to employment that is identical for men and women—is the cause of an "indirect discrimination" which disfavors persons of the female sex, since it disadvantages them in a manner proportionately greater than men in view of a physical difference which is statistically ascertainable and objectively derived from one's sex.

The substantive component of the principle of equality applied in this case also justifies and encourages the passing of legislation designed to ensure the equality of treatment and opportunity. The Constitutional Court has thus appealed to Article 3 in order to justify affirmative action that guarantees privileged treatment for persons or classes of persons who are otherwise in disadvantaged positions. To date, such actions have, in particular, taken the form of laws in favor of women in the professional workplace.

In Judgment 109/1993 the Constitutional Court considered the validity of a statute that provided for affirmative action. In that case, two direct complaints were brought to the Constitutional Court by the Region of Lombardy and by the Autonomous Province of Trento. The Region and the Province alleged that National Statute n. 215 of February 25, 1992, labeled "Positive actions for professional women," violated their respective legislative competences. According to the Region and the Province, the national legislature had no jurisdiction over the subject matter. The Constitutional Court rejected the challenge and, declaring the statute valid, gave an important interpretation of the substantive aspect of the principle of equality.

From the description now concluded, we understand that the contested provisions establish financial incentives in favor of companies with prevalent female participation, with the clear aim of facilitating their development, as regards the most important moments of the production cycle. It is a matter, more precisely, of interventions of a positive character in favor of women, directed to make up for, or in any event to assuage, an evident imbalance that, because of discrimination accumulated in the course of past history as the result of the dominance of certain social behaviors and cultural models, has favored persons of the male sex in positions of entrepreneurship or of business management.

In other words, the ends pursued by the contested provisions are an immediate development of the fundamental obligation which Art. 3, paragraph 2 of the Constitution assigns to the Republic, "to remove those obstacles of an economic or social nature which, by limiting in fact the freedom and equality of citizens, prevent the full development of the human person and the effective participation of all workers in the political, economic and social organization of the country." These "positive actions" are in fact the most powerful instrument at the disposal of the legislator, who, respecting the independence and liberty of single individuals, is inclined to raise the initial threshold of departure for particular classes of socially disadvantaged people—fundamentally those which can be traced to the prohibition of discrimination expressed in Art. 3, paragraph 1 (sex, race, language, religion, political opinions, personal and social conditions)—toward the goal of assuring these very classes an effective status of equal opportunity for social, economic, and political integration.

In the cases at hand the "positive actions" ordered by the contested provisions aim to overcome the risk that differences of a natural or biological character will arbitrarily become discrimination of a social nature. To this end they foresee, in a sector of activity having a personnel that reveals a manifest imbalance to the detriment of persons of the female sex, the adoption of a framework favorable to a class of persons—women—who on the basis of a reasonable evaluation of the legislator have been found to have been subjected in the past to discrimination of a social and cultural order, and who even to this day are at risk of analogous discrimination.

As measures meant to transform a situation of effective inequality of conditions into one characterized by a substantial equality of opportunity, the "positive actions" entail the adoption of differentiated legal frameworks in favor of disadvantaged social classes, notwithstanding the formal principle of equal treatment, established in Art. 3, paragraph 1 of the Constitution. But these distinctions, because they in fact presuppose the historical existence of discrimination pertaining to the social role of specific classes of persons and because they in fact are meant to overcome discrimination affecting personal characteristics (sex) in order to effectively guarantee the primary constitutional value of "equal social dignity", necessitate that their implementation may not be subjected to a lack of uniformity or to exceptions in the different geographic areas or policies of the country.

Article 3, paragraph 2 thus does not contradict the formal component of the principle of equality but instead complements it. By justifying legislation that helps to realize the equality of conditions, even though apparently discriminatory toward certain categories or groups of persons, the substantive component of the principle helps to reaffirm full and effective legal equality as well.

Even though affirmative action has been considered constitutionally valid in Judgment 109/1993 as referred to a statute that favored women in the professional area, more problematic are the cases in which the preferred position of women is taken into consideration in different fields such as political elections. For instance, in Judgment 422/1995, the Court has held unconstitutional parts of Statute 81/1993 that regulated the electoral system of the provinces and the municipalities providing that no lists of candidates to office could include more than two-thirds of candidates of the same gender. The Court evidently adopted a formal reading of Article 3, as specified by Article 51, first paragraph, of the Constitution that provided: "All citizens of either sex are eligible for public offices and for elected positions on equal terms, according to the conditions established by law." Following Judgment 422/1995, Parliament, in order to contrast the very limited participation of women to political life, adopted Constitutional Law 1/2003, which amended Article 51 by adding a new sentence that added some substantive value to the first paragraph. The article now reads: "All citizens of either sex are eligible for public offices and for elected positions on equal terms, according to the conditions established by law. To this end, the Republic shall adopt specific measures to promote equal opportunities between women and men."

3. Personal Liberty

Article 13 of the Constitution establishes the inviolability of personal liberty and subjects any restrictions on liberty to strict judicial control. It restricts provisional detention without judicial authority and requires limits on preventive detention. Overall, the emphasis of Article 13 is clearly focused on the problem of arbitrary detention. The first part of Article 13 states that "no form of personal detention, inspection, or search is permitted, nor any other restriction on personal liberty except by an order of a judicial authority stating a reason, and only in such cases and manner as provided by law."

The "cases and manner" in which a person can be subjected to restrictions of his or her personal freedom can thus be determined only by a detailed legislative act of Parliament. Legislation limiting personal freedom must be complete so as to protect individuals both against the Executive, which cannot issue regulations on the matter (except for regulations implementing parliamentary legislation), and against the misuse of discretionary power by the Judiciary.

Following the Constitution, the Court does not hesitate to declare to be unconstitutional any rules that limit personal liberty without determining precisely the circumstances and manner in which such restrictions can be imposed by the Judiciary. An interesting judgment on this issue is 238/1996. In this case the Court of first instance of Civitavecchia referred to the Constitutional Court the question of whether Article 224, paragraph 2 of the Code of Criminal Procedure violated Articles 3 and 13 of the Constitution. That provision of the Code gives to the investigating judge the power to impose a compulsory blood test on the indicted person and also on certain third parties. In the referral order, the Court of first instance challenged Article 224 as a violation of the right to personal liberty and personal integrity because it did not define precisely the cases and the manner in which the blood test could be ordered and thus granted the investigating authority an overbroad and uncontrolled discretionary power. The ordinary court also challenged the same article of the Code as a violation of Article 3 of the Constitution because it treated both the indicted person and other persons identically, subjecting both to the compulsory blood test. The Constitutional Court struck down Article 224 as a violation of Article 13 of the Constitution, insofar as the Code provision allowed the investigating judge to have an overly broad discretion and uncontrolled power.

> The first test required by the referral is that of the compatibility of the precepts contained in Art. 224, paragraph 2 of the Code of Criminal Procedure with the express prescription of the first applicable standard, Art. 13, paragraph 2 of the Constitution, which subjects every restriction of personal liberty—among which are included detention, inspection, and personal bodily search—to a dual guarantee: the requirement of legality (that these coercive measures are possible "only in such cases and manner as provided by law"); and the requirement of jurisdiction (requiring "an order of a judicial authority stating a reason"). In this way the test places into effect a legal protection that is central to our constitutional design, since it has as its object an inviolable right, that of personal liberty, which forms part of the supreme values and which is inseparable from the essential core of the individual, no differently than the adjoining and closely connected rights to life and physical integrity, with which personal liberty combines to constitute the basis of every other constitutionally protected right of the person.
>
> The drawing of blood certainly entails a restriction of personal liberty whenever it is necessary to carry it out coercively because the person subject to the expert's examination does not spontaneously consent to the taking of the blood sample. And this restriction is even more alarming—and therefore in need of an attentive evaluation by the legislator in its description of the "circumstances and manners" in which it may be ordered by the judge—inasmuch as it not only falls within the sphere of personal liberty but goes beyond it, given that (even if only in a minimal manner) it invades the bodily sphere of the person. . . . And it extracts a part from that sphere, for the purpose of acquiring

probative information in a criminal trial, which even if almost insignificant is certainly more than nothing.

In such a case, therefore, the guarantee of the absolute requirement of legality implicates the need to specify the "cases and manners" in which personal liberty may be legitimately compromised and restricted. This legislative provision may not take the form of a further referral by the law to the full discretion of the judge who is applying it. Instead, it requires a legal framework suitable to anchor the restriction of personal liberty in objectively recognizable criteria.[5]

Restrictions on personal liberty can thus be authorized only by a reasoned judicial order, in compliance with the statutory law. Pursuant to Article 13, third paragraph, of the Constitution, the police authorities may also take provisional measures placing limits on personal liberty, though only "in exceptional cases of necessity and urgency, strictly defined by law." It follows that Parliament must specify the precise circumstances in which the police can impose restrictions on personal liberty so as to prevent them from acting too freely. In any case, these measures are provisional and have to be referred to a judge within 48 hours. If the latter does not ratify them within that 48-hour period, the measures are revoked and declared null and void.

Aside from such provisional measures, personal liberty can be lawfully limited only in certain other specified instances, including through pretrial detention. This is only permissible in compliance with Article 27 of the Constitution ("A defendant shall be considered not guilty until a final sentence has been passed"). Thus, according to the Constitutional Court, pretrial detention can never be used to anticipate the punishment that is to be imposed only after a definitive finding of guilt, and it can only be ordered for serious precautionary reasons or reasons strictly connected to the trial. In this regard, Judgment 64/1970 is illuminating. In this complex case—which originated from referrals by three different criminal courts of first instance—several articles of the Code of Criminal Procedure then in force were challenged as a violation of Articles 13 and 27 of the Constitution. The Court declared the impugned Code provisions to be partially unconstitutional.

In principle, we must recognize that preventive detention—explicitly provided for (within the limits that will be specified below) by the Constitution (Art. 13, last clause)—needs to be regulated in a way that does not conflict with one of the fundamental guarantees of the liberty of the citizen: the presumption of the

---

[5] As a result of this judgment, Statute n. 85 of June 30, 2009, eventually added a new Article 224 *bis* to the Code of Criminal Procedure, which now regulates more precisely how a judge can order physical tests (e.g., blood and DNA) on nonconsenting persons.

defendant's innocence. The rigorous respect for this guarantee—which binds not only the legislator, but also public authorities (judicial police, public prosecutors, and judges) to whom procedural activities are entrusted—necessarily means that preventive detention can under no circumstances have the function of anticipating the punishment that is to be inflicted only after an ascertainment of guilt. This preventive detention, therefore, may only be imposed in order to satisfy requirements of a precautionary nature or requirements strictly relevant to the criminal trial.

From this premise, however, it does not follow that, within the scope of a discretionary political evaluation, the law may not establish conditions under which, where sufficient indications of guilt exist, the judge is under an obligation to issue a warrant of arrest. If and inasmuch as it uses a reasonable evaluation of the existence of a danger derived from the liberty of the person who is suspected of particular crimes, the legislator has the power to decide that, within predetermined time limits, the suspect is to be deprived of liberty. And in fact—aside from the preference for a system that always demands that judges have the power to evaluate on a case by case basis whether freeing the accused constitutes such a danger as to justify his capture and detention—we cannot exclude that the law may (within reasonable but not unappealable limits) presume that a defendant who is accused of a particularly grave crime and who is tainted with sufficient indications of guilt, would be in a condition to place in danger that good which the use of preventive detention is intended to protect.

Indeed, the Code of Criminal Procedure presently in force provides that pretrial detention can be imposed only: (1) for investigation purposes, especially for preserving the authenticity of evidence; (2) in order to prevent the defendant from escaping; (3) in order to prevent the defendant from committing other serious crimes. The need for pretrial detention must be established in every individual case, and it is, therefore, forbidden to order the preventive detention of all persons accused of a particular crime, for instance. In addition, Article 13 of the Constitution provides that the maximum length of time of pretrial detention should be laid down by law, and the Constitutional Court has ruled that the calculation of the length of time, fixed by the Code of Criminal Procedure, must take into consideration the time of imprisonment the accused served abroad while waiting for extradition to Italy or waiting for the execution of a European Arrest Warrant (see Judgments 253/2004 and 143/2008).

In addition to detention for criminal conviction and pretrial detention, Italian legislation envisages precautionary measures limiting personal liberty that can be applied to suspects in order to fight various forms of organized crime. Such precautionary measures can apply to such heterogeneous categories of people as, for instance, *Mafia* suspects and persons involved in crimes related to arms trafficking. More specifically, precautionary measures are provided for by Statutes 575/1965 and 646/1982 concerning the *Mafia* and *Camorra*; Statute 152/1975, enacted in order to fight political terrorism in the 1970s; Statutes 401/1989 and 45/1995, adopted to combat violent behavior in football stadiums and at other sporting events; and Statute 438/2001, which extends the applicability of precautionary measures to persons suspected of taking part in acts of international terrorism. Because these precautionary measures can be taken even in the absence of a crime, and because the cases for which they are established are very vague and give the competent judicial authorities an extremely broad discretionary power, they have been widely criticized.

As for special and "emergency" laws severely restricting personal liberty in various ways such as those mentioned above, the Constitutional Court was called to judge parts of a statute enacted in order to fight the political terrorism that was tormenting Italy during the 1970s and early 1980s. In the important Judgment 15/1982 the Court examined the constitutionality of Decree-Law n. 625 of December 15, 1979 (converted into a Parliamentary act by Conversion Law n. 15 of February 6, 1980), which extended the length of preventive detention for crimes related to political terrorism. Three different courts of first instance suspected such legislation of violating Articles 13 and 27 of the Constitution and referred the question to the Constitutional Court. Although the Court considered the challenged law to be constitutionally legitimate in general, it held that, in order to be considered "reasonable" in accordance with Article 13, an exceptional statute that severely limits personal liberty such as this one must be in force only for a short time period. Moreover, with regard to the law's extension of preventive detention, the resulting maximum time length of the detention must not be excessive. In the end, the Court held the challenged law constitutionally valid, but warned Parliament that such severe preventive measures had to be repealed as soon as the state of emergency finished. In fact, much of the so-called "emergency legislation" adopted during the bloody years of political terrorism is no longer in force.

> The three referrals of the ordinary courts raise two questions which have as their object the same juridical institute—preventive detention—and the same normative text . . . Therefore the relative cases may be united and defined with a single judgment.
>
> 2. The first criticism formulated by the Criminal Court (*Corte d'Assise*) of Torino addresses Art. 10 of the aforementioned decree-law, as confirmed by

the conversion law insofar as it prolongs the maximum duration of pretrial detention for specified crimes by one-third . . .

The question therefore regards the reasonableness of the duration of pretrial detention in the period between the filing of the order to send the case to trial and the first instance of sentencing.

3. Although the data placed into evidence in the cases presented is immediately and profoundly troubling, this question must be declared unfounded.

In the referral order, the ruling expressly refers to Art. 13, paragraphs 1, 2, and 5 and Art. 27, paragraph 2 of the Constitution, but the reasoning is not guided by the principles which those articles contain. Rather, it turns exclusively on the principle of reasonableness, with regard to which the denounced violations become consequential given the absence of any independent reason for them . . .

4. To carry out a control on the reasonableness of the maximum terms of preventive detention, as are established by the contested norm, it is necessary that we first identify and evaluate the *ratio* that led the legislator to provide for the extension of those terms. In this regard, no doubt may be harbored: such an extension is among the "urgent measures for the legal protection of the democratic order and of public safety", as the title of the law textually recites, and is caused by "objective difficulties that exist for the preliminary investigations and hearings concerning the crimes in question", as textually declared in the government report that accompanied the draft of the conversion law. Therefore, just as the need to protect the democratic order and public safety is the *occasio legis*, so are the objective difficulties of the investigations the *ratio*. And it is within this ambit, then, and in relation to its circumstances, that the question should be evaluated.

Specifically, these circumstances can be identified in the immediate reason for the law and in the justifications mentioned above.

With regard to the immediate reason—expressly indicated by the legislator itself as the need to protect the democratic order and public safety against terrorism and subversion—we certainly cannot doubt the existence, consistency, specificity, and gravity of the phenomenon that was meant to be combatted and to which the indictment that the Criminal Court must judge in fact refers. And in truth, it regards a phenomenon characterized not so much and not only by a plan aiming to demolish democratic institutions, as by the effective practice of violence as a method of political struggle, by the high technical level of the actions carried out, and by the capacity for recruitment in the most disparate social environments.

5. Facing an emergency situation such as the one at issue here, if the question is situated in a more ample framework than that offered by the referral in which it was raised, the Parliament and the Government not only have the right and the power, but also the precise and irrefutable obligation to provide for this situation by adopting appropriate emergency legislation.

Consequently it must be recognized that the maximum limits for preventive detention which derive from the extension established by Art. 10 of Decree-Law 625/1979, as modified by Conversion Law 15/1980, and as evaluated in light of the considerations above, may not be considered unreasonable since they are put into effect because of the "objective difficulties that exist for the preliminary investigations and hearings concerning the crimes in question" in trials that have as their object "crimes committed for the purpose of terrorism and to evade the democratic order" . . .

7. At this point, however, two distinct—but upon closer examination convergent—clarifications arise.

If it must be admitted that a legal order in which terrorism dispenses death (including through the ruthless assassination of innocent "hostages") and destruction, causing insecurity and thus the need to entrust the safety of life and of goods to armed security and private police, constitutes a state of emergency, it must nevertheless be agreed that the emergency, in its most proper sense, is a condition that is certainly anomalous and grave, but that is also essentially temporary. It follows that this does legitimate extraordinary measures, but that they lose their legitimacy if unjustifiably prolonged in time.

It must then be observed that, even in a state of emergency, one cannot justify so great an extension of the maximum terms of preventive detention that it would lead to the guarantee [of personal liberty] being substantially thwarted.

As this judgment illustrates, when faced with the various emergency laws severely limiting personal liberty that from time to time have been adopted by the Italian Parliament, the relatively few decisions of the Constitutional Court have generally found the challenged laws to be constitutionally valid, and the Court has been extremely deferential to the legislature (in addition to the case cited above, see, for example, Judgment 38/1985). It has not yet given any indication of making a greater effort to balance liberty and security, derived from the opposition between democracy and terrorism, which has become a part of the opinions of many other constitutional courts around the world since the September 11, 2001, terrorist attacks on New York and Washington, D.C.

4. Freedom of Religion

The Constitution takes religion into consideration in many of its provisions. In addition to the general prohibition of any discrimination based on religious grounds in the formal principle of equality of Article 3, paragraph 1, a number of other articles address religion directly.

Article 19, the central constitutional provision guaranteeing the right to religious liberty for both individuals and communities, protects the freedom both to profess and to propagate religion. As interpreted by the Constitutional Court, this guarantees to every person not only the freedom to adhere personally to a particular religion but also the freedom to divulge one's faith and to induce others to adhere to it, including through the criticism of other people's beliefs (so long as the criticism does not amount to contempt) (see Judgment 188/1975). It also encompasses the so-called negative freedom of religion, or freedom from religion—that is, the right not to profess any religion. In addition, Article 19 explicitly protects freedom of worship, individually and in community, both in private and public spaces, so long as the religious rites are not contrary to public morality.

More than many other constitutional or international human rights documents, the Italian Constitution explicitly recognizes the social dimensions of freedom of religion. In addition to the communal aspects of Article 19 mentioned above, for example, Article 20 protects social groups with religious purposes, whether they are civil associations or religious denominations: "No special legislative limitation or tax burden may be imposed on the establishment, legal capacity or activities of any organization on the ground of its ecclesiastical nature or its religious or worship aims."

Traditionally, in Italy the majority of the population has always been Catholic. For this historical reason, the Italian legal system has acknowledged a special position for Catholicism. In contrast to the constitutional prohibition on the governmental establishment of religion in the United States, the Italian Constitution provides a special constitutional status to the international treaty (Concordat) between the Italian State and the Catholic Church in Article 7. Prior to the adoption of the 1948 Constitution, relations between the Italian State and the Roman Catholic Church were already based on Concordats in the form of the Lateran Treaties signed in 1929. These treaties were subsequently amended, and today relations between the State and the Catholic Church are regulated by the amended Concordat of 1984, colloquially known as Villa Madama agreements.

In parallel to that special status given to the Concordat with the Catholic Church, Article 8 of the Constitution provides that other religious confessions may be freely organized and shall be treated equally under the law, and may choose to formalize their relations with the State by entering into their own special agreements. The fact that the Constitution thus provides for agreements with all religious confessions—that is, a Concordat with the Catholic Church and a series of "understandings" with other religions (the most recent of these have been with the Church of Jesus Christ of Latter Day Saints (Mormons), the Holy Orthodox Archdiocese of Italy and the Exarchate of Southern Europe (jointly), the Apostolic Church, and the Buddhist and Hindu communities)—does not mean that the theoretical equality enjoyed by all religions will lead to a unique legal treatment of the relations between the State and every different confession, but does imply that the adoption of rules governing relations between the State and religious communities will vary in accordance with the variety of ad hoc bilateral agreements. Thus, the challenge of constitutional justice is rather a question of when and how to limit such "inequalities."

In recent years, the main problems related to the constitutional protection of freedom of religion have originated, on the one hand, in the flows of immigrants from outside the European Union introducing a wider variety of religions among the population and, on the other hand, in the broader diffusion of secular ideologies in the public sphere. In response, the Constitutional Court has developed and repeatedly affirmed the principle of *laicità*,[6] understood not as the indifference of the State to religious experience generally, but rather as the equidistance and impartiality of the law with respect to all religious confessions.

The Court has explicitly recognized *laicità* as a supreme and inviolable constitutional principle. The first and most important decision establishing this principle is Judgment 203/1989. In this case, the Court of first instance of Firenze referred to the Constitutional Court the question whether the Villa Madama agreements violated Articles 2, 3, and 19 of the Constitution. The specific article challenged established (consistently with the prior Concordat) that the Catholic religion was to be taught in public schools, but that "[r]especting the freedom of religion, conscience, and education of parents, everyone must freely decide whether to take advantage or not of the teaching of the Catholic religion." The Constitutional Court, although finding the contested article to be constitutionally valid, declared that the principle of *laicità* is inviolable and that as such cannot be infringed even by constitutional laws or by acts of the European Community.

This Court has established and consistently observed that the supreme principles of the constitutional order "prevail over other laws or constitutional

---

[6] Although *laicità* is sometimes translated into English as "secularity," "secularism," or "laicity," or with the French word *laicité*, none of these terms adequately captures the somewhat distinctive meaning of the term in Italian constitutional jurisprudence, so we have chosen to preserve the Italian word in this book.

norms, such as when the Court maintained that even the prescriptions of the Concordat, which enjoy particular constitutional protection under Art. 7, paragraph 2, are not excluded from scrutiny for conformity to the supreme principles of the Constitutional order (*see* Judgments 30/1971, 12/1972, 175/1973, 1/1977, and 18/1982) and also when the Court affirmed that the laws executing the EEC Treaty may be subject to the jurisdiction of this Court "in reference to the fundamental principles of our Constitutional order, and to the inalienable rights of the human person (*see* Judgments 183/1973 and 170/1984)" (citing Judgment 1146/1988).

Therefore the Court cannot exempt itself from extending the test of constitutionality to the denounced norm, where there is a question of conflict with one of the supreme principles of the constitutional order, given the standards invoked: Art. 2, 3, and 19. In particular in the challenged subject matter, Art. 3 and 19 become evident as values of religious liberty that specify a dual prohibition: a) that citizens not be discriminated against for religious reasons; and b) that religious pluralism not limit the negative liberty to refrain from professing any religion.

4. These values combine with others (Art. 7, 8, and 20 of the Constitution) to give structure to the supreme principle of *laicità* of the State, one of the characteristics of the form of the State delineated in the Constitution of the Republic.

The principle of *laicità* which emerges from Art. 2, 3, 7, 8, and 20 of the Constitution does not imply the State's indifference to religions but rather the State's guarantee to safeguard the freedom of religion in a system of confessional and cultural pluralism.

As a consequence of the principle of *laicità*, the Constitutional Court has repeatedly intervened to affirm the equality of treatment of various religions, for instance with regard to blasphemy laws. In this area two decisions are particularly relevant. In Judgment 508/2000, the Court ruled on a constitutional challenge to Article 508 of the Criminal Code. A remnant of the regime of the 1929 Concordat, this provision of the Criminal Code established the crime of contempt of State religion. The Constitutional Court struck it down as a violation of Articles 3 and 8 of the Constitution.

According to the fundamental principles of equality of all citizens without distinction on the basis of religion (Art. 3 of the Constitution), and of equal liberty under the law of all religious confessions (Art. 8 of the Constitution), the position of the State must be one of equidistance and impartiality with respect to the latter. The greater or lesser number of adherents of this or that religious confession is not relevant, nor is the greater or lesser degree of social reactions that result from a violation of rights of one or another of these religious confessions (Judgments 925/1988, 440/1995, and 329/1977). Each person who identifies with a faith, no matter what the confession to which he belongs, demands equal protection of conscience (*see* again Judgment 440/1995). Nevertheless the possibility remains for the State to regulate in a bilateral way, and therefore in a specific and differentiated way, relations with the Catholic Church through the Concordat (Art. 7 of the Constitution) and relations with religious confessions other than Catholicism with "understandings."

Such a position of equidistance and impartiality is the reflection of the principle of *laicità* that the Constitutional Court has extracted from the system of constitutional norms, a principle that rises to the level of a "supreme principle" (Judgments 203/1989, 259/1990, 195/1993, and 329/1997), characterizing the form of our State as a pluralistic one in which diverse faiths, culture, and traditions coexist in equal liberty (Judgment 440/1995).

Five years later, with Judgment 168/2005, the Constitutional Court also held Article 403 of the Criminal Code, which provided for the crime of contempt of the Catholic religion by offending a Catholic person or a Catholic minister, to be invalid. Again in this case, the Constitutional Court found the Criminal Code in conflict with Articles 3 and 8 of the Constitution because Article 403 established a sanction that was more severe in the case of contempt of the Catholic religion than in cases of contempt of religions other than Catholicism.

In the last decade this Court, repeatedly called upon to pronounce on criminal protection of religious sentiment, has taken under examination . . . the incriminating matters provided for in Art. 402, 404, and 405 of the Criminal Code, accepting, with reference to Art. 3 and 8 of the Constitution, the questions of constitutionality raised by the disparity of treatment between the Catholic religion and other religions . . .

The constitutional requirement of the equal protection of religious sentiment that underlies the equalization of the sanctions for offenses against the Catholic religion with those against other religious confessions, as already affirmed by this Court in Judgments 329/1997 and 327/2002, is attributable, on the one hand, to the principle of equality before the law without regard to religious difference as provided by Art. 3 of the Constitution, and on the other hand by the principle of *laicità* or non-confessionality of the State (*see* Judgments 203/1989, 259/1990, 195/1993, 329/1997, 50/2000, 327/2002), implying, among other things, equidistance and impartiality toward all religions in accordance with Art. 8 of the Constitution, which requires the equal liberty of all religious confessions under the law.

Other circumstances in which the Constitutional Court has intervened to affirm the equality of treatment of various religions are the oath taken by witnesses in legal proceedings (Judgment 149/1995), and tax incentives and exemptions in favor of religious entities (Judgment 235/1997).

In recent years, similarly to what happened earlier in the United States, many disputes have arisen regarding the display of religious symbols in public areas. While in the American cases the problems originated with such controversies as the posting of the Ten Commandments in courtrooms or the display of Christmas scenes in parks and public squares, in the Italian cases the problems originated almost exclusively from the presence of crucifixes in polling stations, courtrooms, and classrooms.

In particular, the presence of the crucifix in the classroom of a public primary school has been the subject of a very complex and controversial dispute that originated in the Veneto Administrative Court and involved the Council of State, the Constitutional Court, and even the European Court of Human Rights. For the importance of its subject matter and for its long and multilevel procedural history, the crucifix case provides a good example of the workings of the Italian system of constitutional adjudication and of the relationships between the various courts involved in constitutional litigation, even though it regards a question on which the Constitutional Court issued an order of a procedural nature without ever deciding the merits of the case.

The case began in 2002, when the parents of two students enrolled in a primary public school in the town of Abano Terme, in the Veneto Region, asked the local School Board to remove the crucifix from their children's classrooms. After the decision of the Board not to remove the crucifix, the parents filed a petition with the Administrative Court contesting the decision. The parents challenged the decision of the Board as infringing the supreme and inviolable principle of *laicità*, the principle of equality affirmed in Article 3 of the Constitution, freedom of religion—which includes the right not to profess any religion—protected by Article 19 of the Constitution, and Article 9 of the European Convention on Human Rights, which recognizes freedom of thought, conscience, and religion.

The Veneto Administrative Court in 2004 referred to the Constitutional Court the question of whether the rules that include the crucifix among the furniture of the public schools' classrooms conflicted with the principle of *laicità* as affirmed in the jurisprudence of the Constitutional Court, and with Articles 2, 3, 7, 8, 19, and 20 of the Constitution. The Constitutional Court ruled that it did not have jurisdiction, declaring the question raised by the Administrative Court inadmissible because the sources of law that provided for the crucifix in the classrooms were not legislative but only consisted of administrative regulations. The Constitutional Court has the power to review only statutory law and acts with the same force of statutes, not "secondary legislation," such as administrative rules and regulations (see Chapter 2, section 5).

As a consequence of the surprising restraint of the Constitutional Court, the proceedings in the Administrative Court resumed, and in 2005 the applicant's complaint was dismissed. The Administrative Court held that the crucifix was a symbol of Italian history and culture, and therefore of Italian identity; a symbol of the principles of equality, freedom, and tolerance; and even (paradoxically, one cannot deny) a symbol of the State's secular basis.

The decision of the Administrative Court was appealed to the Council of State, the court of last resort for administrative matters, which dismissed the appeal in 2006. The Council of State held that, in Italy, the crucifix symbolized the values that characterized Italian civilization (tolerance, mutual respect, dignity of the person, affirmation of one's rights, consideration of one's freedom, the autonomy of one's moral conscience vis-à-vis authority, human solidarity, and the refusal of any form of discrimination), and their Christian origins. In that sense, when displayed in classrooms, the crucifix could serve a highly educational symbolic function—even from a "secular" perspective distinct from the religious perspective to which it specifically referred—irrespective of the religion professed by the pupils.

The litigation over the presence of the crucifix in public schools did not end in the Italian courts. Soile Lautsi, the mother of the two children, filed an action with the European Court of Human Rights in Strasbourg. The applicant alleged in her own name and on behalf of her children that displaying the crucifix in the children's public school constituted interference incompatible with her right to ensure that they receive education and teaching in conformity with her religious and philosophical convictions within the meaning of Article 2 of Protocol n. 1 to the European Convention on Human Rights, which provides:

> No person shall be denied the right to education. In the exercise of any functions which it assumes in relation to education and teaching, the State shall respect the right of parents to ensure such education and teaching in conformity with their own religious and philosophical convictions.

The applicant further alleged that displaying the crucifix also infringed her freedom of belief and religion, protected by Article 9 of the Convention, which provides:

1. Everyone has the right to freedom of thought, conscience and religion; this right includes freedom to change his religion or belief and freedom, either alone or in community with others and in public or private, to manifest his religion or belief, in worship, teaching, practice and observance.

2. Freedom to manifest one's religion or beliefs shall be subject only to such limitations as are prescribed by law and are necessary in a democratic society in the interest of public safety, for the protection of public order, health or morals, or for the protection of the rights and freedoms of others.

In November 2009, the Second Chamber of the Strasbourg Court unanimously held that the Italian State, by allowing the display of the crucifix in the classroom of a public school, had violated the rights of Soile Lautsi and her children, as protected by Article 2 of Protocol n. 1 taken together with Article 9 of the Convention.[7] The decision was severely criticized in Italy among certain political and social sectors, and led to a very bitter debate in public opinion. On one side of the spectrum were those who viewed the public display of the symbol of a religion followed by the majority of the population, as is the crucifix, as a violation of freedom of religion of the persons who do not recognize this symbol, either because they follow other religious beliefs or none. On the opposite side of the spectrum were those who considered the cross as a legitimate expression of the national identity, the mere display of which did not in any way violate basic guarantees of religious freedom or education; and those, whether believers or not, that did not feel offended by the presence of a religious symbol in the public buildings.

The Italian Government asked for the case to be referred to the Grand Chamber (a panel of 17 judges of the European Court of Human Rights, which has the discretion to review decisions rendered by the Chambers), which granted the request. Testifying to the importance of the case, the Grand Chamber gave leave to 33 members of the European Parliament acting collectively, to many nongovernmental organizations, and to 10 Member States of the Council of Europe, to intervene in the case with their written (and in the case of the other States, oral) arguments. In March 2011, the Grand Chamber issued a judgment reversing that of the Second

---

[7] ECtHR, Second Chamber, case of *Lautsi and Others v. Italy*, Application no. 30814/06, Judgment, 9 November 2009.

Chamber, and holding by 15 votes to 2 that there had been no violation of the Convention.[8]

71. . . . [I]t is true that by prescribing the presence of crucifixes in State-school classrooms—a sign which, whether or not it is accorded in addition a secular symbolic value, undoubtedly refers to Christianity—the regulations confer on the country's majority religion preponderant visibility in the school environment. That is not itself sufficient, however, to denote a process of indoctrination on the respondent State's part and establish a breach of the requirements of Art. 2 of Protocol n. 1 . . .

72. Furthermore, a crucifix on a wall is an essentially passive symbol and this point is of importance in the Court's view, particularly having regard to the principle of neutrality. It cannot be deemed to have influence on pupils comparable to that of didactic speech or participation to religious activities . . .

74. Moreover, the effects of the greater visibility which the presence of the crucifix gives to Christianity in schools needs to be further placed in perspective by considering the following points. Firstly, the presence of crucifixes is not associated with compulsory teaching about Christianity. Secondly, according to the indications provided by the Government, Italy opens up the school environment in parallel to other religions. The Government indicated in this connection that it was not forbidden for pupils to wear Islamic headscarves or other symbols or apparel having a religious connotation; alternative arrangements were possible to help schooling fit in with non-majority religious practices; the beginning and end of Ramadan were "often celebrated" in schools; and optional religious education could be organized in schools for "all recognized religious creeds". Moreover, there was nothing to suggest that the authorities were intolerant of pupils who believed in other religions, were non-believers or who held non-religious philosophical convictions.

In addition, the applicants did not assert that the presence of the crucifix in classrooms had encouraged the development of teaching practices with a proselytizing tendency, or claim that [Soile Lautsi's two children] had ever experienced a tendentious reference to that presence by a teacher in the exercise of his or her functions.

---

[8] ECtHR, Grand Chamber, case of *Lautsi and Others v. Italy*, Application no. 30814/06, Judgment, 18 March 2011.

75. Lastly, the Court notes that the first applicant retained in full her right as a parent to enlighten and advise her children, to exercise in their regard her natural functions as educator and to guide them on a path in line with her own philosophical convictions. [Internal citations removed.]

In the end, the Grand Chamber found the question to fall within the scope of the margin of appreciation to be accorded to the State, essentially remanding the controversy to the Italian legislature and courts. It is very likely, therefore, that the domestic Italian legal system will be writing further chapters in this tale in the not-too-distant future.

5. Life, Reproduction, Health

5.1 RIGHT TO LIFE

The right to life, which is solemnly announced by the Universal Declaration of Human Rights and by the European Convention on Human Rights, is not expressly provided for by the Italian Constitution, but can be considered the first and most important of the inviolable rights protected by Article 2. The right to life can also be inferred from Article 27, paragraph 4 of the Constitution, which prohibits capital punishment.

The fundamental relation between Articles 2 and 27, paragraph 4 of the Constitution is stressed by Judgment 223/1996. The case—that reached the Constitutional Court after a referral from the Administrative Court of the Lazio Region—was about an Italian citizen convicted of first-degree murder by a trial court of Dade County, Florida, and detained in Italy. According to the Administrative Tribunal, Article 698, paragraph 2 of the Code of Criminal Procedure and Statute 225/1984 (which ratified the extradition treaty between Italy and the United States) violated Articles 2 and 27 of the Constitution because it permitted extradition for a crime that was punishable with the death penalty—even though assurances were given by U.S. authorities that capital punishment would not be applied. The Constitutional Court struck down the challenged norms, underlining the inviolability of the right to life, and stating that the mere fact that a legal system provides for capital punishment contrasts with the prohibition against it enshrined in the Italian Constitution.

[T]he prohibition of the death penalty is given special significance in the first part of the Constitution, like that given to inhuman punishments. Introduced by the fourth paragraph of Art. 27, it implies the principle—"which may be said to be Italian in many ways" (words taken from the Commission's report from the Constituent Assembly, in the section dedicated to civil relations), and which, "though reiterated during periods and regimes of freedom in our country, has been dismissed in periods of reaction and violence"—which manifests itself in the constitutional system as the guarantee of life, a fundamental good and the first of the inalienable human rights recognized under Art. 2.

The absolute quality of this constitutional guarantee affects how the authority granted to all the public entities in the republican system is exercised as well as the types of authority that allow for international cooperation for purposes of mutual legal assistance. Therefore, Art. 27, paragraph 4, read in light of Art. 2 of the Constitution, provides an essential guideline for evaluating the constitutional validity of both the general law governing the concession of extradition (Art. 698, paragraph 2 of the Code of Criminal Procedure) and the laws giving legal effect to international treaties on extradition and legal assistance.

5—This Court has held elsewhere that any involvement by the Italian State in the execution of punishments, "which could not be inflicted in Italy in peacetime under any theory or for any type of crime", is a violation of the Constitution in and of itself (Judgment 54/1979).

Moreover, for the Constitutional Court, the right to life belongs to a category of rights that "assumes a privileged position within the legal order because it pertains to the very essence of those supreme values upon which the Italian Constitution is based" (Judgment 1146/1988).

5.2 REPRODUCTIVE FREEDOM

The question of the right to life of a fetus—and contemporarily the right to abortion of a mother—first reached the Italian Constitutional Court in 1975, the same year of the German *Bundesverfassungsgeright*'s decision on abortion[9] and only two years after *Roe v. Wade*.[10]

With Judgment 27/1975 the Constitutional Court struck down Article 546 of the Criminal Code, which permitted abortion only when necessary to save the life of the mother and punished both the mother and the doctor for abortions performed in any other circumstance. The case was referred to the Court by the trial court of Milano, which contested the validity of Article 546 of the Criminal Code under Article 31, paragraph 2, and Article 32, paragraph 1 of the Constitution. The former

---

[9]   Judgment of the First Senate of 25 February, 1975.
[10]   410 U.S. 113 (1973).

establishes that "the Republic protects motherhood, childhood and youth encouraging the institutions necessary for that purpose," and the latter that "the Republic safeguards health as a fundamental right of the individual and as a collective interest." In reaching its decision—extremely brief if compared with *Roe v. Wade* and other European examples—the Court balanced the right to life of the fetus, that is not yet a person, with the right to life and health of the mother, who is a fully developed person, and concluded that Parliament cannot place an absolute priority on the fetus's constitutional right to life where this would deny adequate protection to the pregnant woman's rights.

> The Court holds that the protection of the conceived [*concepito*],[11] which already holds an important place under civil law (Art. 320, 339, and 687 of the Civil Code), has a constitutional foundation. Art. 31, paragraph 2 of the Constitution expressly requires the protection of "maternity" and Art. 2 more generally recognizes and guarantees the inalienable rights of human beings, a legal status we must apply to the conceived, albeit with its own particular characteristics.
>
> Nevertheless, this premise—which, taken as it is, justifies legislative intervention intended to provide for criminal sanctions—must be considered in conjunction with the fact that the constitutionally protected interest concerning the conceived may come into conflict with other goods that also benefit from constitutional protection. As a consequence, the law cannot give to the former a total and absolute preeminence that detracts from the adequate protection of the latter. Herein lies the constitutional defect, which, in the opinion of this Court, nullifies the current criminal regulation of abortion.
>
> The decision under review specifically denounces Art. 546 of the Criminal Code, under Art. 31 and 32 of the Constitution, which provide criminal sanctions for whoever performs an abortion on a consenting woman, and for the woman herself, "even when the danger of pregnancy to the physical wellbeing and mental stability of the pregnant woman have been verified, but where they do not satisfy the conditions of the state of necessity provided for by Art. 54 of the Criminal Code . . .
>
> The right of someone who is already a person—like the mother—not only to life, but also to good health, is not at this time equivalent to the protection of the embryo, which has yet to become a person.

---

[11] *Concepito* is literally translated as "the conceived," for which there is no adequate English.

Judgment 27/1975 opened the way to Statute 194/1978 regulating "the social protection of motherhood and the voluntary termination of pregnancy," modeled after the law regulating abortion adopted in France in 1975.[12] Because of the political turmoil the new statute provoked, and because the Constitutional Court was called to judge its validity, a very brief description of the main features of the statute is required.

The first article of the statute sets forth the general principles that guide the interpretation of the new legislation: "The State recognizes the right to a willing and responsible procreation recognizes the social value of motherhood and protects human life from its beginnings. The voluntary termination of pregnancy is not a means of birth control. The State, the Regions and the local authorities will create and develop social and medical services in order to prevent abortion from being utilized to limit the numbers of births." After establishing the principle of respect for human life, the statute then specifies the circumstances under which it will tolerate derogation from that principle, referring to these circumstances as a "state of necessity." The statute also distinguishes, in order to apply the "state of necessity," between termination of pregnancy before and after the first 90 days—a distinction that easily recalls the well-known trimester framework of *Roe v. Wade*.

Within the first 90 days, abortion is lawful when there is a danger to the physical or psychological health of the woman. The health of the woman must be considered in terms of her economic, social, and family situation, and the possibility that the child may be born with malformations must also be taken into consideration. The procedure for obtaining an abortion requires that both a doctor and the woman sign a document that certifies the pregnancy of the woman and her request to terminate it. After a waiting period of seven days from the time of the signature of the document (although the statute provides exceptions to this rule), the abortion will be performed under the national healthcare system—that is, without financial costs for the woman. After 90 days, abortion may be performed only when a physician certifies that the pregnancy constitutes a serious danger to the woman's life or physical or mental health. When the fetus may be viable, abortion is permitted only to save the life of the mother, and the physician must then take any appropriate action to save the life of the fetus. In any case, when the woman is a minor, the statute requires parental or judicial consent.

The enactment of Statute 194/1978 fuelled an intense debate between pro-choice and pro-life advocates, which both started the necessary proceedings to hold a public referendum in order to abrogate the new law. More precisely, on one hand, the Radical Party proposed a referendum in order to eliminate from the statute all the rules regarding certification and a waiting period. On the other hand, the Pro-Life

---

[12] Statute n. 75-17 of January 17, 1975.

Movement proposed a referendum to abrogate all kinds of legal abortions with the only exception being the case in which abortion is needed to save the woman's life. With Judgment 26/1981 the Constitutional Court admitted the referendum, which, that same year, upheld the statute.

The public referendum was not the only attempt made in order to contest the validity of Statute 194/1978. In fact, the Constitutional Court was called to decide whether the statute was a violation of those articles of the Constitution protecting human life, motherhood, and family. With Judgment 108/1981 the Court declared inadmissible the various challenges brought by 11 different courts against the statute. Through its restrained decision, the Court seemed very respectful of the popular will that resulted from the referendum that had upheld the statute.

The role played by the Constitutional Court in the abortion story did not end in 1981, because in 1997 the Court was called again to judge the admissibility of a new referendum. The new referendum, the purpose of which was to abrogate part of Statute 194/1978 in order to limit substantially the possibility for women of obtaining an abortion, never took place because the Court, recalling its own precedents, declared the referendum not admissible and left Statute 194/1978 untouched once again (see Judgment 35/1997).

Interesting questions, although very technical and complex, related to the health of the pregnant woman, were also raised in connection with Statute 40/2004 regulating medically assisted reproduction techniques. The Administrative Court of Lazio and the Trial Court of Firenze contested the constitutional validity of Article 14, paragraphs 2 and 3 of the statute because they limited to three the number of embryos to be produced and prohibited, save for exceptional and unforeseeable circumstances, the freezing of the embryos. The Constitutional Court, with Judgment 15/2009, struck down the challenged paragraphs as a violation of the right to health of the woman, protected by Article 32, and as a violation of the principle of equality established by Article 3 of the Constitution.

[I]t must be observed that the prohibition found at Art. 14, paragraph 2, by forbidding the creation of any number of embryos more than are strictly necessary for a single and contemporaneous implantation, and in any case forbidding the creation of more than three, renders it necessary to increase the number of cycles of fertilization (also contrary to the principle that the process of assisted reproduction be gradual and minimally invasive found in Art. 4, paragraph 2), since three embryos do not always give rise to a pregnancy. Indeed, the chances of success vary depending on the characteristics of the embryos, the individual circumstances of the woman who undergoes medically assisted reproduction, and the woman's age, the advancement of which gradually reduces the probability of a pregnancy.

Therefore, the legislative limitation under scrutiny ends up, on the one hand, favouring an increased risk of the damage these hyper-stimulations can cause by necessitating the repetition of the ovarian stimulation cycles described above whenever the first implantation attempt did not produce a positive result. On the other hand, it prejudices the health of both the woman and the fetus in cases where the chances of successful implantation are greater, since, in the case of multiple pregnancies, selective reduction of the embryos is prohibited in Art. 14, paragraph 4, except for abortion. The legislation fails to recognize that a doctor may evaluate an individual case on the basis of the most advanced and legitimate technical/scientific knowledge, and make a case-by-case determination of the number of embryos to implant, in order to assure that a serious attempt at assisted reproduction is undertaken and that risks to the health of both woman and fetus are reduced to the minimum possible.

Here we note that constitutional jurisprudence has repeatedly pointed out the limitations placed on legislative discretion by advances in knowledge due to scientific and experimental discoveries, which form the basis of the practice of medicine, and which are constantly evolving. Therefore, when it comes to medical care, the basic rule must be the autonomy and responsibility of the doctor, who, with the patient's consent, makes the necessary professional determinations (Judgments 338/2003 and 282/2002).

The provision limiting the creation of a number of embryos to three, in the absence of any consideration of the subjective conditions of the woman who undergoes medically assisted reproduction, decidedly conflicts with Art. 3 of the Constitution, analyzed under the dual framework of reasonableness and equality, to the extent that the legislature applies a uniform rule to different situations. It also contradicts Art. 32 of the Constitution as prejudicial to the health of the woman, and potentially to that of the fetus as well.

In order to appreciate the multilevel nature of the protection of fundamental rights, it is worth noting that another provision of the same Statute 40/2004 was contested in front of the European Court of Human Rights. In the case *Costa and Pavan v. Italy*,[13] the Strasbourg Court unanimously held that Article 13, which bans access to embryo screening, is a violation of Article 8 of the Convention, which establishes the right to respect for private and family life. The reasoning of the Court is

---

[13] ECtHR, Second Chamber, case of *Costa and Pavan v. Italy*, Application no. 54270/10, Judgment, 11 February 2013.

extremely interesting because, given the factual situation, it underlined the inconsistencies between Statute 40/2004, which regulates medically assisted pro-creation techniques, and Statute 194/1978, which regulates "the social protection of motherhood and the voluntary termination of pregnancy."

> The Court considered that the applicants' desire to resort to medically-assisted procreation and PID in order to have a baby that did not suffer from cystic fibrosis was a form of expression of their private and family life that fell within the scope of Art. 8. The fact that the law did not allow them to proceed in this manner therefore amounted to an interference with their right to respect for their private and family life which was "in accordance with the law" and pursued the legitimate aims of protecting morals and the rights and freedoms of others.
>
> The Italian Government justified this interference by the need to protect the health of the mother and child and the dignity and freedom of conscience of the medical professions, and to avoid the risk of eugenic abuses. The Court observed first of all that the notions of "embryo" and "child" must not be confused. It could not see how, in the event that the foetus proved to have the disease, a medically-assisted abortion could be reconciled with the Government's justifications, considering, among other things, the consequences of such a procedure for both the foetus and the parents, particularly the mother. . . .
>
> The Court observed that the inconsistency in Italian law—prohibiting the implantation of only those embryos which were healthy, but authorising the abortion of foetuses which showed symptoms of the disease—left the applicants only one choice, which brought anxiety and suffering: starting a pregnancy by natural means and terminating it if prenatal tests showed the foetus to have the disease. The Court accordingly considered that the interference with the applicants' right to respect for their private and family life was disproportionate, in breach of Art. 8.

Eventually the Italian Administration asked the Grand Chamber of the European Court of Human Rights to reconsider the decision of the Second Chamber, but the request was rejected on February 11, 2013.

In 2013 Statute 40/2004 was again challenged by the Courts of first instance of Milano, Firenze, and Catania. More precisely, the referring Courts contested Article 4, prohibiting medically assisted pro-creation of the "aetherologus" kind. With Judgment 162/2014, in which the Constitutional Court operated an important and complex balancing of the various rights involved, Article 4 was struck down.

> 4—In the case at bar the issues raised in reference to articles 2, 3, 29, 31, and 32 of the Constitution are well-founded in the ways laid out below.

5—Scrutiny of the challenges should be carried out, and with regard for all of these parameters jointly, since medically assisted procreation involves "numerous constitutional needs" (Judgment 347/1998) and, consequently, Statute 40/2004 has a bearing on multiple interests of the same rank. These, in their entirety, require a "balancing among themselves that assures a minimum level of legislative protection" to each (Judgment 45/2005), this Court having already held that the "protection of the embryo is not absolute, but limited by the need to identify a fair balance with the needs of procreation" (Judgment 51/2009).

The questions touch upon ethically sensitive issues, concerning which finding a reasonable point of equilibrium between the opposed needs concerning the dignity of the human person belongs "primarily to the evaluation of the legislature (Judgment 347/1998)"; however, it remains subject to judicial review, with the aim of verifying whether the balancing of these needs and the values that give rise to them is reasonable.

5.3 HEALTH

At this point, Article 32 of the Constitution must be read in its entirety. The first paragraph, as already mentioned, provides that "the Republic safeguards health as a fundamental right of the individual and as a collective interest," but the same paragraph also provides that the Republic "guarantees free medical care to the indigent." Notwithstanding the wording of this provision, Parliament established, with Statute 883/1978 and subsequent amendments, the National Health Service committing itself to ensuring the physical and mental health of the entire population, regardless of social and individual backgrounds. In this respect, the right to health is a right that creates a positive burden for public authorities and, as such, is subject to budgetary limits.[14] Consequently, health care may vary, depending on the economic situation. However, the level of health care can never fall below a minimum standard, which guarantees the essential content of the right to health. In this regard, following the 2001 reform of Title V of the Constitution, which assigned the subject matter of "health" to the concurrent legislative powers of the State and the Regions (Art. 117, paragraph 3 of the Constitution), the central State still retains the exclusive legislative power in relation to the "determination of essential levels of services concerning the rights and social entitlements to be

---

[14] Important judgments on health care are discussed *infra*, in section 7. For the relation between the right to health and budgetary problems, see especially Judgment 445/1990 also discussed *infra*.

guaranteed throughout the national territory" (Art. 117, paragraph 2, letter m) of the Constitution).

The need to protect health as a collective interest may also require people to submit to certain medical treatments such as, for instance, mandatory vaccinations. In this regard, however, the Constitution provides that health care can only be imposed by law and that any such law cannot violate "the limits imposed by the respect for the human person" (Art. 32, paragraph 2 of the Constitution). The constitutional case law has also established the right to compensation from the State when, following compulsory vaccination, an individual has suffered personal injuries.

Discussing Article 32 of the Constitution in its various components, Judgment 118/1996 is fundamental for two reasons. First of all, it clarifies the distinction between the individual and social dimensions of the right to health; second, it establishes important principles related to medical treatment and to the right to compensation in case of injuries derived from compulsory medical treatment.

The case reached the Constitutional Court by referral of a trial court of Firenze, which challenged Articles 2 and 3 of Statute 210/1992 that regulated compensation for persons permanently injured by compulsory vaccinations or blood transfusions. Articles 2 and 3 established that the amount of damages for injuries derived from compulsory vaccination had to be calculated from the day in which the request was filed; they established also that for those who had already suffered injury before the enactment of the statute, damages were to be calculated from the day in which the statute came into force. For the judge *a quo*, such norms violated Article 32 of the Constitution because they "did not provide a compensation which is full and complete for those who had suffered injuries before the enactment of the statute." The Constitutional Court struck down Articles 2 and 3 of Statute 210/1992.

4. The constitutional regulation of health consists of two facets, the individual and subjective on the one hand (health as a "fundamental right of the individual"), and the objective and social on the other (health as an "interest of the community"). One of these can, at times, conflict with the other, as often happens in dealing with the relationship between a whole and its parts. In particular—as in the case at hand—it may happen that the pursuit of the community's interest in health, through healthcare treatments such as obligatory vaccinations, compromise the individual right to health when such treatments can inflict undesired consequences upon the individuals who receive them, which are detrimental beyond the bounds of what is normally considered tolerable.

These treatments are permitted under Art. 32, paragraph 2, of the Constitution, which reserves their use to government lawmakers and conditions them upon a necessary respect for the human person and, as this Court held in Judgment 258/1994, upon the requirement that lawmakers provide for all possible precautionary measures to avoid the risk of complications. However, such risks are not always avoidable, and this is where the individual dimension and the collective one come into conflict. The case that gave rise to the present judgment of constitutionality is an example. The polio vaccine carries a risk of infection that is predictable in the abstract because it has been statistically observed; however, as a concrete matter, the individuals who will be damaged by this occurrence cannot be predicted. Under the circumstances, the law, which imposes the obligation to receive the polio vaccine, makes a deliberate evaluation of the collective and individual interests involved, nearly to the point of making one of the so-called "tragic choices" of law: the choices a society decides it must undertake for the sake of some good (in this case the eradication of polio), which entails the risk of some harm (in this case the infection which, although extremely rarely, will strike some number of its members). The tragic element lies in the fact that suffering and wellbeing are not evenly distributed among all, but impact only some in order to benefit others.

Until the advancement of science and medical technology succeeds in completely eliminating any risk of complication—a circumstance not yet attained in the case of the polio vaccine—the decision to make the vaccine mandatory will belong to this category of public choice.

5. In a legal order such as ours, which is based on the recognition of the fundamental value of the person as an individual (Art. 2 of the Constitution), the characteristics of the polio vaccine described above implicate a further condition for constitutionality in addition to those required by Art. 32, paragraph 2 of the Constitution. It is nearly tantamount to a reinforcement of the reservation of power to the lawmaker found in that paragraph, which was explained in this Court's Judgment 307/1990, a decision that provides the necessary reference point for the present decision.

In that case, the Constitutional Court affirmed that the significance given by the Constitution to health as a collective interest, although normally sufficient on its own to "justify the restriction of human self-determination, which is inherent to each person's right to health as a fundamental right," that is, sufficient to prohibit individuals from exempting themselves from an obligatory measure (*see* also Judgment 258/1994), is not sufficient when damaging consequences for the individual's right to health could ensue. Without prejudice to the importance of conscientious objection to medical treatments, which must be recognized, it is possible that, in the name of the duty of solidarity with others, whoever must undergo healthcare treatments (or, as in the case of polio vaccinations, which are given in the first months of life, whoever exercises parental power or protection) will be deprived of the ability to freely decide. But no one can simply be called upon to sacrifice their own health for the health of others, even if for all others. The coexistence of the individual and collective dimensions of the constitutional regulation of health, as well as the duty of solidarity that binds the individual to the community, but also the community to the individual, dictate that a specific amount of support, consistent with an equitable indemnification for damages, be accorded to those injured as a result of conforming to obligatory healthcare treatments. It bears adding that this compensation is due based on the bare, objective fact—not involving culpability—that an inevitable injury was inflicted on some individual by a circumstance that bestows a benefit upon society as a whole: such compensation is due irrespective of any proper reparations, which may be requested by the interested party, where the conditions provided by Art. 2043 of the Civil Code are met.

6. In short, negative health impacts caused by healthcare treatments may give rise to one of the following three consequences: a) the right to reparations for suffering, recognized by Art. 2043 of the Civil Code, in cases of culpable behaviour; b) the right to equitable indemnification, which derives from Art. 32 of the Constitution, in combination with Art. 2, in cases where the injury, not having been caused by tort, was the consequence of the performance of a legal obligation; and, c) the right, under Art. 2 and 38 of the Constitution, to an amount of aid specified by the legislature, in the exercise of its constitutionally legitimate discretionary powers, in all other cases.

Parliament answered Judgment 118/1996 by enacting a new Statute (238/1997), which also was challenged as a violation of Article 32 of the Constitution. But in this case, the Constitutional Court saved the law, holding that the exact amount of damages for injuries deriving from obligatory vaccination is a political question and rests within the discretion of the legislative body to determine (Judgment 27/1998). Notwithstanding Judgment 27/1998, the Court has been called upon in other cases to decide the issue of the amount of damages for persons permanently injured by obligatory medical treatment, and in every case the Court, although holding the challenged legislation valid, urged the legislative body to enact new rules (see Judgments 423/2000 and 38/2002). Parliament, as often happens with social rights, has not yet followed the Constitutional Court's suggestion.

5.4 END OF LIFE

At present, one of the most debated issues regarding health care and obligatory treatment pertains to end-of-life problems—that is, to problems concerning the thin line that divides aggressive medical treatment from euthanasia. It is believed that Article 32 of the Constitution, while protecting the right to health care, also protects the freedom to refuse medical treatment, even when such a refusal may lead to a premature death.

The question of the refusal of life-saving medical treatment has arisen in tremendously dramatic situations where patients, due to the clinical condition in which they lie, are unable to express their will. One of these was the very important case of Eluana Englaro, a young woman who lived for more than 15 years in a permanent vegetative state before her father asked that hydration and artificial feeding be disconnected.

The *Englaro* case, decided by the Supreme Court of Cassation, is interesting for several reasons. First of all, it is interesting for the intense political struggle and heated social debate it provoked, which closely recall those raised in the United States by the tragic case of Terri Schiavo.[15] Second, because the case shows the relationship between the Constitutional Court (to which belongs the interpretation of the Constitution) and the Court of Cassation (to which belongs the final interpretation of the law). Finally, because the Court of Cassation, in deciding such a difficult case, not only quoted the European Court of Human Rights but also made extensive reference to foreign case law, explicitly citing the Supreme Court of New Jersey,[16] the U.S. Supreme Court,[17] the German *Bundesgerichtshof*,[18] and the House of Lords;[19] the Englaro judgment, therefore, represents a rare Italian example of explicit judicial constitutional dialogue.

The case of Eluana was brought to the Supreme Court of Cassation by her father and legal guardian, Beppino Englaro, after he was denied by the trial judge and Court of Appeal of Milano the possibility of disconnecting his daughter's feeding tube.

The Court of Cassation reversed the decision and remanded the case to the Court of Appeal stating the principle of law (that is the correct interpretation of the law) that the Court of Appeal had to follow. The reasoning of the Court of Cassation is important because—reading the law in light of Articles 2, 13, and 32 of the Constitution and considering also that there is no statute regulating so-called "living will/advance directives"—it clarified the content of the right to refuse

---

[15] The Terri Schiavo case was a legal struggle involving prolonged life support that lasted from 1990 to 2005. The issue was whether to carry out the decision of the husband of Teresa Marie "Terri" Schiavo to terminate life support for her. Terri was diagnosed by doctors as being in a persistent vegetative state. The highly publicized and prolonged series of legal challenges presented by her parents and by state and federal legislative intervention effected a seven-year delay before life support finally was terminated.

[16] *In re Quinlan*, 70 N.J. 10, 335 A.2d 647 (1976), and *In re Nancy Ellen*, 108 N.J. 394, 529 A.2d 434 (1987).

[17] *Vacco v. Quill*, 521 U.S. 793 (1997), and *Cruzan v. Director*, 497 U.S. 261 (1990).

[18] Judgment of March 17, 2003.

[19] *Airendale NHS Trust v. Bland*, (1993) AC 789 HL.

medical treatment and the limits within which a legal guardian can ask to discon-
nect life-supporting systems of a person in a permanent vegetative state.

6. It is important to note that informed consent is usually the foundation and
legitimization of healthcare: without informed consent, a doctor's interventions are strictly forbidden, even when they are in the best interest of a patient.
The practice of informed consent is a form of respect for the freedom of the
individual, and is a means of pursuing his or her best interest.

The principle of informed consent—which communicates a value choice in
the way of conceiving the doctor-patient relationship, in the sense that this
relationship appears to be founded, first of all, on the rights of the patient and
on the patient's freedom to self-determination when it comes to therapies,
rather than the rights of the doctor—has a firm foundation in law under Art.
2 of the Constitution, which protects and promotes the fundamental rights
of the human person, identity, and dignity; under Art. 13, which declares the
inviolability of personal freedom, in which lies "the power of the person over
his or her own body" (Constitutional Court, Judgment 471/1990); and under
Art. 32, which protects health as a fundamental right of the individual, in
addition to its value as an interest of the collective, and allows for the possibility of mandatory healthcare treatments. Under Art. 32 the institution of
such treatments is reserved to lawmakers, and is conditioned upon a necessary
respect for the human person and the requirement that lawmakers take every
possible precaution to minimize the risk of complications.

. . .

The principle of informed consent is well-established in the precedents set
by this Court.

. . .

6.1 Informed consent involves not only the ability to choose among the various possible medical courses of action, but also the option to refuse treatment
and make an informed decision to terminate treatment at any stage of life,
including the final one.

. . .

The complete picture given above of the values at stake, essentially based
on the free use of health as a good by the directly interested party, in full possession of his or her faculties of reason and desire, is altered when an adult
individual is not able to communicate his or her will on account of complete
incapacity and has not, before falling into such a condition and while in complete possession of his or her mental faculties, indicated, through a prior declaration of intent, which therapies would be desired and which rejected if he

or she were to fall into an unconscious state. In this situation, the fundamental and absolute value of the rights involved demands the implementation of immediate protection and requires that the judge perform a delicate reconstruction of the criteria for judgment within the framework of constitutional principles (*see* Constitutional Court, Judgment 347/1998).

. . .

7.3 Given that the guardian's responsibility to care for the person takes the shape of giving informed consent to medical treatment intended for the incompetent person, the issue then becomes to determine the boundaries of the legal representative's interventions.

. . .

According to this Court, the use of representative power, since it must be oriented toward protecting the represented individual's right to life, only allows for cessation of medical treatment in extreme cases . . .

. . .

It follows that the contested decision is struck down, and we remand the case to a different Section of the Milan Court of Appeal. That Court will make a decision according to the following legal principle:

"In the case that the patient languish for a very long time (for example, more than fifteen years) in a permanent vegetative state, resulting in an extreme inability to engage with the outside world, and he or she is artificially kept alive via a nasogastric tube, which provides nourishment and hydration, upon the request of the guardian representative, and in dialogue with the special caregiver, a judge may authorize the termination of such medical treatment (but not barring the application of measures recommended by science and medical practice in the interest of the patient), exclusively when the following prerequisites are met: (a) a rigorous clinical evaluation has determined that the vegetative state is irreversible, and there is no medical basis, under internationally recognized scientific standards, for even the minimum possibility, however slim, of some recovery of consciousness and return to perception of the outside world; and b) the request truly expresses, based on clear proof that is unequivocal and convincing, the patient's own voice, obtained from his or her previous declarations or even from his or her personality, lifestyle, and convictions, corresponding to his or her view of human dignity before falling into an unconscious state. Where either of these prerequisites does not exist, the judge must withhold authorization, and must give unconditional precedence to the right to life, independent of the patient's state of health, autonomy, and ability to will and understand, and of whatever perception others might have of his or her quality of life."

6. Family

The Italian Constitution deals with the family and with family relations in many articles. Particularly important are Articles 29, 30, and 31. The former qualifies the family "as a natural society founded on marriage"; Article 30 governs the relationship between parents and children, "even if born out of wedlock"; and the last gives public authorities the responsibility of promoting economic measures and other provisions in order to foster the development of families and also gives public authorities the responsibility of protecting "motherhood, childhood and youth encouraging the institutions necessary for that purpose." In addition, the term "family" is used in several other articles: Article 36 provides that the salary of an employee must provide a free and decent life for himself and his family; Article 34 mentions families as recipients of grants to ensure the right to education; finally, Article 37 protects the "essential role in the family" of the working woman.

The wording of Articles 29 and 30 evidently reflects the compromise between the secular and Catholic cultures that characterized the debate during the Constituent Assembly on many issues, such as the indissolubility of marriage and the status of children born out of wedlock. Evidence of the compromise between the two opposing cultures may also be found, for instance, in the presence of specific restrictive clauses regarding equality between spouses, which can be established by law "to guarantee the unity of the family" (see Article 29, paragraph 2), or in the equality between legitimate children and children born to unmarried parents, to whom the law must ensure every legal and social protection, as long as "compatible with the rights of the members of the legitimate family" (see Article 30, paragraph 3).

The constitutional provisions related to family have never been subject to reform, but over the past 60 years they have been interpreted in very broad ways, which have carried many away from their literal meaning. This creative interpretation, on the one hand, takes stock of the profound changes in Italian society, while, on the other hand, it proceeds by a proper, systematic reading of the rules governing family relations in light of Articles 2 and 3 of the Constitution. More specifically, the provisions limiting equality between spouses and limiting equality among children have been interpreted, both by the Constitutional Court and by Parliament—since the important legislative reform of 1975 that amended parts of the Civil Code concerning family law—having in mind the principle of equal dignity of all individuals and that of formal equality, without distinction, regardless of sex and personal and social conditions proclaimed by Article 3 of the Constitution.

Regarding spouses, some fundamental judgments of the Constitutional Court have declared unconstitutional all the numerous rules that differentiated the position of the wife from that of the husband. In Judgment 126/1968 the Constitutional Court held that Article 559 of the Criminal Code violated Article 29 of the Constitution because it punished adultery only when committed by a wife.

The principle that a husband may violate the obligation of marital fidelity with impunity, while a wife must be punished—more or less severely—recalls the remote past when a woman, considered to be legally incompetent and deprived of many rights, was subjugated to the power of her husband. Much has changed in social life since that time: women have acquired the entirety of rights, and their participation in the economic and social life of the family and of the entire community has become much more intense, to the point of finally reached full equality with men. Meanwhile, this disparate treatment as concerns adultery has remained unchanged, notwithstanding the fact that in some highly developed States the principle of legislative non-interference in this delicate subject matter has prevailed . . .

Instead, the relationship between spouses is regulated by Art. 29 of the Constitution, which recognizes the rights of the family as a natural society founded on marriage, affirms the moral and legal equality of spouses, and provides that this equality may be subject to limitations only in order to vouchsafe family unity. By sanctioning both the equality of the spouses and the unity of the family, the Constitution proclaims the prevalence of unity over equality, but only if and when the equal treatment of spouses is a threat to unity.

As this Court has pointed out elsewhere, there is no doubt that the needs of the organization of the family are among the important factors that limit the principle of equality, and that make the husband, to this day, without creating any inferiority on the part of the wife, the point of convergence of the family unit and its position in society in some regards. This undoubtedly gives the legislature, in order to guarantee family unity, some authority to adopt defensive measures against negative and destructive influences. Nevertheless, these considerations neither explain nor justify the discrimination permitted by the contested law.

The question of punishment for adultery is one of legislative politics. However, since the current criminal law violates the principle of equality of spouses, which remains the general rule, the relevant question becomes whether it is essential to family unity. Only an affirmative answer would render the sacrifice of this basic principle of our legal order acceptable.

This Court holds, in keeping with the realities of today's society, that discrimination, far from being useful, is of severe detriment to the harmony and unity of the family. The law, by giving no importance to adultery by a husband while punishing that of a wife, places the latter in an inferior position: her dignity suffers; she is compelled to tolerate injury and infidelity; and the criminal system offers her no protection . . .

Judgment 126/1968, with which the Court overruled a previous decision (64/1961), is particularly relevant because it mirrors the changing culture of the late 1960s that would pave the way for the 1970 statute that introduced divorce in the Italian legal system and culminate in the already mentioned family law reform of 1975.

More recently, the Constitutional Court, with Judgment 61/2006, had the opportunity to evaluate the constitutional legitimacy of the articles of the Civil Code that establish that children born within wedlock take the family name of the father even when the parents do not agree. More precisely, the Court was called to judge the constitutionality of Articles 143 *bis*, 236, 237 second paragraph, 262, and 299 third paragraph of the Civil Code, which do not allow a child to acquire the family name of the mother even when both parents consent. The Constitutional Court, with Judgment 61/2006, rejected the challenge and confirmed two important precedents (Judgments 176/1988 and 586/1988). The Court, though recognizing that the Civil Code provided for a nonreasonable disparity of treatment between husband and wife, concluded that the question of the attribution of a mother's name to her children is a "political question" and invited the legislative body to regulate the subject matter following the principle of equality between man and woman and of the equal dignity of husband and wife. Parliament, notwithstanding the Court's suggestion, had not yet amended the Civil Code. At the very beginning of 2014, the European Court of Human Rights recognized that Italy violated Article 14 (prohibition of discrimination) of the European Convention on Human Rights, taken together with Article 8 (right to respect for private and family life) of the Convention. The Court held that the decision to name a child based on transmission of the father's name was based solely on discrimination on the ground of the parents' sex, and is therefore incompatible with the principle of nondiscrimination.[20]

Regarding children, legislative reform and rulings of the Constitutional Court have eliminated all discrimination between legitimate and illegitimate children in personal and property relationships with their parents.

Furthermore, the Constitutional provision stating that "it is the duty and right of parents to support, raise, and educate their children, even if born out of wedlock" (Art. 30, paragraph 1) has been subject to systematic interpretation in light of Articles 2 and 3 of the Constitution, and has acquired an autonomous meaning

---

[20] ECtHR, Second Chamber, case of *Cusan and Fazzo v. Italy*, Application no. 77/07, Judgment, 7 January 2014.

from the context in which it is located. Moreover, the issue of filiation has progressively become a base for the construction of a system of constitutional guarantees in favor of minors, known as the status of the constitutional rights of the child. Again, a coordinated reading of the rules laid down in Articles 2, 3, 30, and 31 of the Constitution has given rise to constitutional rulings in accordance with the numerous international conventions to which Italy is part, the so-called principle of the best interest of the child. Finally, with respect to any substantial or procedural legal relationship in which a minor is involved, the legislative body and the interpreter, each in its own area, operate a balance of interests such that the real interest of the minor is ensured with preference over that of any other subject.

In the discussion of the status of children, Judgment 494/2002 is particularly important. In this case the Court held unconstitutional the provisions of the Civil Code that prohibited incestuous children from bringing an action for a judicial declaration of paternity and maternity. The case was referred to the Constitutional Court by the Court of Cassation, which challenged the validity of the first paragraphs of Articles 251 and 278 of the Civil Code as a violation of Articles 2, 3, and 30, third paragraph, of the Constitution. In its opinion, the Constitutional Court takes into account the legislative history of the rules governing the status of incestuous children and also interestingly takes into consideration Article 29 of the Constitution, which is the general provision that recognizes the rights of the family as a natural society founded on marriage.

The regulation of the condition of—to use the expression used in law until the present—"incestuous children," that is, children resulting from sexual relations between individuals belonging to the same family circle, as defined by Art. 252, first paragraph, of the Civil Code (the marriage of whom is prohibited by Art. 87 of the same), is left over from the traditional, radical disfavor that existed toward children born outside of marriage. From this disfavor derives the fact that it is forbidden to attribute a formal legal value to their biological link with their natural parents, either through recognition or declaration of the public authority. The original tradition of excluding the moral rights of children born outside of marriage, inspired by the Napoleonic Code (Art. 171–173) and reiterated by the laws of post-unification Italy, was weakened, and then overcome with regard to natural children born to parents bound in marriage to other people. Art. 252 of the 1942 Civil Code introduced the recognition of "adulterous" children, but only on the part of the parent who at the moment of conception was free of the bonds of marriage. The Family Law reforms enacted with Statute n. 151 of May 19, 1975 then abolished this limitation. Thus, children born in violation of the duty of conjugal fidelity were rendered recognizable by their natural parents in every case and, under Art. 269 of the Civil Code, an action for judicial declaration of paternity and maternity can be brought against them.

Concerning "incestuous children," however, the 1975 reform continued the tradition of excluding them from recognition and from any judicial declaration of natural paternity or maternity. The current Art. 251, in conformance with the corresponding article in the 1942 Civil Code, establishes that "children born to persons between whom exists a bond of kinship, even if only by blood, of direct descent to infinity or parallel descent to the second degree, or of a bond in law of direct descent may not be recognized by their parents." Under Art. 269, the same is true of judicial declarations. Consequently, investigation into the paternity or maternity of the offspring of the individuals described is not permitted (Art. 278, first paragraph, Civil Code).

. . .

5. From this regulation, to the detriment of the offspring of parents related in the ways described by Art. 251 of the Civil Code, derives a perpetual and irremediable *capitis deminutio*, as an objective consequence of third party behavior—a discrimination compounded, even in the usage of the legislature, in the expression "incestuous children." The violations of the right to a *status filiationis*, attributed to Art. 2 of the Constitution, and of the constitutional principle of equality—as the equal dignity of all citizens and as a prohibition of legislative discrimination based on personal and social conditions—are self-evident and need no words of explanation. Invoking legislative discretion to the contrary, in reference to Art. 30, fourth paragraph of the Constitution, which authorizes the law to dictate rules and limits for establishing paternity, is unacceptable: it is not the principle of equality that must bow to legislative discretion, but the opposite.

. . .

The Constitution contains a clause of general recognition of the rights of the family, as a natural society founded upon marriage (Art. 29, first paragraph). This permits the requirement of behavior conforming to this recognition and the establishment of consequences and measures, even criminal ones, in response to conduct that compromise family identity, as happens in the case of incest. But the adoption of sanctions over and above these parameters, involving individuals who bear no responsibility whatsoever—as is the case of children of incestuous parents, who merely bear the consequences of their parents' behavior and are designated by fate, by dint of their very existence, to be involuntary signs of an inconsistency in the family order—would only be justified under a "totalitarian" idea of the family. The Civil Code itself takes into consideration hypotheses of involuntariness in reference to parents, before whom the defense of the family as an institution gives way to individual positions: the first paragraph of Art. 251, aiming to allow recognition, attributes significance to the good faith of incestuous parents, and the second paragraph of Art. 278 dispenses with the prohibition on establishing maternity and paternity in cases of *force majeure* (rape and sexual aggression). The Constitution does not support an idea of the family unit which is an enemy to individuals and their rights: in this case, the right of the child to formal recognition of a *status filiationis*, where compelling reasons to the contrary in the child's own best interests do not exist, as affirmed elsewhere by this Court (Judgment 120/2001), is a fundamental element of personal identity, and is protected by Art. 2 of the Constitution in addition to Art. 7 and 8 of the cited Convention on the Rights of the Child. It follows from this last regulation, in keeping with what has been defined as the "paternal principle" that this treaty proclaims, that the value of "social institutions," primary among which is the family, lies in the purpose assigned to them, that is, to permit, or more precisely, to promote the development of the personality of human beings.

If the claims maintained by the Court in Judgment 494/2002 are commonly shared, the relationship between Articles 2 and 29 of the Constitution is very controversial when the issues of the protection of the de facto family and of same-sex marriage are raised.

As to the first issue, Article 2 seems to protect a de facto family that shows a certain degree of stability, although such protection would be difficult to define in its exact content and is still less extensive than that offered to the legitimate family, to which the Constitution confers a superior dignity because of the features of stability, predictability, and reciprocity of rights and duties arising from marriage (see Judgment 310/1989). More precisely, the jurisprudence of the Constitutional Court follows two different paths depending on whether, within the context of a de facto family, the rights of the children or the rights of the partners are taken into consideration. In the first case, the Court is particularly sensitive to the rights of children born to de facto unions, in accordance with the already mentioned constitutional imperative of equal treatment of all children (see Judgment 394/2005). In the case of partners' rights, the Court tends to deny that there is perfect equivalence between de facto families and legitimate families, except in some special instances; for example, with Judgments 404/1988 and 559/1989 the Constitutional Court upheld the rights of cohabiting partners to succeed in the right to lease a house and an apartment in the allocation of public housing.

As for the issue of same-sex marriage, the Constitutional Court, in Judgment 138/2010, has made clear that the idea of family protected by Article 29 of the

Constitution is the traditional one, based on the marriage of a man and a woman. On the other hand, for the Court, the concept of "social formation" as protected by Article 2 of the Constitution also refers to homosexual unions, seen as the stable cohabitation of two persons of the same sex. At the same time, the recognition of same-sex couples cannot be reached by judicial decision, and it is for Parliament to determine the forms of such recognition. Presently, Parliament has not yet regulated on the subject, and Italy is one of the very few countries within the European Union in which same-sex couples, and also de facto unions, have no status. Reasoning similar to that of the Italian Constitutional Court was adopted, a few months later, by the European Court of Human Rights in *Schalk and Kopf v. Austria*.[21]

The issue of same-sex marriage reached the Constitutional Court after referrals from the Trial Court of Venezia and the Court of Appeal of Trento that challenged the articles of the Civil Code that were interpreted as permitting marriage only between a man and a woman (Arts. 93, 96, 98, 107, 108, 143, 143 *bis*, 156 *bis*) as violating Articles 2, 3, 29, and 117, first paragraph of the Constitution.

8.–Art. 2 of the Constitution provides that the Republic recognizes and guarantees the inviolable rights of man, both as an individual as well as in social groupings in which he or she expresses his or her personality and requires compliance with the mandatory duties of political, economic and social solidarity.

Accordingly, social grouping must be deemed to include all forms of simple or complex communities that are capable of permitting and favoring the free development of the person through relationships, within a context that promotes a pluralist model. This concept must also include homosexual unions, understood as the stable cohabitation of two individuals of the same sex, who are granted the fundamental right to live out their situation as a couple freely and to obtain legal recognition thereof along with the associated rights and duties, according to the time-scales, procedures and limits specified by law.

However, the Court finds that the aspiration to this recognition—which necessarily postulates legislation of a general nature, aimed at regulating the rights and duties of the members of the couple—cannot solely be achieved by rendering homosexual unions equivalent to marriage. It is sufficient in this regard to examine even on a non-exhaustive basis the legislation of the Countries that have to date recognized the aforementioned unions in order to ascertain the diversity within the choices made.

---

[21] ECtHR, First Chamber, case of *Schalk and Kopf v. Austria*, Application no. 30141/04, Judgment, 24 June 2010.

It therefore follows that, for the purposes of Article 2 of the Constitution, it is for Parliament to determine—exercising its full discretion—the forms of guarantee and recognition for the aforementioned unions, whilst the Constitutional Court has the possibility to intervene in order to protect specific situations . . .

9.–The question raised with reference to the principles indicated in Art. 3 and 29 of the Constitution is groundless . . .

In view of the above, it is true to say that the concepts of family and marriage cannot be considered to have been "crystallized" with reference to the time when the Constitution entered into force, because they are endowed with the flexibility that is inherent within constitutional principles, and are therefore be interpreted taking account not only of the transformations within the legal system, but also the evolution of society and customs. However, such an interpretation cannot go so far as to impinge upon the core of the provision, modifying it in such a manner as to embrace situations and problems that were not considered at all when it was enacted.

In fact, as is clear from the *travaux preparatoires* cited, the question of homosexual unions remained entirely extraneous to the debate conducted within the Assembly, even though homosexuality was by no means unknown. When drafting Art. 29 of the Constitution, the delegates discussed an institution with a precise articulation and which was regulated in detail under civil law. Therefore, absent any different references, the inevitable conclusion is that they took account of the concept of marriage defined under the Civil Code which entered into force in 1942 and which, as noted above, specified (and still specifies) that married couples must be comprised of persons of the opposite sex. The second clause of the Article also makes provision to this effect, in asserting the principle of the moral equality of the married couple, focused in particular on the position of the woman to whom it wishes to guarantee equal dignity and rights within the marital relationship.

This meaning of the constitutional precept cannot be overcome through interpretation, because to do so would not involve a simple re-reading of the system or the abandonment of a mere interpretative practice, but rather the implementation of a creative interpretation.

It must therefore be reasserted that the norm did not take account of homosexual unions, but rather intended to refer to marriage within the traditional meaning of that institution.[22]

---

[22] The translation is from the official website of the Italian Constitutional Court.

The Constitutional Court recently addressed an interesting issue closely related to that of same-sex marriage. Articles 2 and 4 of Statute 164/1982 provided that if a wife or husband changes her or his sex physically and legally, the marriage is necessarily and automatically dissolved. Said provisions were contested by a couple after one of the spouses had changed sex because they didn't want the marriage to be dissolved. The Court of Cassation raised the question of the possible contrast of Statute 164/1982 with Articles 2, 29, and 117, first paragraph of the Italian Constitution and with Articles 8 and 12 of the European Convention for the Protection of Fundamental Rights and Freedoms. In Judgment 170/2014 the Constitutional Court held that in case of change of sex, the couple must retain the right to keep a relationship with legal effect, although the marriage is dissolved. The statute was then declared unconstitutional because it lacked a provision protecting the relationship after the change of sex.

7. Social Rights

The Italian constitutional framework gives social rights a special place, laying the groundwork for the construction of the welfare state. Philosophical personalism, Catholic social teaching, and socialist theories all favored state intervention, in light of the necessity of protecting and promoting human dignity. Moreover, in the Constituent Assembly, the socialists, the communists, and the Catholics were all deeply persuaded that a rapid recovery from the destruction of the war required a weighty state presence in the market and in the provision of health care,[23] education, and housing. The efforts of the state were understood as an indispensable part of democratic life and the development of the country. Thus, in enshrining the right to receive an education, to have a family, to bear children, to have a job, or to receive health care, the Constitution gives the State not only the power but even the affirmative responsibility to actively intervene in these fields by promoting housing, establishing schools and hospitals, encouraging higher rates of savings, and so on.

The Framers understood the promotion of inalienable rights, equality, and social rights as a unitary whole. Social rights were seen to represent the public institutions' most effective instrument to promote both individual and group rights and to foster substantive equality. It was, therefore, for the sake of individual rights and in the name of substantive equality that the Constitution promoted interventions in favor of the weaker social classes, in order to promote their full participation in social life. In the constitutional text, inalienable rights, dignity, equality, social rights, and

---

[23] The issue of health care is discussed *supra*, section 5.3.

the welfare state can all be understood as facets of a single relational conception of human beings, which prompts a duty of solidarity.

This is particularly evident in a series of Constitutional Court decisions that expanded the protection accorded to people in need. Judgment 215/1987 sees the State as in charge of the duty to remove obstacles to the enjoyment of the right to education:

> The effectiveness of mandatory education is guaranteed in the second paragraph [of Article 34] by the fact that it is provided free of charge. That of higher education is also guaranteed to whoever is capable and deserving, but lacking in means, through scholarships, grants to families, and other provisions (third and fourth paragraphs). These provisions focus on economic obstacles, since the founders were well aware that such obstacles are the main component of unequal starting points in life, and that it was, therefore, essential to provide express prescriptions in order to guarantee the effectiveness of the principle contained in the first paragraph. This does not imply, however, that the application of the principle may be permitted to run into limits and obstacles of other kinds, as the suppression of these other limits is put forward as a general duty of the Republic in Art. 2 and 3, second paragraph. To reach such a conclusion would be to deny the obvious fact that school attendance and the acquisition of a complete education are fundamental tools for the "full development of the human person," the achievement of which is the goal of these provisions.

Another meaningful example pertains to legislative measures intended to address the needs of persons with disabilities, addressed in Judgment 203/2013.[24] The Constitutional Court struck down those parts of the law that limited the number of relatives who had the right to take a leave of absence from their job in order to assist disabled persons. The Court stated that the constitutional system requires the most effective protection of persons in need, and that such protection includes their right to enjoy human relationships. Consequently, people with disabilities had the right to be assisted by their family members, and the limitation of the category of relatives was unconstitutional:

> [T]his development [in the Court's jurisprudence] is in keeping with the principles asserted in the case law of this Court, which has for some time been clear in its view that protection for the mental and physical health of the disabled is also premised on the provision of supplementary financial benefits to families,

---

[24] Judgment 203/2013 is also discussed in Chapter 3, section 4.

"the role of which remains fundamental in the provision of care and assistance to the disabled", which also include the leave of absence under examination.

Stressing the essential role of the family in the provision of assistance to and socialisation of the disabled, the Court wishes to highlight the fact that in order to ensure full protection for the weak it is necessary to provide not only healthcare services and rehabilitation, but also care and social inclusion and above all to ensure continuity within the constitutive relationships of the human personality.[25]

As this language indicates, the conception of social rights enshrined in the Constitution stems from a fundamentally *relational* conception of individual persons and their rights. Another particularly illustrative example of this idea can be found in a case in which the Constitutional Court was called to judge whether the obligation to wear a helmet imposed on motorcyclists violated their freedom of movement (Judgment 180/1994). The Court articulates a conception of individual health as inextricably linked to other people's rights and interests:

We cannot accept the theory that underlies these conclusions: that is, that the interference of the State in the life of a citizen is only permitted where a third party's right to health is threatened, while when "the collective has a mere interest in the health of an individual," "every imposition or limitation" on the rights of liberty, like freedom "of movement and of development of personality in general," would be invalid.

The assumption that limitations on the right to freedom of movement are only permitted under Art. 32 of the Constitution when the right to health of a third party is also at stake, with sanctions in cases of disobedience, is unacceptable. Especially when, as in the case under examination, measures (which are also not too heavy) are put in place for drivers of two-wheeled motor vehicles, the decision of the legislature, in its discretion, to prescribe particular ways of behaving and punishing disobedience with the aim of minimizing damaging consequences caused by road accidents, in particular mortality and crippling injury, appears to be in conformity with the Constitution, which considers the health of the individual also to be an interest of the collective. There can be no doubt that consequences such as these have an impact in terms of social costs for society as a whole, since it is not realistic to envision that an individual, in refusing to observe the specified preventative measures, could renounce at the same time the assistance of public health structures and services designated

---

[25] The translation is from the official website of the Italian Constitutional Court.

for persons with disabilities. The measures intended to soften the consequences that may derive from traumatic accidents involving two-wheeled motor vehicles, therefore, appear to be dictated by the necessity that the prescriptions imposed by the rules in question not seem to unreasonably limit the "expression of personality." We must also observe that the rules in no way limit freedom of movement, understood as the ability to move from one place to another, which is the freedom protected by Article 16 of the Constitution (also invoked by the referring judge). Rather, it merely dictates a few procedures to be followed by whoever wishes to use certain vehicles. Therefore, if the prescription is intended to prevent injuries to people, which is undeniably an interest of society, it must, even in this case, be unaffected by the claims at bar.

The constitutional directives on social rights played an increasing role in the decades following the adoption of the 1948 Constitution. The Constitutional Court was able to develop the text further so as to encompass increasing numbers of rights (for example, the right to personal self-determination), each of which also has social dimensions and social implications in the context of a welfare state. On the one hand, this has magnified the dignitarian and social reading of the Constitution itself. On the other hand, the recognition of new individual and collective rights stemming from the Constitution has heightened the role of public institutions generally and dramatically increased their financial obligations because the expansion of rights has also raised the expectations that the public institutions will intervene to make the enjoyment of such rights effective.

This has often generated a tension between the Court and the legislature. As the Court has extended the scope of the welfare state through its decisions—for instance by mandating more beneficiaries of public services than those initially included in particular State and local interventions—it has concretely depended on the legislature to give effect to its judgments by increasing the budget for this purpose.

The interdependence of the Court and legislature with regard to social rights is particularly evident in decisions that pertain to the right to health care, which traditionally absorbs a sizable portion of public resources. In Decision 445/1990, for example, the Court acknowledges the immediate applicability of the right to health, but also acknowledges the role that must be given to the legislature:

As constitutional case law has consistently held, the right to health is recognized and guaranteed by Art. 32 of the Constitution as a "primary and fundamental right that (. . .) dictates full and complete protection." This protection, however, manifests in a variety of subjective legal situations depending on the nature and kind of protection that the constitutional order grants to the good of a person's physical and psychological wholeness, as well as balance in relation to the relevant concrete legal relationships. For this reason, this Court has held that, when viewed in light of the defense of the physio-psychological wholeness of the human person faced with assaults or other injurious conduct by third persons, the right to health is a right *erga omnes*, directly guaranteed by the Constitution and, as such, directly protectable and actionable by legitimate individuals *vis-à-vis* the perpetrators of illicit behaviors. At the same time, this Court has always specified that, in light of the right to healthcare, the right to health is subject to a "determination of the tools, the times, and the modes of implementation" of the relative protection by the legislature.

This last aspect of the right to health, which is the one implicated by the constitutional issues under examination, entails that, as with all rights that impose a positive duty, the right to medical care, being based on programmatic constitutional principles that are oriented toward a specific goal, is guaranteed to every person as a constitutional right. This right is conditioned by the way the legislature chooses to implement it, balancing the interest it protects against other constitutionally protected interests and also considering the objective limits it encounters in doing so (e.g. the organizational and financial resources available at the time). This principle, which is common to every other constitutional right imposing a positive obligation on the State, certainly does not imply that the supreme protection assured by the Constitution is degraded to the level of a purely legislative protection. Rather, it entails that the implementation of the constitutionally-mandated protection of a particular good (health) occurs gradually, according to a reasonable balancing with other interests or goods which also enjoy constitutional protection, and with the real, objective possibility to dispose of the necessary resources to carry out the implementation. This balancing is subject to the scrutiny of this Court, according to the forms and methods proper to the use of legislative discretion, and according to which each person in the objective conditions established by the regulations on the provision of health services has a "full and unconditional right" to benefit from the health services provided, in conformity with the law, as a public service to citizens.

Nevertheless, this generally cautious approach of the Constitutional Court, which carves out a pivotal role for the Legislative Branch in balancing rights and financial constraints, has superseded the previous orientation, well-established in the 1980s and early 1990s, which tended to favor a more expansive approach toward social rights, regardless of their financial implications.

The guarantee of social rights and its associated fiscal implications have also figured importantly in the waves of decentralization in Italy. As explained in more detail in Chapter 6, the powers of the regional and local governments were increased twice in the 1970s, once in the 1990s, and again in the 2001 constitutional reform, which granted the Regions significant competences, especially in the field of health care.

Given the special importance that it accords to social rights, the Constitution ensures that an "essential level" of social rights is enjoyed throughout the country, reserving a special role for the central government. It is the State's responsibility to determine "the essential level of benefits relating to civil and social entitlements to be guaranteed throughout the national territory." Judgment 20/2010 provides a snapshot of the constitutional framework:

> As a consequence of the allocation of competences between the State and Regions carried out by the amendment of Part II, Title V of the Constitution, to the former is reserved, among other things, the power of "determination of the essential level of benefits relating to civil and social entitlements to be guaranteed throughout the national territory" (Art. 117, second paragraph, point m), Const.). The allocation of this exclusive power to the State involves the establishment of the structural and qualitative levels of services, which, since they involve the fulfillment of civil and social rights, must be guaranteed, as a general matter, to all those who have the right. Therefore, exclusive competence may be invoked in regard to specific services for which State norms define the essential level of provision of benefits.

The huge public debt and the inefficiencies generated in this system have become apparent over the decades, and have progressively led to a reconsideration of the sustainability of social rights and of the welfare system itself.

As to the sustainability of social rights, starting in the early 1990s public institutions have tried to put a cap on increasing public debt, in part due to the pressure of the European Union, which wanted to secure the performance of the euro through fiscally sound state budgets. This led to the 2012 constitutional reform, which required balanced budgets and which also contributed to a new attitude in the Constitutional Court. The Court became particularly concerned about the financial sustainability of social rights, and it began to temper its expansive attitude toward social rights. It has curbed its decisions, foreseeing the financial implications that these can entail.

This new attitude has led to some significant shifts in the Court's jurisprudence. One decision that was much discussed and criticized for having dramatically changed the case law over night was Judgment 310/2013, issued at the height of the global economic and financial crisis, when the Italian state was trying to moderate its deficit and debt, including by cutting the salaries of public employees. A few months earlier, the Court had found that the freezing of the salaries of Italian judges was unconstitutional. This time, the Court justified the extended freezing of the salary of university professors by invoking the overriding necessity of budgetary savings and its relationship to the duty of solidarity:

not concerning themselves, so easier to freeze

The limitation and optimization of public spending, through which a policy of rebalancing the budget may be realized, entail onerous sacrifices, like those under examination, which are justified under the current situation of economic crisis. In particular, by reason of the current, necessary, long-term budgetary projections, these sacrifices cannot but involve time periods that are longer (though certainly still determinate) than those in previous decisions of this Court, which were handed down with regards to the budgetary measures of 1992.

The contested norms, therefore, pass the reasonableness test, in that their goal is budgetary saving involving the entire division of public employment, in keeping with solidarity—albeit with the differentiations necessitated by the various professional categories composing it—and for a limited time period, which involves a greater number of years in consideration of the multi-year program of the budgetary policies.

The inefficiencies and growing expenses that all levels of government were facing, in trying to implement an ever expanding welfare state in a time of budgetary constraint, also contributed to a broader shift in the constitutional culture in the last 10 to 15 years, in which a new conception of "welfare" took shape. Both academic scholarship and political platforms have resurrected the idea of subsidiarity as a principle that could govern the relationship between the public and private spheres, including with respect to many of the interventions designed to guarantee social rights. This principle, which was formally inserted into the Constitution in 2001 in Article 118, affirms, among other things, that public institutions must address a social issue if and only to the extent that they can achieve social justice more effectively than individuals and private groups.

The principle of subsidiarity sheds new light on the role of civil society in the age of the modern welfare state. Individuals and groups are an active part of welfare policies through their spontaneous efforts. Only when these don't succeed, may public powers step in. It remains to be seen what the Constitutional Court will make of this shift in the constitutional text and culture; thus far the Court's jurisprudence has not significantly engaged the principle of subsidiarity as it applies to the protection and realization of social rights.

8. Citizens and Migrants

The Italian constitutional text reflects the traditional understanding of Italy as a country of emigration rather than of immigration. The only relevant wording on this subject is to be found in Article 35, which recognizes the freedom to emigrate and which grants protection to Italian workers abroad. Italians fled to other states massively after the unification of the country in the late nineteenth century as well as after each of the two world wars of the twentieth century. Even European integration led to the deployment of Italian workers abroad; many Italians, taking advantage of international agreements specifically made with this purpose, went to Belgium to work as miners. It is no surprise, then, that Article 35 of the Constitution also says that the Republic "shall promote and encourage international agreements and organizations which have the aim of establishing and regulating labour rights."

The law on citizenship has consistently reflected an approach based on the criterion of *ius sanguinis,* and thus the prevailing path for achieving citizenship has been through family lineage. This was also intended to provide those Italians who emigrated and their descendants the possibility of retaining Italian citizenship even if they were born and lived abroad. This traditional approach has never been changed, although it has been called into question several times. The normal way through which foreign nationals can acquire Italian citizenship now is only after 10 years of residency in the Italian territory.

It was only in the late 1970s and early 1980s that Italy began to experience significant waves of immigration, both documented and undocumented. Geography has made the Italian peninsula a destination as well as a European hub for masses of immigrants coming from practically everywhere in the Mediterranean area. While the 1990s saw the arrival of thousands of Albanians after the fall of the communist regime, in the last decade immigrants and refugees from North Africa and the Middle East have arrived in huge numbers, seeking shelter and economic opportunity.

These noncitizens do not have the right to vote in Italy. Article 48 of the Constitution, which says that "[a]ll citizens, male and female, who have attained their majority, are voters," has usually been interpreted as endowing *only* citizens with the right to vote. Noncitizens can therefore participate in elections only once they have become Italian citizens.[26]

While the rights to citizenship and to vote have not changed even after the country has become more the destination than the origin of migration, since the 1990s

---

[26] This interpretation of Article 48 is disputed, however, especially with reference to regional and local elections, which, according to some critics, are not covered by the article and therefore should not be constitutionally limited to citizens.

the Italian political institutions have repeatedly legislated in the field of immigration, intermittently reshaping the normative framework for immigration in more restrictive or more permissive ways.

In this evolving normative landscape the protection of the human rights of immigrants has steadily increased over time. For instance, until the 1990s the Constitutional Court largely deferred to the legislature to draw a balance between social stability and the human rights of the undocumented. Judgment 353/1997 exemplifies this approach:

> The demands of human solidarity cannot be met without a correct balancing of the values at stake, which task has been undertaken by the legislature. The State cannot forgo the unavoidable task of overseeing its own boundaries: the rules established as a function of an orderly migratory stream and a suitable reception of people into the country must, therefore, be respected, and neither circumvented nor even only disregarded time and again through essentially discretionary evaluations. This is because they serve as a defense of the national collective and, taken together, as a protection of those who have observed them and could be damaged by tolerance of illegal situations.

More recently, the Court has reconsidered the rights of immigrants against the background of the Constitution, drawing largely from the jurisprudence of the European Court of Human Rights. This has led to new understandings of the status of noncitizens as well as of the constitutional principle of equality, with powerful implications for immigration and welfare policies alike.

Article 3 of the Constitutional text formally commands an equal protection only of the rights of citizens: "All *citizens* have equal social dignity and are equal before the law, without distinction of sex, race, language, religion, political opinion, personal and social conditions. It is the task of the Republic to remove those economic and social obstacles which by limiting in fact the freedom and equality of *citizens* ..." (emphasis added). The Constitutional Court has, however, basically overcome the formal distinction between citizen and noncitizen by developing a strong protection of immigrants' human rights. This package of rights does not pertain solely to refugees but also to immigrants moving to Italy for reasons of employment, and even to undocumented immigrants. In sum, the Constitutional Court has committed itself to an affirmative interpretive effort to expand the rights of immigrants, whatever their legal status might be.

The intervention of the Court has been twofold. On one hand, it made it absolutely clear that, strictly speaking, the legislature *can* differentiate the treatment of

Italian citizens and noncitizens, so long as it is outside the scope of a limited set of inviolable human rights:

> Only where the enjoyment of the inalienable rights of man is concerned does the constitutional principle of equality refuse to tolerate discrimination between citizens and foreigners . . . [It is] legitimate for the legislature to introduce norms that only apply to those who have the requisite citizenship—or, conversely, only to those who lack it—provided that the exercise of those fundamental rights is not compromised (Judgment 432/2005).

On the other hand, according to the Court's case law, any discrimination between citizens and noncitizens must survive the test of reasonableness, a criterion that the Court has elaborated, drawing from the constitutional principle of equality as enshrined in Article 3 (as discussed earlier in this chapter).[27] According to this scrutiny, national and regional policies can legitimately treat citizens and noncitizens differently only if the condition of citizenship is concretely related to the field of regulation. Conversely, if citizenship is made a prerequisite for the enjoyment of a right or a service provided by public institutions, but the situation that is regulated affects citizens and noncitizens alike, then the insertion of the citizenship criterion is arbitrary and illegitimate.

This approach has had a strong impact on national, regional, and local welfare policies. Such policies often originally addressed only citizens, for both budgetary and political reasons: since social policies have suffered from severe budget constraints, and non-immigrants do not have the right to vote, cutting services for them has a smaller impact on political opinion and on voting preferences. According to the Court, however, benefits and services cannot be conferred only to citizens if there is no reasonable justification for excluding noncitizen immigrants from such treatment. The Court has therefore expanded many social rights to noncitizen immigrants.

This reasoning has been applied largely to long-term immigrants, whose equivalence to citizens has been explained by reference to their stable, non-episodic presence in the national or local territory. Judgment 187/2010, for example, says:

> However, precisely when considering the legislation in question, this Court did not fail to stress that the Italian legislature is without doubt permitted to enact legislation intended to regulate the entry of non-Community nationals and their stay in Italy, provided that this is not manifestly unreasonable or in breach of international law obligations. It also added that "it is also possible to subject the award of particular benefits—not intended to remedy

---

[27] *See also* Chapter 3, section 2.

serious urgent situations—to the requirement that the legal basis entitling the foreign national to reside within the territory of the State demonstrates its non-occasional nature and that it will not have a short duration, provided that this is not unreasonable; however—this Court went on—once the right to reside under the aforementioned conditions is not under discussion, it is not possible to discriminate against foreign nationals by imposing upon them particular restrictions on the exercise of fundamental human rights, which are on the other hand granted guaranteed to Italian nationals".[28]

In some instances similar reflections have led the Court also to strike down some pieces of legislation that excluded short-term noncitizen residents coming from non-EU countries from some social benefits:

That absolute exclusion of entire classes of persons based either on the failure to possess European citizenship, or the fact that the individual has not been resident for at least thirty six months does not respect the principle of equality since it introduces arbitrary grounds for distinction into the legislative framework, since there is no reasonable correlation between these conditions for eligibility to receive the benefit (European citizenship in conjunction with residence for at least thirty six months) and the other particular prerequisites (consisting in situations of need or discomfort directly relating to the person as such) Constituting the prerequisite for eligibility to receive the social services which, by their very nature, do not tolerate distinctions based either on citizenship or particular classes of residence aimed at excluding precisely those individuals who, on the facts, are the most exposed to situations of need or discomfort which such a social services system aims to supersede by pursuing an eminently social goal.[29] (Judgment 40/2011)

The Constitutional Court, in so doing, has expanded the rights of immigrants as well as imposed on the State a special duty: policies that discriminate between citizens and noncitizens need to be appropriately justified.

It is not by chance that this trend of the Court has taken place in the field of social rights and the welfare system: since these are conceived as ways to redress social inequalities and to meet the necessities of people in need, here the principles of equality and solidarity converge to expand rights.

---

[28] The translation is from the official website of the Italian Constitutional Court.
[29] The translation is from the official website of the Italian Constitutional Court.

5 Powers and Conflicts

1. Relation of Powers and the Unique Role of the Judiciary

As a parliamentary Republic, Italy has a form of government clearly distinguishable from that of the United States, and closely comparable in many ways to that of the United Kingdom. It is characterized in general by a close constitutional and political link between the Legislative Branch and the Executive Branch, which consists of the Prime Minister (or, as the office is denominated in Italy, the "President of the Council of Ministers") and the other Ministers of his cabinet. In order to take office, a new Executive, or "Government," must first be appointed by the President of the Republic and then must present itself before the two Chambers of Parliament in order to obtain a vote of confidence (*mozione di fiducia*). Conversely, when Parliament withdraws its confidence in the Executive, the Prime Minister must immediately deliver his resignation to the President of the Republic.

The expression "separation of powers" in Italy accordingly does not refer to the distribution of powers typical of the United States, but rather to a cooperative constitutional structure focused on Parliament as the core of the legal and institutional architecture. More than a clear-cut "separation" of the constitutional powers

(Legislative, Executive, and Judiciary), Italy has a constitutionally regulated "relation" among them, with the Constitution defining either their reciprocal competences and limitations or the procedures for determining these relationships.

In principle, the ideal image of Italy's constitutional structure centers on Parliament, the only democratically representative body elected by popular vote. Each public power depends directly on Parliament: the Executive needs parliamentary confidence; the President of the Republic is elected by Parliament (together with some Representatives from the Regions); and "Judges are subject only to the law" (i.e., the enacted statutory law of Parliament), according to Article 101 of the Constitution.

Nevertheless, it must be recognized that, in fact, this picture of the Italian parliamentary system, which is totally centered on the pivotal position of the Legislature relative to both the Executive and the Judiciary, is increasingly distant from the reality of constitutional practice. In recent decades the Executive has dramatically increased its role and influence in the institutional system, relegating Parliament more and more to a peripheral role in lawmaking. The expanding role of the Executive Branch as the key policy-maker is consistent with a common trend among European parliamentary or semi-parliamentary systems more generally—including the United Kingdom, Spain, Germany, and France—and is part of a much wider crisis of the institutions of representative democracy in Europe as a whole (characterized by the decline of political parties and Parliaments). At the same time, an important and more distinctively local phenomenon in the Italian constitutional system has been the dramatic increase in the Judiciary's influence on Parliament, the Executive, and the overall political system, which has multiplied the conflicts between Judiciary, on one hand, and the Executive and Legislature, on the other.

The Judiciary has a unique position among the constitutional powers in the Italian legal framework. Whereas cooperation among the political branches of the constitutional system is a hallmark of the Italian constitutional system, as noted above, the original design of the Constitution intended to define a more clear-cut separation of the Judiciary from the other powers in order to shield the former. This choice has a historical explanation. After the end of the Fascist regime, the main concern was to protect the Judiciary from any undue influence of the political branches, an influence that might undermine the fair and impartial administration of justice. This independence was the key principle of the constitutional design concerning the Judiciary: a few articles after affirming "judges are subject only to the law," the Constitution also establishes that "[t]he Judiciary is a branch that is autonomous and independent of all other powers" (Art. 104). The Constitution then establishes the High Council of the Judiciary, a new body to govern the Judiciary and to remove judicial authorities from Executive control. All the constitutional principles concerning the Judiciary revolve around the idea of its independence from political powers as a *conditio sine qua non* for fairness and impartiality in the administration of justice.

Inversely, in the original text of the Constitution the political institutions were also protected against any possible arbitrary use of judicial authority. For this reason, the Constitution grants the President of the Republic, the members of Government, and members of Parliament a set of prerogatives insulating them from the Judiciary. These prerogatives are also a historical legacy that dates back to the epoch when a parliamentary democracy incrementally took the place of the monarchy: all through the nineteenth century, European countries followed the British model and steadily endowed their Parliaments with increasing numbers of competences that had been previously reserved to the Crown. During this progressive shift from monarchy to democracy it was necessary to guarantee the autonomy of Parliament from any interference by the King or by those powers dependent on the King, including judges. Since then, a series of safeguards was designed to hinder the Judiciary from prosecuting politicians without the consent of a political body.[1] To a great extent, these prerogatives derive from that time of transition from monarchy to parliamentary democracy.

The President of the Republic, as a general principle "is not responsible for acts performed in the exercise of his functions" (Art. 90). In a way, the old principle that "the King can do no wrong," and therefore cannot be prosecuted, is applicable to the President of the Republic. The ordinary Judiciary has no power over him within the scope of his exercise of the powers of his office. This means both that normally he is as legally responsible as any ordinary citizen for all the crimes or torts committed outside his presidential functions, and that any prosecution or suit for those wrongs is suspended during the period of time in which he is in office, and will continue only as soon as he is no longer occupying the position of President. There are, however, some important exceptions to this rule: the traditional principle of absolute immunity of the Head of State is tempered by constitutional provisions concerning the crimes of "high treason" and "offences against the Constitution," for which the President may be impeached by Parliament and submitted to the judgment of the Constitutional Court. In those cases, a special jurisdiction is set up for judging the President (or Ministers), following a very special procedure (see Chapter 2, section 3.2 on the jurisdiction of the Constitutional Court). This special procedure

---

[1] For those readers less familiar with criminal procedure in typical continental European civil law systems, it may be helpful to recall that the investigation and prosecution of crimes is considered a judicial activity, undertaken by an investigating magistrate. That is, prosecutors are part of the Judicial, not Executive, Branch of the Government, unlike in the United States, for instance.

has never been employed against a President of the Republic and has only been used once against a Minister in the *Lockheed* case at the end of the 1970s.

As to the members of the Government, an interesting change occurred at the end of the 1980s. The original text of the Constitution conferred on the Constitutional Court exclusive jurisdiction over "ministerial offences"—that is, cases concerning criminal acts committed by the members of the Government in the exercise of their governmental duties. In 1989, however, Constitutional Law n. 1 of January 16, 1989, amended Articles 90 and 96 of the Constitution to allow ordinary judges also to exercise jurisdiction over cases against members of the Government. This was the first of a set of constitutional reforms in the name of the principle of equality— "all citizens are equal before the law"—that tended to dismantle all sorts of special treatment for politicians with respect to their legal liabilities. Article 96 of the Constitution now reads: "The President of the Council of Ministers and the Ministers, even if they resign from office, are subject to ordinary courts for crimes committed in the exercise of their duties, provided authorization is given by the Senate of the Republic or the Chamber of Deputies, in accordance with the norms established by Constitutional Law." Parliament can still stop criminal proceedings against members of Government, but only on the basis of a finding that the accused has acted in pursuit of a prominent public interest in the exercise of his duties.

In recent years, especially during the Governments led by Silvio Berlusconi, a number of pieces of legislation were passed by Parliament in an attempt to expand once again the immunities of Government members, but the Constitutional Court has struck them all down, stating that additional safeguards can only be reintroduced with a constitutional amendment.[2] In effect, the Constitutional Court has prevented a simple legislative majority from expanding the immunity of its members to the detriment of the balance of power between the political and judicial branches set in the Constitution, while still leaving open, however, the possibility of changing the rules with the supermajority necessary to approve a constitutional amendment.

A third group of immunities concerns the members of Parliament. Again in this case the provisions of the Constitution were originally more generous, and accorded a rich set of prerogatives to Deputies and Senators. For instance, Article 68 included a requirement that judicial authorities obtain the prior, formal authorization of Parliament in order to subject any member of Parliament to any civil or criminal process. In 1992 a series of investigations conducted primarily by the court of first instance of Milan (commonly known as *"Mani Pulite"* or "Clean Hands")

---

[2] *See* Judgment 24/2004 on Statute 140/2003 ("Lodo Schifani"); Judgment 262/2009 on Statute 124/2008 ("Lodo Alfano"); and Judgment 23/2011 on Statute 51/2010 (on "Legittimo impedimento").

uncovered widespread corruption among politicians of the time. After these investigations, Constitutional Law n. 3 of October 29, 1993, modified Article 68 to remove the requirement of parliamentary consent, and since then it has been relatively common for a politician to be subject to both civil and criminal process in the ordinary courts.[3]

The one significant parliamentary immunity to have survived the *"Mani Pulite"* era is the guarantee in Article 68 that "members of Parliament cannot be held accountable for the opinions expressed or votes cast in the performance of their function." Thus, the expressed opinions and the votes of politicians fall out of the reach of judicial process. This is the main area where, according to the Constitutional Court, the historic principle of the "independence and autonomy of the Chambers from the other organs and powers of the State" (Judgment 1150/1988) has survived.

Given this complex structure, the Constitutional Court plays a major role in making the constitutional machinery effective. It is the ultimate supervisor and the guarantor of the institutional framework, and ensures that all the applicable procedures and limits are respected. The Constitutional Court in Italy is in this way not only the "judge of the laws" but also the "judge of powers." We can understand better how the Court's jurisprudence shapes the relation of constitutional powers by examining one set of reciprocal binary relationships at a time.

2. Executive vs. President of the Republic

The role of the President of the Republic exemplifies the Italian constitutional system's distinctive "relation of powers" principle, in contrast to its American "separation of powers" counterpart. While in a presidential (or semi-presidential) system the President is the head of one of the three divided powers (the Executive), and works in a condition of clear separation with regard to the other powers, the Presidency of the Republic according to the Italian Constitution is an institution that operates in a permanent constitutional relationship with the other powers. The President is the Head of the State and, together with the Constitutional Court, is the "guarantor" of the Constitution; his only interest should, in principle, be the correct functioning of the constitutional system. Therefore, he must remain in an important way *super partes*, meaning he is not a representative of the political majority of Parliament, nor of the Executive, but stands outside of the partisanship of the other political branches. For that reason the President is not directly elected

---

[3] The prior consent of the Chamber to which the member of Parliament belongs is still necessary for certain purposes: to arrest him or her; to search his or her person or domicile; for wiretapping or otherwise monitoring his or her conversations or communications; or to seize his or her mail.

by the people but by a two-thirds majority of a joint session of Parliament that also includes Representatives of the Regions.[4]

To begin to form an understanding of the intense networking activity that the President undertakes in this role, consider that, with respect to the Executive, the President both appoints the President of the Council of Ministers and the other Ministers that together constitute the Government, and formally promulgates all the legal acts approved by the Executive (decree-laws, legislative decrees, regulations). With respect to the Legislature, the President promulgates all the parliamentary laws, with only a limited veto power over them (he can refuse the promulgation only once, requiring a new vote from Parliament, but in case of a second approval he is obligated to promulgate the law); at the same time, he has the ultimate power to dissolve Parliament and call for a new general election in case of institutional deadlock. With respect to the Judiciary, the President of the Republic also serves *ex officio* as President of the High Council of the Judiciary, the principal body through which the Judiciary exercises its constitutionally established powers of self-governance.

In this daily interaction among constitutional powers, the Constitutional Court's case law becomes the vehicle for establishing the proper borders between them. For instance, in one of the most significant disputes involving the relations between the President and the Executive (in this case, acting through the Minister of Justice), the Constitutional Court was called to adjudicate the meaning of Article 87 of the Constitution, which provides that "the President may grant pardons and commute punishments," and its relationship to Article 89, commonly known as Executive "countersignature" power, according to which "a writ of the President of the Republic shall not be valid unless countersigned by the proposing Ministers, who shall be accountable for it."

The combination of those two constitutional articles requires, on its face, that a pardon require a presidential decree that is proposed and countersigned by the Minister of Justice. This provoked a conflict in 2004 when the Ministry of Justice refused to act according to the decision of the President of the Republic to pardon a convicted terrorist. The reason for the conflict was, obviously, a difference in political opinion about the acceptability of that act of clemency, but the dispute immediately shifted to legal and constitutional ground because the President appealed to the Constitutional Court against the Minister of Justice:

> The appeal disputes—based on the claim that the power to grant pardons is reserved "expressly and exclusively to the Head of State by Article 87 of the Constitution"—the Justice Minister's refusal "to formulate a proposal for a

---

[4] After the fourth vote, an absolute majority suffices for election.

pardon" and draft the relevant decree of pardon, in spite of the fact that the President of the Republic, in a note of 8 November 2004, had expressed his decision to pardon the interested party. (Judgment 200/2006)

The opposing positions of the two conflicting parties were straightforward: on the one hand, on the basis of Article 89, the Minister of Justice asserted that each presidential act, including a pardon, has to be *proposed* by a Minister; on the other hand, referring to Article 87, the President argued that only the President has the power to grant pardons, and that "the Justice Minister's claim that he has the 'exclusive right to make proposals' has no basis in constitutional law."

To decide the case, the Court therefore needed to assess:

> which type of relationship exists between the Head of State, as the holder of the power to grant pardons, and the Minister of Justice who, on account of his responsibility for preliminary inquiries and hence, by extension, through his participation in the complex procedure to which the exercise of the power under examination is subject, is called upon to draft the decree which gives concrete form to the clemency measure, as well as to countersign it and subsequently to oversee its implementation.

Even in a constitutional system of the civil law tradition, in order to fully understand the true shape of the form of government, history and customs matter, not only written constitutional rules. So, the Court in its decision draws a long and detailed history of the power to grant pardons in Italy, starting from the personal prerogative of absolute sovereigns, passing through the Albertine Statute (see Chapter 1) and the constitutional monarchy, up until the Constituent Assembly and the Republican era:

> It is therefore important for the resolution of the question before the Court to identify the inherent purpose of the power to grant pardons, in particular in the light of the practices, which have developed during the Republican period in relations between the Head of State and the Minister of Justice.

To trace the exact boundary between the presidential and executive roles, the Court, therefore, started from the *purpose* of the power in question. The mere reading of the text of the Constitution is not sufficient to grasp that purpose, so the Court turns its focus on the practical use of the pardon power. Institutional experience reveals that the pardon power can be seen in two different ways: as an instrument of criminal or prison policy—and therefore clearly within the scope of executive prerogatives—or as humanitarian and exceptional measure—and therefore evoking the "*super partes*" role of the President.

> Indeed, whilst up until the mid 80s of the last century particularly frequent recourse was made to this instrument, so much so as to legitimize the idea of its possible use for prison policy purposes, a reduction in its use occurred from 1986 onwards—at the same time, not by chance, as the entry into force of Law n. 663 of October 10, 1986 (Amendments to the law governing incarceration and the implementation of measures which deprive or restrict personal freedom): a striking example of this can be found in the comparison between the 1,003 pardons granted in 1966 against the mere 104 granted in 1987, with the number falling even further over the following years, ending up as low as several dozen. . . .
>
> This meant that the institution of pardon was restored—correcting the practice, in some ways contrived, which had evolved during the course of the first decades in which Art. 87 of the Constitution applied—to its role as an exceptional instrument intended to satisfy extraordinary needs of a humanitarian nature.

According to the Court, then, both historically and today the pardon power is better understood as serving humanitarian ends rather than political expediency. This view gives a more sound constitutional account of a presidential power that, per se, otherwise constitutes a clear derogation from the principles of the rule of law and of equality before the law: it is an *extra ordinem* act of justice that aims to mitigate the full effect of the law when, in certain situations, it could amount to a violation of human rights or the rehabilitative aim of criminal punishment.[5] On this basis, the Court in its decision upholds that the substantive decision to pardon is vested exclusively in the President as a *super partes* institution.

Nevertheless, in a regime of relation of powers this alone is not sufficient.

> Having said this, it is still necessary—in order to resolve the present dispute—to clarify which tasks are reserved to the Minister of Justice within the ambit of the procedure leading up to the granting of a pardon.

The provisions of the Constitution must not be interpreted in ways that render them meaningless, and the text says expressly that any act of the President of the Republic

---

[5] Article 27 of the Italian Constitution requires that "[p]unishments . . . shall aim at re-educating the convicted."

must be countersigned by the proposing Minister to be valid. The Constitutional Court therefore has to delineate the boundaries of the corresponding power of the Ministry of Justice within the pardon process.

The Court points out that "a pardon is the result of a full-scale procedure consisting of a range of official acts and stages."

It can start in the Judiciary, generally with the Parole Board (*Magistrato di Sorveglianza*), who collates all the relevant facts of the case and the observations of the Prosecutor General at the Court of Appeal and transmits them to the Minister of Justice, together with a reasoned opinion.

These elements also include—in addition clearly to those contained in the trial court's sentence, the individual's criminal record and any offences he has been charged with—declarations by the injured parties or close relatives of the victim concerning restitution for the harm caused and the granting of clemency along with, as part of an assessment of the individual's character, information pertaining to his family and financial circumstances, as well as the behavior of the interested party. . . .

Where on the other hand the initiative is taken by the President himself, the Head of State may request the Minister to open the procedure for the granting of a pardon; also in this case the Minister of Justice is under a duty both to commence and conclude the requested preliminary inquiries, drafting the relevant proposal.

In the above cases, any refusal by the Minister would in essence preclude the exercise of the power to grant a pardon, with the resulting limitation of a power, which the Constitution attributes—in relation to the final decision—to the Head of State. Accordingly, where the President of the Republic has requested the conclusion of the preliminary inquiries or has directly taken the initiative to grant a pardon, the Minister of Justice, who may not refuse to commence and conclude the preliminary inquiries, thereby bringing about a procedural standstill, may only inform the Head of State of the procedural or substantive grounds which in his opinion stand in the way of the granting of the measure.

To accept that the Minister may either refuse to conclude the necessary preliminary inquiries or may in any case remain inactive would be tantamount to asserting that he enjoys an inadmissible power of constraint, or a kind of veto, in relation to the conclusion of the procedure leading to the emanation of the decree of pardon desired by the Head of State.

The Court aligned itself with the long-standing position prevailing in scholarly commentary by affirming that the relation between the President of the Republic and the Executive described by Articles 87 (pardon power) and 89 (countersignature power), cannot be interpreted in a single and unique way. Rather, it has to be considered as a relationship with "variable geometry": as far as the countersignature, in particular, is concerned, while it may be necessary in order to complete the procedure, generally speaking it takes on a different value depending on the type of procedure that it completes or, more precisely, for the validity of which it is a prerequisite. It is, of course, clear that the countersignature plays a substantive role when the act presented for signature by the Head of State is governmental in nature and, therefore, an expression of the powers vested in the Executive, while it instead has a merely formal value where the act is an expression of the powers vested in the President of the Republic (for example, with regard to the right to send messages to the Houses of Parliament and to appoint life senators or judges to the Constitutional Court). Such acts must be treated in the same way as the right to grant pardons, which Article 87 of the Constitution recognizes only to the Head of State.

3. Executive vs. Parliament

Generally speaking, in a parliamentary system it is difficult for a Constitutional Court to closely scrutinize relations between Parliament and the Executive. The reasons are rooted in the very nature of parliamentary regimes, where the political majority of Parliament must necessarily support the Executive at all times. This is a major difference with presidential systems, which frequently have permanent conflicts between the Legislature and the Executive. In parliamentary systems, instead, it is more unusual for a political conflict between Parliament and the Executive to arise, and it is even less common for such a conflict to reach the courts. Disagreements between Parliament and the Executive are typically settled politically—that is, either through informal channels of moral persuasion or pressure, or, in the extreme case, through a no-confidence vote that dissolves the Government.

Although it is difficult to find cases involving "conflicts of attributions" (see Chapter 2) between Parliament and the Executive, there is a wide area of constitutional justice through which we may more indirectly perceive a jurisprudence applicable to this relationship of constitutional powers: the area of the sources of law. One of the most important areas of connection between the legislative and executive powers in Italian constitutional law lies in the constitutional rules of procedure regarding those sources of law that have primary force in the hierarchy of legal norms.

In the Italian constitutional system Parliament does not have a monopoly on legislative power; the Government can also make laws by two instruments that were intended to be exceptional: legislative decrees (*decreti legislativi*) and decree-laws (*decreti-legge*), according to Articles 76 and 77, respectively, of the Constitution. Legislative decrees are forms of a delegated lawmaking power: Parliament can pass a delegation law (*legge delega*) entrusting the Executive to adopt one or more acts (legislative decrees) that have legal force. Decree-laws, instead, are forms of lawmaking through emergency powers that the Executive can exercise in "extraordinary cases of necessity and urgency," according to Article 77 of the Constitution. Within 60 days of the publication of a decree-law, Parliament has to "convert" the measure into an ordinary law—otherwise the decree is nullified from its very beginning.

Obviously, if either the Executive or the Legislature makes use of these legal instruments in violation of the constitutional rules of procedure or competence applicable to them, then the governmental act or parliamentary law in question can be subject to the judicial review of the Constitutional Court and may be found unconstitutional. Such cases do not necessarily involve "material" unconstitutionality (the violation of substantive Constitutional norms) but rather "formal" unconstitutionality (the violation of procedural norms of the Constitution). Many decisions regarding legislative decrees and decree-laws can be understood as reliable tests of the effective constitutional regulation of the relationships between Parliament and the Executive.

In particular, today the decree-law presents one of the most constitutionally problematic sources of law, just as it did earlier in Italy's constitutional history (see Chapter 1). In the practice of the Italian government today, there is still a huge gap between constitutional theory and reality. The letter of Article 77 of the Constitution describes decree-laws as truly "exceptional" acts that the Executive may adopt only under certain specific circumstances (i.e., in "extraordinary cases of necessity and urgency"), but the concrete institutional experience is astoundingly distant from that formal ideal. Extremely slow and complex parliamentary procedures, which are often directed toward producing wide-ranging discussions more than timely decisions, have made the decree-law the only reasonably expeditious legislative track for the Executive.

For this reason, since the 1980s the use of decree-laws has expanded abnormally and in clear violation of the requirements of Article 77. In Italy today more than two-thirds of the overall legislative acts derive from decree-laws or legislative decrees. In effect, the conversion of previously issued decree-laws has become the "ordinary" lawmaking procedure, while the constitutionally prescribed legislative process has been reduced to a residual parliamentary power.

This reality tends to put Parliament in an increasingly submissive position with respect to the Executive. In contrast to an ordinary bill, a decree-law is already a valid legislative act, effectively in force since its publication, at the time of its consideration by the two Houses of Parliament. The Chamber of Deputies and the Senate only have 60 days to approve or disapprove of it. Moreover, in recent years the Government has increasingly resorted to asking for a vote of confidence in connection with the legal conversion of decree-laws—that is, the Executive threatens to resign if the conversion is rejected, and thereby tries to force approval. Overall, therefore, it is clear that this praxis of emergency decrees is altering the respective roles and positions of Parliament and the Executive Branch in the Italian constitutional system.

In this context, the Constitutional Court has had to intervene several times to review the constitutionality of decree-laws and the related conversion laws. One of the Court's most important decisions in this field is Judgment 360/1996.

The controversy arose during a period in the 1990s when the situation became so out of control that the Executive reached the shocking record of adopting more than one decree-law per day (the monthly average in 1995 was approximately 34 decree-laws). Consequently, Parliament was inundated with decree-law conversion bills from the Executive. This, in turn, triggered a vicious circle: the more the Executive introduced decree-law conversion bills for consideration, the less Parliament had time to examine and approve them, and the more difficult it became for Parliament to make any decision within the maximum 60-day period. In order to avoid automatic nullification of its decrees, one or two days before the expiration date the Government would re-adopt another identical decree-law and gain an additional 60 days of validity, thus creating chains of identical decree-laws over as much as two or three years without Parliamentary action—a practice known as "reiteration."

Parliament, by definition ruled by the same political majority as the Government, consented to this abuse and never brought a conflict of attribution against the Executive directly to the Constitutional Court. A serious constitutional reaction therefore had to wait until the Judiciary raised the issue through the incidental method of access to the Constitutional Court. By the fall of 1996, a great number of lower courts challenged the constitutionality of those reiterated decrees.

The Court in this case was fully aware that the institutional system of legal sources was in a condition of true constitutional crisis, and in Judgment 360/1996 it declared the reiteration of decree-laws to be unconstitutional.

This praxis has more and more degenerated and *obscures constitutional principles of primary relevance* as the ones provided by Art. 77 of the Italian Constitution, principles whose violation or elusion can affect not only the regular development of law-making processes, but also fundamental equilibriums of the form of government . . . The praxis of reiteration, moreover, if diffused and prolonged over time as happened in recent times, affects the institutional equilibriums, altering the same form of government and the ordinary attribution of legislative power to the Parliament (Art. 70 of the Italian Constitution). Moreover this praxis if diffused and prolonged, ends in wounding the certainty of law in the relationships among citizens, because of the impossibility of predicting neither the duration in time of the reiterated norms nor the final outcome of the conversion process: with even more dangerous consequences when the decree influences the domain of fundamental rights sphere or—as in the case—the criminal law. [Emphasis added.]

That was only the first act in the decree-law drama, however. In compliance with the Constitutional Court's decision, the Government ceased the reiteration of decree-laws, but it did not refrain from issuing new ones. The Court's order simply resulted in forcing Parliament to convert each decree-law on time. The overall number of decree-laws adopted did decrease, and eventually stabilized at the current number of approximately three per month, on average.

At this point, another, more radical question of constitutionality arose: How was it possible that an "exceptional" and "extraordinary" legislative tool, intended for circumstances of emergency, had come to be used on such a regular basis? The real constitutional problem is that, in many cases, decree-laws are enacted in the flagrant *absence* of those requisites of "extraordinary necessity and urgency" specified by Article 77 of the Constitution. The constitutional defect does not stem from the connection of two (or more) identical decree-laws, but rather affects each decree-law at its very origin.

The issue of decree-laws lacking the requisite urgency was not new for the Court. Since the 1980s lower courts had asked the Constitutional Court to review the constitutionality of such decrees. The older case law and scholarly commentary—for instance, in the Fascist period (see Chapter 1)—tended to consider the evaluation of necessity and urgency to be a "political question" best left to Parliament. The Court had thus refrained from scrutiny of decree-laws on the basis of Article 77 prerequisites.

In Judgment 29/1995 the Court overruled its precedents, saying that:

[T]he pre-existence of a state of affairs entailing the necessity and urgency of taking action through an exceptional instrument, as the decree-law, constitutes a requisite of constitutional validity of the adoption of such an act, so as the possible *evident absence* of that pre-requisite amounts to either a constitutional defect of the decree-law—adopted out of the constitutional discipline—*or a procedural defect (vizio in procedendo) of the conversion law itself, having wrongly evaluated the presence of non existing validity requisites and, therefore, converted into a law an act that couldn't be a legitimate object of conversion.* [Emphasis added.]

In the case before the Court, this passage was merely *obiter dictum* and, therefore, the Court did not annul the challenged decree-law, but it did articulate two seminal principles for future cases. First, in order to find a decree-law unconstitutional, the absence of Article 77 prerequisites must be "evident." The Court thus maintained a certain degree of discretion on the part of the Executive to assess the reasons for urgency, taking into consideration only major violations and applying a fairly flexible level of judicial scrutiny.

Second, and more important, the Court found that a decree-law's violation of Article 77 requirements would transfer to the associated conversion law. Until that decision, it was assumed that Parliament's conversion of a decree-law into a statute "legalizes" the decree and cures it of any constitutional vice. As the Constitutional Court had reaffirmed in the same decision on reiteration of decree-laws quoted above (Judgment 360/1996), "the procedural defects of the decree-law are healed when the Chambers of the Parliament, through the conversion law, accepted as theirs the contents of the decree." In other words, according to the Constitutional Court's earlier jurisprudence the Government's violation of constitutional procedures was "constitutionalized" by Parliament's subsequent approval—meaning that the procedural part of the Constitution would somehow give way to the power of the political majority. With its 1995 decision, instead, the Court took the opposite course, finding that procedural unconstitutionality cannot be "healed" by the conversion law, and that the latter remains unconstitutional because its content is based on an illegitimate decree.

Although the Court enunciated this shift in Judgment 29/1995, it never applied the new principle to strike down a conversion law until 2007. For more than 10 years, the Court never found an "evident" absence of the Article 77 prerequisites, and instead used its wide margin of judicial discretion to "save" Executive actions from unconstitutionality.

The first occasion on which the Court found the "evident absence" test to have been satisfied was in Judgment 171/2007. In that case, the Court of Cassation raised the question of the constitutionality of a decree-law (Art. 7, paragraph 1 of Decree-Law n. 80 of March 29, 2004, Urgent provisions governing local authorities) converted into law (Law n. 140 of May 28, 2004). The decree-law in question repealed a requirement in the Consolidated Law on Local Authorities that required removal of a Mayor after his conviction for the offence of "improper use of State assets." The facts involved the Mayor of Messina (Sicily), who was removed from office after a criminal court found him guilty of improper use of State assets. The Mayor challenged the act of removal, and during the pendency of the case on appeal the Executive (ruled by same political party as the Mayor) issued the decree-law, with the clear aim of changing the applicable law before the final Court decision.

The Court of Cassation asked the Constitutional Court to assess what "extraordinary cases of necessity and urgency" justified using a decree-law to change the Law on Local Authorities (aside from the unconstitutional, and therefore unmentionable, aim of modifying the law in order to interfere with a very likely adverse judicial decision). If the Executive desired to change the law on the discipline of local authorities—the Court of Cassation reasoned—then it could have introduced an ordinary bill and allowed Parliament to discuss it in the ordinary course. Instead, the Government used a decree-law for which there was an "evident absence" of the "urgency" required by Article 77.

Surprisingly, the Constitutional Court followed the reasoning of the Court of Cassation, and went even further, using the occasion to write what is known as a "doctrinal" decision—that is, it situated the judgment regarding the single decree-law within a broad analysis of the Italian form of government and of the Court's long and contradictory case law.

> There is a broad consensus that the framework establishing the sources of law is one of the principal elements which characterizes the form of government within constitutional systems. It is an integral part of the system for the protection of fundamental values and rights. In the States which draw inspiration from the separation of powers and the subjection of the courts and the administrative apparatus to the law, the adoption of primary legislation is reserved to the bodies, or single body, on which power is conferred directly by the people.
>
> The Italian Constitution adheres to these principles where it provides that "legislative power is exercised collectively by the two Houses of Parliament" (Art. 70)....
>
> Before moving on to an examination of the merits of the case it is necessary to resolve the question, which logically comes before this, of the eventual remedying effect of the conversion law since, as mentioned above, after the question of the constitutionality of Art. 7, paragraph 1, letter a) of Decree-Law 80/2004 had been referred to this Court, the decree-law was converted, with amendments—which did not however concern the contested provision—by Law 140/2004.
>
> On this point, the Court asserted in Judgment 29/1995 the principle that after the relevant decree-law has been converted into law, the failure to

comply with the requirement of "extraordinary circumstances of necessity and urgency" translates into a procedural defect in the law in question. . . .

A different approach was on the other hand adopted, without any specific reasons being given in favor, in Judgments 330/1996, 419/2000, and 29/2002 and, on one specific ground, by Judgment 360/1996.

The Court finds that it must reiterate the first principle pointed out.

There are various arguments which support this conclusion.

First, whilst the constitutional provision which governs the enactment of primary legislation (laws and other measures with the force of law) places particular emphasis on the relationship between organs of State—which might suggest that there is no margin for further control following parliamentary approval and the conversion into law of the decree—it must not be forgotten that such provisions also serve the purpose of protecting rights and are characteristic of the structure of the constitutional system as a whole. The assertion that the conversion law in any case remedies any defects in the decree would imply the concrete attribution to ordinary legislation of the power to modify the constitutional division of competences between Parliament and the Government as regards the production of primary legislation.

In addition, where consideration is given to the fact that in a parliamentary Republic, such as Italy, the Government must enjoy the confidence of the Houses of Parliament and it is considered that the decree-law involves a particular acceptance of responsibility, it must be concluded that the constitutionality of the provisions of the conversion law cannot be assessed as such—*i.e.* insofar as they do not have a substantive effect on the normative content of the provisions of the decree, as in the case before the Court—in isolation from those of the decree itself. In fact, the decree's immediate effectiveness, which makes it capable of creating even irreversible changes to society and to the legal order, places particular conditions on Parliament's activities when converting the decree into law compared to the constraints on ordinary legislative activity, thus also making clear the rationale for the constitutional provision which confers on the Government the responsibility for the issue of the decree. Parliament thus ends up making its own assessments and debating with reference to a situation which has been changed by legislation introduced by a body which as a rule, as the holder of executive power, is not entitled to enact legislation with the force of law.

Despite this precedent (followed by other important judgments, including 181/2008, 22/2012, and 32/2014), the situation did not change substantially. The Governments in power, regardless of political orientation (both conservative and progressive party coalitions), have continued to adopt an incredibly stable and continuous number of decree-laws that are clearly outside of the original constitutional scheme. What accounts for the ineffectiveness of constitutional justice in Italy on this issue?

In part, an explanation can be found in the intrinsic difficulty of rigid constitutions to ensure the observance of their procedural provisions—there is a sort of inevitable weakness of the constitutional review of legislative acts for formal flaws. Formal flaws can trigger a chain reaction, transmitting the parent measure's unconstitutionality to all the subsequent norms approved on its basis. The downstream consequences can be copious and important (such as recent decree-laws on which the operation of entire financial systems are based). As Gustavo Zagrebelsky realistically observes, constitutional judges very often hesitate to annul norms that only have formal flaws and not substantive ones, and they strike down formally flawed laws only if they are also substantively flawed.[6]

However, there are two additional, more structural reasons that explain this "flexibilization" of the constitutional distribution of lawmaking powers and the limited role of constitutional adjudication.

First, the value of *time* in rule-making is increasing, and today the timeliness of laws is often more important than their content. Taking action late can be tantamount to not deciding on or regulating a phenomenon at all.

Second, many parliamentary procedures are still fundamentally linked to an archaic idea of the statutory law enacted by Parliament as the principal normative act of the legal order. This law must be approved article by article, subjected to a final vote, examined by a commission and then by the entire House. That basic structure, inherited from nineteenth-century parliamentary procedures in liberal democracies like that of the United Kingdom, was transposed unchanged into the Italian Constitution and into the Italian Parliament's internal regulations. The structure certainly worked well as long as the function of Parliament was mainly one of discussion (within consociationalism political contexts). Beginning with the great geopolitical changes of the early 1990s, and the introduction of obligatory harmonization of economic policies at the European level during the same period, Parliament's function evolved. Discussion and dialogue gave way to what has been called by a former Speaker of the Chamber of Deputies (Luciano Violante) a "deciding democracy." In contemporary democracies where it has become necessary to ensure efficiency and coherence of Government directives, especially in decisions of an economic nature, the traditional structure of parliamentary lawmaking

---

[6] In this connection, although considered less effective, the *preemptive* review for constitutionality (such as that operated by the French *Conseil Constitutionnel*, performed prior to the law's entry into force) appears to be more incisive.

reveals certain limitations. Decree-laws, capable of entering immediately into force, became the preferred instrument for making timely decisions.

It is important to highlight that the inadequacy of the constitutional system of sources of law is a phenomenon that does not concern only Italian and other national constitutional systems; a similar trend is taking place on the European level. Some of the most significant recent decisions at the European level—such as the adoption of the European Stability Mechanism and the related European Stability Facility and the so-called "Fiscal Compact"—were the result of direct and *sui generis* international agreements between certain EU members, rather than through the usual processes of EU lawmaking such as those that generate regulations and directives. There are surprising analogies between the reasons for these developments within the Italian constitutional system and those within European law. First, the European constitutional system as a whole is undergoing a powerful intergovernmental shift. Member State executive branches are regaining a great deal of strength within the European Union's system of governance despite efforts to counter this force with a more thorough realization of the principle of subsidiarity. The value of time is a second issue that links European developments to the great proliferation of urgent decree-making in Italy. To cite one example, the necessity of timeliness led the Eurozone States to adopt the European Financial Stability Facility by means of an "executive agreement," an immediately binding international agreement that enters into force when signed by governments without need for ratification by national parliaments. To effectively guarantee the repayment of the Eurozone States' debts, it would have otherwise been necessary to amend the Lisbon Treaty (to overcome the ban on European institutions guaranteeing or taking on the debts of Member States established in the European treaties), and that, in turn, would have required a long and complex treaty amendment process, according to a timeframe that the financial markets would never have been able to sustain. The need to provide an immediate response to the markets' requirements favored a legal act that could immediately enter into force. Only after this immediately effective act was the necessary amendment to the Lisbon Treaty adopted—much like a conversion law in the Italian Parliament.

4. Judiciary vs. Parliament

As noted at the outset of this chapter, since the early 1990s the relationships between the Judiciary and the political bodies have become more and more confrontational, and a number of conflicts of attribution have been raised before the Constitutional

Court, confirming Justice Valerio Onida's observation (released during the 2005 Constitutional Court Presidential Press Conference) that the Court is increasingly becoming a "court of conflicts."

In these cases, the Court has adopted a strict interpretation of the constitutional provisions on parliamentary privileges and immunities, considering them to be exceptions to or derogations from the general rule that all citizens shall be equally subject to the law. Judgment 390/2007 exemplifies the Constitutional Court's approach. The case involved the so-called "indirect wiretapping" of a member of Parliament. Article 68 of the Italian Constitution says that:

> Members of Parliament cannot be held accountable for the opinions expressed or votes cast in the performance of their function. In default of the authorization of his House, no member of Parliament may be submitted to personal or home search, nor may he be arrested or otherwise deprived of his personal freedom, nor held in detention, except when a final court sentence is enforced, or when the member is apprehended in the act of committing an offence for which arrest *flagrante delicto* is mandatory.
>
> Such an authorization shall also be required in order to monitor a member of Parliament's conversations or communications, or to seize such member's mail.

Therefore, in order to record the phone communications of a member of Parliament, an authorization of the Chamber is required.

> [I]n the scope of the constitutional system, the legal texts which set forth immunity and privileges [to protect the purpose of Parliament], notwithstanding the principal of equal treatment under the law—a principle [that lies] "at the origin of the formation of the legal State" (Judgment 24/2004)—must be interpreted as closely as possible to the normative text. This requirement is accentuated by the movement—accomplished by the Constitutional Law n. 3 of October 29, 1993, a modification of Art. 68 of the Constitution—to a system exclusively based on specific authorizations *ad acta*: a system in which every single constitutional provision attributes significance to a specific interest linked to the purpose of Parliament and fixes, in equal time, the limits in which this interest deserves protection, establishing what traits a determined procedural act must present, so that its subjection to the procedure of *nulla osta* of that political organ is justified.

The Constitutional Court goes on to affirm that the immunities are meant only to protect the politician from "persecutions" by the Judiciary; they are not intended to impede the due course of justice.

> Art. 68 of the Constitution seeks to suggest a safe haven for parliamentarians from illegitimate judicial interference with [Parliament's] exercise of its representative mandate; to protect it, in other words, from the risk that investigative instruments of particular invasiveness or acts which would be conditional or coercive of its fundamental liberties could be used with a prosecutorial scope, or would in other ways be foreign to the effective requirements of jurisdiction. The necessity of authorization decreases, in fact, when the limitation on the liberty of a member of Parliament is connected to positions or situations—like the execution of an irrevocable judgment of guilt or the flagrancy of a crime for which obligatory arrest is required—which exclude, in and of themselves, an ability to be configured to the aforementioned circumstances ... From this perspective, prior authorization [from the Chamber]—contemplated by the constitutional norm—provides a control on the legitimacy of the act of authorization, notwithstanding consideration of the prejudice that its execution would entail for the single parliamentarian. The protected good identifies itself, in fact, with the need to assure the correct exercise of judicial power towards members of Parliament, not to assure their substantive interests (privacy, honor, and personal liberty), potentially compromised by accomplishing the act; these interests find a safeguard in precedents, also constitutional, established for the associated members in general.

That is why, for example, the Constitutional Court considers that wiretapping of Deputies and Senators requires a specific authorization of the Chamber and the Senate only if they are directed toward the parliamentarian (direct wiretapping), whereas a similar authorization is not needed if wiretapping is directed toward a common citizen that happens to talk on the phone with a parliamentarian (indirect or unintended wiretapping).

Having established that the immunities are narrowly aimed at protecting politicians only from the "persecutory intent" of the Judiciary, the Constitutional Court retains the power to review the decisions of Parliament concerning the immunities of its members, in order to assure that parliamentarians are not unduly removed from legitimate exercises of judicial authority. The Constitutional Court has, therefore, frequently needed to resolve conflicts between the Judiciary and Parliament. In particular, a significant number of controversies reach the Constitutional Court each year concerning conflicts between Parliament and the Judiciary over the "unchallengeability" (*insindacabilità*) of the opinions and votes of members of Parliament. Article 68 of the Constitution provides that "Members of Parliament cannot be held accountable for the opinions expressed or votes cast in the performance of their function," and the Constitutional Court has asserted its competence to assess whether a Chamber has correctly used its power to declare that Article 68 protects any one of its members from judicial process. Again, Judgment 390/2007 (but in the same vein, see Judgment 1150/1988) clarifies the point:

> Inasmuch as it is allocated within the limits of the circumstances indicated by Art. 68, paragraph 1 and legitimately exercised only within these limits, the evaluative power of the Chamber is not arbitrary or subject solely to an internal rule of self-restraint. In our Constitution, which recognizes the inviolable rights of man (among which are the rights to honor and reputation) as fundamental values of our legal order and provides for a judicial organ for constitutional guarantees, the aforesaid power is subject to a control on its legitimacy—operating with the instrument of the conflict of attributions, as governed by Art. 134 of the Constitution and Art. 37 of the Constitutional Law 87/1953—and therefore is limited to the faults that intrude upon and constrain the sphere of judicial authority. When the judge in a civil case for damages, filed by a person who is aggrieved by defamatory declarations made by a Deputy or Senator in an extra-parliamentary context, considers that the Chamber's decision asserting the absence of legal responsibility of the specific member who is subject to judgment, is the result of an illegitimate exercise (or, as others express it, an "evil use") of the Chamber's power of evaluation, the judge may invoke the control of the Constitutional Court.

Many questions have arisen regarding the scope of the freedom of opinion and vote of the members of Parliament. The Constitutional Court's settled case law (beginning with Judgments 10/2000 and 11/2000) holds that Article 68 of the Constitution covers opinions expressed by members of Parliament not only within the Chambers but also outside of them, provided that such activities are strictly connected with their activity in Parliament.

> The prerogative of Art. 68, paragraph 1 of the Constitution does not cover all opinions expressed by a member of Parliament in the sphere of his political activities, but only those bound by a "functional nexus" with the activity carried out "in his quality" as a member of the Chambers. . . .
> It is settled that opinions manifested in the course of the work of the Chamber and its various organs, in carrying out any one of the many functions

executed by the same Chamber, or manifested in acts, even individual ones, constitute an expression of the powers specific to the parliamentarian as a member of the assembly. Instead, the political activity undertaken by the parliamentary member outside of this scope cannot be said in and of itself to be a performance of the actual parliamentary member's function in the precise sense to which Art. 68, paragraph 1 of the Constitution refers.

In the normal development of democratic life and political debate, the opinions that the parliamentarian expresses outside of these responsibilities and outside of the proper activities of the Assembly, represent rather an exercise of the freedom of expression common to all. One cannot extend to those opinions the same immunity that the Constitution, notwithstanding the general principle of legality and justiciability of rights, grants to the opinions expressed in the exercise of the parliamentarian's functions, without distorting the nature of the immunity.

The boundary line between, on the one hand, the protection of the autonomy and the liberty of the Chambers and, to that end, of the freedom of expression of their members, and on the other, the protection of constitutionally recognized rights and interests which are susceptible to being harmed by the expression of opinions, is fixed by the Constitution through the functional delimitation of the scope of the privilege. Without this delimitation, the application of the prerogative would transform it into a personal privilege (Judgment 375/1997), which would confer on parliamentary members a sort of favored personal status with regard to the scope and the limits of their liberty of expression of thought, and would thus also lead to possible distortions of the principle of equality and of equal opportunity between citizens in the dialectic of politics.

Nor can we accept, without frustrating this limitation, a definition of the "function" of the parliamentary member that is so generic as to include the political activity that the member carries out in any context, and in which his position as a member of the Chamber is irrelevant.

In short, the Court seeks to preserve both the autonomy of Parliament and the immunity of its members from any interference by the Judiciary and also to limit parliamentary immunity in order to avoid the risk of unequally "privileging" the Deputies and Senators relative to other citizens. To this end, the Court has tried to give greater definition to the requirement that the protected opinions be expressed "in connection" with the exercise of parliamentary duties.

[W]e must specify the meaning of "functional nexus" that must be found between the statement and the political activity in order to retain its unquestionable nature. It is not simply the subject matter or context that connects parliamentary activity and statements, but the identification of the statement itself as an expression of parliamentary activity. (Judgment 11/2000)

In a different opinion, the Court also clarified that:

> The statements could therefore be covered by immunity only inasmuch as they are substantially reproductions of an opinion expressed in a parliamentary context. In fact, the opinion expressed in the exercise of the parliamentary function is not protected by immunity only on the specific occasion in which it is expressed within the seat of parliamentary, falling outside of the sphere of privilege if it is reproduced in a different context. Immunity encompasses not only the specific occasions in which the opinions are manifested in the seat of parliamentary, but the historical content of this, even when publicly disseminated, in every place and through every means. The activities and acts of Parliament precisely in order to ensure to the fullest the freedom of political debate are normally characterized by publicity and are naturally directed towards the entirety of the Representatives. This entails that immunity must be extended to other contexts and occasions in which the opinions may be reproduced outside of the seat of Parliament.
>
> But immunity is limited to that historical content. Therefore, in the case of reproduction outside of Parliament, in order to retain its unchallengeable nature (*insindicabilità*), it is necessary that there be a substantive identity of content between the opinion expressed in Parliament and that expressed externally.
>
> That which is required, obviously, is not a specific textual coincidence, but a substantive correspondence of content. (Judgment 10/2000)

5. Judiciary vs. President of the Republic

The Constitutional Court's regulation of relations between the Judiciary and the President of the Republic was illustrated quite interestingly in a dispute involving the accidental recording of four phone calls, totaling 18 minutes, between the President of the Republic and a Senator who was being investigated for possible involvement in organized crime. Believing the conversations to be irrelevant to their investigation, the public prosecutors[7] in the case decided to eliminate the irrelevant

---

[7] Again, it is useful to recall here that prosecutors in Italy are members of the Judiciary, as typical of civil law systems.

wiretaps from the trial dossier in accordance with the provisions of the Code of the Criminal Procedure. That procedure requires a judicial hearing in closed chambers, with the participation of the public prosecutors and the private attorneys of the parties; in that hearing the parties have full access to all the recordings before their removal and destruction. In other words, the Code of the Criminal Procedure required a judicial examination of the content of recordings regarding the President of the Republic in order to establish whether or not they were relevant for the trial, prior to any decision to remove and destroy them.

The President of the Republic argued that wiretapping of the President is always illegal in any case, whether relevant or irrelevant, intentional or accidental: "As a consequence, the recordings we are discussing, could not be in any way evaluated, used or transcribed, and the judge should request their immediate destruction in accordance with Art. 271 of the Code of the Criminal Procedure inasmuch as they were undertaken 'outside of cases authorized by law'." (Judgment 1/2013). According to that article of the Code of the Criminal Procedure, the results of illegal recordings cannot be utilized in any way, and, consequently, the judge must order their immediate destruction without any evaluation of their content. Because the public prosecutors did not agree with the President's position, however, the President filed a constitutional complaint against the prosecutors over this conflict of powers.

In this case, as in the "pardon power" case (see section 2, above), where the conflict was between the President and the Executive, the distinct place of the President in the constitutional distribution of powers is important: the Presidency does not belong to any of the three basic branches (Legislative, Executive, Judicial) but is, instead, a "*super partes*" power.

The Constitutional Court reaffirmed, in this case, that:

[T]he reconstruction of the entirety of the attributes of the President of the Republic in the Italian constitutional system highlights that the Constitution places him outside of the traditional powers of the State, and naturally above all the political actors. Hence he exercises responsibilities that intrude on each one of the cited powers, with the goal of safeguarding, simultaneously, their separation and their equilibrium. This singular characteristic of the position of the Presidency reflects the nature of its attributes, which do not imply the power to adopt decisions on the merits of certain specific matters, but give him instruments to induce the other constitutional powers to correctly carry out their proper functions, from which the relative decisions on the merits must flow.

The Court, therefore, went on to analyze the reciprocal relation between the Judiciary and the President by following a functional approach, starting from the aim of the President's power. The general scope of the Presidency, according to the Court, is to guarantee the physiological equilibrium of the constitutional system.

> To effectively carry out the proper role of guarantor of the constitutional equilibrium, and of "magistrate of influence" the President must consistently weave together a network of connections with the goal of harmonizing possible positions in conflict and bitter debates, indicating to the various Heads of the constitutional organs the principles on the basis of which one can and must find solutions, that are as widely held as possible, to the diverse problems that arise from time to time.
>
> From this perspective, it is indispensable that the President continually join to his formal powers—which are expressed by issuing specific and timely acts, as expressly provided for by the Constitution—a discrete use of that which has been defined as "the power of persuasion." This is essentially composed of informal activities, which may precede or follow the adoption of specific measures of his own or by other constitutional organs, either to evaluate institutional possibilities in advance, or to test afterwards their impact on the system of relations between the powers of the State. The informal activities are hence inextricably connected to those that are formal.

The Court here recognizes that one of the key constitutional features of the President of the Republic is his power of moral persuasion, which implies the need for the President to keep informal relations with all the constitutional actors in order to help orient their decisions without either replacing them or depriving them of their legal competences.

> [T]he discretion and the confidentiality of the communications of the President of the Republic are therefore co-essential to his role in the constitutional order. . . . [T]he President of the Republic must be able to count upon the absolute confidentiality of his own communications, not just with regard to a specific function but for the efficacious exercise of them all. . . .
>
> [Moreover,] it should still be remembered that as the Head of State he presides over the Supreme Council of Defense and has the command of the Armed Forces, and since he is called to maintain, even in these indicated roles, relations and communications of a confidential character it is not necessary to give particular examples.

Following this reasoning, the only possible conclusion seems to be that the wiretapping of the President is always and per se illegal.

The Court, however, had to face another robust objection as well. Telephone interceptions, as violations of the freedom of communication protected by Article 15 of the Constitution, are constrained by two basic principles: (1) the principle of the rule of law, meaning that wiretapping in order to be legal has to be regulated by a prior parliamentary statute; and (2) the principle of due process, meaning that it can be legally ordered only by a judicial warrant. But there is no general constitutional prohibition on the Judiciary's use of investigative techniques such as phone interceptions, not even with respect to persons representing the other constitutional powers—for example, under specific and detailed constitutional regulations,[8] judges can wiretap a member of the Legislature or Executive. There is no similar, specific regulation for the President of the Republic, however. Thus, the Constitutional Court needed to address the argument that the lack of a constitutional prohibition, together with the basic principle of equality, justified using the same techniques against the President of the Republic. The argument posited that, rather than distinguish the position of the President of the Republic from that of a Deputy or a Senator, and interpret the absence of a specific regulation as a general prohibition, the Court could extend the regulations applicable to the investigation of similar constitutional actors to the President as well. Otherwise, the result would create an irrational privilege rather than ensure the President's privacy in the exercise of his functions. In other words, according to the prosecutors, the consequence of recognizing absolute presidential immunity would be to remove him completely from the reach of the judicial power, like an absolute monarch of the past.

The Constitutional Court, nevertheless, upheld the President's claim, saying that there are fundamental differences between the President and the members of either the Legislature or the Executive.

> The position of the subjects just indicated and that of the President of the Republic differ ... in two distinct characteristics. In the first place, the President possesses only the functions of bringing together and balancing, which do not imply in his daily activities, making political decisions of the kind for which he must respond to those who elected him or to those who gave him their trust. Instead they require that he establishes a connection between the Heads of the highest institutions, exercising those powers of advancement,

---

[8] Article 68 of the Italian Constitution says that judges can order the wiretapping of members of the Chamber of Deputies or of the Senate, asking for a previous authorization to the respective Chamber; Article 10 of Constitutional Law 1/1989 extends this regulation to members of the Executive. (*See also supra*, section 4.)

persuasion, and moderation, of which we were speaking before, which necessarily require discretion and confidentiality. Conversely, and not by chance, the Constitution does not contemplate any instrument to remove the prohibition on using invasive manners of fact-finding with respect to the President, unlike those which affect members of Parliament and components of the Executive, for whom it is possible to carry out such forms of control if the Chamber in charge concedes the required authorization in accordance with the various ways in which the subject is regulated.

In the normative framework, moreover, every reference to institutional subjects from whom it would be possible for the judicial authority to request an authorization concerning the President of the Republic, is defective. The absence of a framework cannot be overcome by interpretation, not even on the part of this Court, since an obligatory constitutional solution is evidently lacking. The identification of a subject competent to give authorization of the kind could be done only by a norm of constitutional rank, which is unable to be substituted by any other type of source, and even less by a pronouncement of a constitutional judge.

That is, the Court argues that the lack of constitutional regulation of the interception of presidential communications cannot be replaced merely through the exercise of the Court's interpretive power; the lacuna is too large. Instead, if Parliament wants to regulate in this area, providing a special procedure to allow judges to wiretap the President of the Republic, it should amend the Constitution.

The absence of provisions for acts of authorization similar to those contemplated for the members of Parliament and the Ministers, and the lack, moreover, of explicit limitations for categories of crimes established by constitutional norms, cannot lead to the paradoxical consequence that the communications of the President of the Republic benefit from a protection inferior to those of other aforementioned institutional subjects, but rather must lead to the more coherent conclusion that the silence of the Constitution on this point expresses the absolutely obligatory . . . confidentiality of presidential communications.

This absolute obligation follows from the position and the role of the Head of State in the Italian constitutional system and cannot be tied to a specific and explicit norm, since there is no legal provision that points to an institutional subject in charge of giving an authorization to override the privilege. It is therefore not a question of a gap, but on the contrary it is a logical presumption of a juridical-constitutional nature, of the untouchable quality of the sphere of communications of the supreme guarantor of equilibrium among the powers of the State. . . .

On the basis of what has been said up until now, the solution to the present conflict must be grounded on the affirmation of the presiding judicial authority's obligation to destroy, within the shortest time period, the accidental recordings of the telephone conversations of the President of the Republic.

In the Constitutional Court's resolution of the dispute, the *relation* of powers again prevails over the *separation* of powers—even if, as is the case here, the President needs a special status in order to perform his "relational" role, can only be guaranteed through strict protection from the judiciary power.

Somewhat paradoxically, the Italian system's orientation toward a general principle of cooperation among the powers leads the Constitutional Court to separate them, reaching a result that more closely resembles what might be expected in a presidential system like that of the United States.

6 Regionalism

1. Not "Federal" but "Regional"

If we were to differentiate *unitary* and *federal* States along a continuous linear spectrum, it is increasingly difficult to find clear examples that reside at the two opposite poles of that spectrum. On the contrary, the vast majority of constitutional systems in the world today would need to be classified somewhere in the middle of that spectrum. The difference between federal and unitary states seems to be losing its original significance, in favor of a form of "compound state," in which one finds a varying and dynamic equilibrium between central and peripheral powers.

The Italian "regional State" can be said in a sense to have anticipated this trend, embodying a very peculiar balance between central State, Regions, and local "autonomies"[1] (i.e., Municipalities, Provinces, and Metropolitan Cities). Within the Italian constitutional system, the distribution of powers between the central

---

[1] Notwithstanding the somewhat awkward neologism, we will use "autonomies" in English both to capture the literal word in Italian and as a term of art in Italian constitutional structure.

State and the 20 Regions (15 "ordinary" Regions and 5 "special" Regions[2]) follows a very peculiar scheme, quite different from both classical federal systems and paradigmatical unitary States.

As we have already pointed out (see Chapter 1, section 3.1), the choice of the regional system was the result of a compromise between two opposite visions within the Constituent Assembly. On the one hand, Christian Democrats, deeply oriented by Catholic social teaching, emphasized the primacy of society over the State and consequently favored a wide recognition of the political autonomy of local authorities. On the other hand, the Communist Party was strongly committed to the exclusivity of the political representativeness of the national Parliament, and thus in principle opposed any subdivision of powers or subtraction of political functions from the central State. Similarly to all the fundamental issues in the Italian Constitution, the final result was a "noble compromise" well depicted by Article 5 of the Italian Constitution: "The Republic, one and indivisible, recognizes and promotes local autonomies."

This article represents a very deliberate and careful use of legal language. The article begins by reaffirming the uniqueness and indivisibility of the Republic, a principle that puts this "regional" system clearly outside the family of "federal" systems, at least insofar as the latter are defined as "divided" States. Yet, immediately after this opening, the article uses the verb to "recognize" in reference to the local "autonomies." This verb has a clear meaning within Italian constitutional language, as previously seen with respect to the "recognition" of fundamental rights in Article 2. One can "recognize" only what is already existing; therefore if the Republic "recognizes" a local entity (and does not simply guarantee, or promote, or protect it), this implies that the entity in question preexists the Republic and cannot be at the mercy of the State. Thus, in the Italian constitutional vision it is generally understood that although local authorities should always be regulated, they must never be eliminated. This permanence and conceptual priority of local units distinguishes the Italian regional model clearly from the family of the classically "unitary States."

In any case, however, a fundamental constitutional difference between the State and the Regions always remains: only the central State is an expression of the "sovereign power" of the Italian people, while Regions are expressions of the "autonomy" of their respective populations.

---

[2] The 15 "ordinary" Regions are: Piedmont, Lombardy, Veneto, Liguria, Emilia-Romagna, Tuscany, Umbria, The Marches, Latium, Abruzzi, Molise, Campania, Apulia, Basilicata, Calabria. The five "special" Regions are: Valle d'Aosta, Trentino-Alto Adige, Friuli-Venezia Giulia, Sicily, Sardinia.

To understand exactly what this distinction means we have to make reference to some leading cases of the Constitutional Court. Probably the most relevant is Judgment 365/2007. This case was brought before the Court by the State against a law of the Region of Sardinia establishing a "Special Committee for the new Regional Charter of Autonomy and Sovereignty of the People of Sardinia." The problem was the use of the term "sovereignty" in reference to the people of the Sardinia Region. Unlike in the United States, for example—where the several states can still be said to retain (a limited form of) "sovereignty, in Italy sovereignty can belong to the central State only. Accordingly, the Constitutional Court declared the regional law to be unconstitutional:

> Through the use of the term "sovereignty", the law attempts to attribute a structure to the Region that differs profoundly from the existing one and is characterized by institutions more appropriate and suitable for a federal model, which is normally the result of historical processes in which the territorial entities that comprise the federal State retain forms and institutions that are marked by their prior condition of sovereignty.

The Court concedes that the absoluteness of State sovereignty today is deeply challenged, mainly by international and supranational legal orders, but at the same time it strongly reaffirms that "the internal sovereignty of the State keeps its essential structure intact, undamaged even by the significant expansion of the many functions attributed to the Regions and territorial entities by the Constitution." For that reason the Court confirms the significance of the constitutional distinction between "sovereignty" and "autonomy":

> Art. 5 and 114 of the Constitution and Art. 1 of the Charter of the Special Region of Sardinia all use (and not by chance) the term "autonomy" or its related adjective to describe the space left by the Republican system to the individual choices of the various Regions. On the other hand, it is well known that the Constituent Assembly, which introduced regional autonomy into our system for the first time only after extensive and heated debate, was absolutely firm in its rejection of concepts that may even only appear to be broadly derived from federal, or even confederal, models.

An obvious consequence of this constitutional framework is that some of the "key" legislative competences, that in a federal state are typically split between the national and the subnational levels, in Italy are vested entirely in the central State and excluded from the scope of regional authority. For example, only Parliament can legislate on civil law (that is, on areas within the scope of the civil code) and criminal law issues. There is, moreover, only a unitary judiciary, with no form of regional or local judges.[3]

Another peculiar feature of the Italian regional system is its flexibility. Even though the relationship among central State, Regions, and local authorities is established by the text of Constitution (especially in Part II, Title V), it is extremely dynamic. The "theoretical" system created with the 1948 Constitution is in fact totally different from the "living" system that effectively existed during the 1970s or 1980s, or that has been in place since 2001.

There are two reasons for such great variability. First, Part II, Title V of the Constitution was profoundly and extensively amended in 2001. Second, the concrete life of the regional system is not determined by constitutional rules alone. The Constitutional Court, through its power of judicial review, has been a key actor in the translation of the constitutional values into a precise political reality.

While in some sense a truism, because all constitutional rules acquire their meaning in important part through their interpretation and enforcement, in the case of the rules governing the regional system the role played by Italian constitutional adjudication is even more relevant and influential than in other constitutional areas. Here the Court is virtually a constitutional "coauthor": because many of the constitutional provisions about the regional system are so broadly framed, and because of the persistent absence of implementing legislation by the Parliament, the Court has had to play a more active role in giving effective meaning to the constitutional principles through its jurisprudence. It is not an accident that since the 2001 reform, Constitutional Court decisions regarding disputes between the State and Regions have outnumbered decisions on other constitutional issues.[4] Therefore, in order to have a more genuine idea of how the relations between the center and periphery really works, one must examine both the new constitutional text introduced in 2001 and the main jurisprudential doctrines regarding the regional system that have been developed in the last decade.

2. The 2001 Constitutional Reform of the Regional System

The major reform of Title V of the Italian Constitution, entitled "Regions, Provinces, Municipalities," which Parliament approved in 2001,[5] deeply modified

---

[3] The "Regional Administrative Tribunals" are "regional" only in the sense that their jurisdiction is limited to regional territory, but they are State courts.

[4] *See* Appendix III.

[5] Constitutional Law 3/2001 (Amendments to Title V of the Second Part of the Constitution).

the original model of the 1948 Constitution and completed the reform of regionalism initiated only a little earlier by Constitutional Law 1/1999 (amending the constitutional rules governing the Ordinary Regions' Charters) and Constitutional Law 2/2001 (which extended similar rules to the Regions enjoying special autonomy). The explicit aim of the 2001 revision was to strengthen the role of local authorities vis-à-vis the central State. The political intent of the constitutional change was to move in the direction of a more "federal" model, even if the result was not entirely successful in doing so.

The new constitutional architecture is built on three main pillars. The first, and probably the most symbolic change, is the revision of Article 114 of the Italian Constitution. In its original version, Article 114 said that "[t]he Republic is *divided into* Regions, Provinces and Municipalities"; the new formulation states instead that "[t]he Republic is *composed of* the Municipalities, the Provinces, the Metropolitan Cities, the Regions and the State" (emphasis added). The change marks a significant shift in the meaning of the word "Republic." There is no longer a strict identity between the Republic and the (central) State. Rather, the Republic becomes an overarching term embracing all public authorities, from Municipalities to Provinces, Metropolitan Cities, Regions, and including the State itself. Therefore, both Regions and the State are equally constitutive elements of the greater entity that is the Italian Republic. In this way all levels of public authority are put on the same constitutional plane, with only functional distinctions among them.

The second pillar is the revision of the distribution of legislative powers between the State and Regions (the only authority, other than the State and the Autonomous Provinces of Trento and Bolzano, vested with any legislative powers). The change moves toward a federal-like organization. The constitutional amendment identifies three different categories of lawmaking power: (1) the *exclusive enumerated* legislative powers of the State in the matters listed under the Article 117, paragraph 2;[6] (2) the *concurrent enumerated* legislative powers of both State and Regions in the matters listed under the Article 117, paragraph 3;[7] and, finally, (3) the *residual* legislative power of Regions in all the matters not included in the previous two lists (on their minor practical relevance, see section 4.2.2, below). The reform also removed the power of the State to challenge the constitutionality of regional laws *prior to* their promulgation and publication, limiting this executive power to the possibility of bringing a regional law before the Constitutional Court only *after* its entry into force.

---

[6] *See* Art. 117, paragraph 2 of the Italian Constitution, in Appendix I.
[7] *See* Art. 117, paragraph 3 of the Italian Constitution, in Appendix I.

In addition, the 1999 and 2001 reforms also modified the power of the Regions to enact their Charters (a kind of regional Constitution). Prior to the reforms, the Charters provided the general rules about the Regions' internal organization, and they were discussed by the Regional Council but only approved by the Parliament with a national law. With the 1999 and 2001 reforms, the Charter became a regional law and it can provide not merely for some organizational principles but also the "form of government" of the Regions: "Regional Charters are adopted and amended by the Regional Council.... This law does not require the approval of the Government commissioner."

The third pillar, the reform of administrative powers, was also a remarkable change. The original criterion for the distribution of administrative powers between the State and the Regions was the so-called "paralleling" doctrine, which established that wherever Regions had legislative power they also had administrative powers. The central State could only intervene in these regional competences in case of "strictly local interests," to delegate administrative functions to more local authorities (Municipalities or Provinces). The new Article 118 of the Italian Constitution begins from a totally different principle: "Administrative functions are attributed to the Municipalities, unless they are attributed to the Provinces, Metropolitan Cities and Regions or to the State, pursuant to the principles of subsidiarity, differentiation and proportionality, to ensure their uniform implementation."

Thus, the level of public authority of the Republic that is in the first instance generally endowed with administrative powers is the Municipality, except for those functions that—for reasons of subsidiarity or differentiation or proportionality—need to be assigned to a higher authority (Province, Metropolitan City, Region, or State). Here the subsidiarity principle operates—to borrow an image from Italian legal literature[8]—as an "elevator" that lifts administrative functions up from the local level towards higher levels (until the central State) only as necessary "to ensure their uniform implementation."

Very important changes were introduced by the 2001 constitutional revision in other areas as well (financing powers, relationships with the European Union, substituting powers by the central Government), but these three pillars support the main features of that reform.

Notwithstanding the overall movement in this reform away from the central authority of the State, the Constitutional Court has continued to deny that Italy has in any significant sense become a federal system. According to the Court, despite all the main features of the 2001 reform, the Italian constitutional system still is focused on the "State's *peculiar* position," as it emphasized in Judgment 274/2003:

> Of particular relevance in this regard are Art. 114, which places the State and the Regions on the same plane as constitutional entities of the

---

[8] R. Bin, G. Pitruzzella, *Diritto costituzionale*, XV ed., Giappichelli, Torino, 2014, p. 103.

Republic, alongside Municipalities, Metropolitan Cities, and Provinces; Art. 117, which overturns the previous criteria, explicitly enumerating the legislative powers delegated to the State and establishing a residuary clause in favor of the Regions; and, lastly, Art. 127, which makes the central Government's recourse against regional laws subsequent and no longer only preventative.

However, it is crucial to note that, in the new constitutional order arising from the reform, a unique position is still reserved to the State, inferable not only from the proclamation of the principle found in Art. 5 of the Constitution, but also from the repeated evocation of national unity. This is manifested by the call to respect the Constitution, as well as by the duties which derive from the European system and international obligations, which limit all legislative powers (Art. 117, first paragraph of the Constitution), and by the recognition of the need to protect the legal and economic unity of the system itself (Art. 120, second paragraph). This unity necessarily implies that some entity—the State—exists within the system for the purpose of assuring its fulfillment.

Art. 114 of the Constitution in no way requires total parity among the listed entities [Municipalities, Provinces, Metropolitan Cities, Regions and the State], the powers of which differ significantly: it suffices to note that the State alone has power to amend the Constitution, and that the Municipalities, Metropolitan Cities and Provinces (with the exception of Autonomous Provinces) do not have legislative power.

3. Statutory Autonomy

The basic organization of each Region is established by its Charter. The Italian constitutional system provides for two different kinds of Charters corresponding to the two types of Regions, ordinary Regions and special Regions.

As far as the five so-called "special Regions" (Trentino-Alto Adige/Südtirol, Friuli-Venezia Giulia, Valle d'Aosta/Vallée d'Aoste, Sicily, and Sardinia) are concerned, they had their own basic laws—"special Charters"—approved by a constitutional law of the State (Article 116, paragraph 1 of the Constitution). They provide specific rules and legal principles that differ from the general structure of the regional powers outlined in the Constitution, to be applied in each of those Regions. They partially depart from other constitutional provisions in order to provide these Regions with "special forms and conditions of autonomy"; however, the special Regions cannot amend all the constitutional provisions but only those falling within their specific competence.

As far as the ordinary Regions are concerned, the Constitutional reform of 2001 significantly increased their power to adopt their own Charters, granting them the capacity of determining their own institutional architecture and their basic organization. To be more precise, the "mandatory" content of the Regional Charters encompasses the form of government and other basic principles for the organization of the Region as well as procedures for popular participation in the regional deliberations, such as referenda on regional laws and administrative measures, the rules concerning the publication of regional laws and regulations, and the Council of local authorities as a consultative body on relations between the Regions and local authorities.

In addition to addressing this fundamental content prescribed by the Constitution itself, a good number of Regions have enriched their Charters with other principles expressing the legal and political purposes to which the Region is committed. The Constitutional Court has, however, held that this additional content goes beyond the limits of the Regions' statutory powers and by consequence does not have any legally binding force. In Judgment 372/2004—concerning some general provisions of the Charter of Tuscany such as the extension of the right to vote to immigrants, the recognition of forms of cohabitation other than the marriage, the respect for ecological balance, the protection of the environment and of cultural heritage, the conservation of biodiversity, the promotion of a culture of respect for animals, the protection of the historic and artistic heritage and of the landscape, and the promotion of economic development—the Court ruled:

> The pronouncements under review, despite having been inserted into a Charter, may not be given any legal effect, and belong more appropriately to the category of convictions that express the various political sensibilities present within the regional community at the time the Charter was ratified.... [W]e are not dealing here with Constitutional charters, but with regional sources endowed with "a reserved and specialized jurisdiction", that is, with regional Charters which, even if constitutionally guaranteed, must still be "in harmony with the precepts and principles derivable from the Constitution" (Judgment 196/2003). If we accept these premises concerning the non-binding and non-mandatory character of this kind of statutory pronouncement, it follows that they may have a cultural or even political function, so to speak, but certainly not a prescriptive one.

Thus the Constitutional Court does not regard Regional Charters to be comparable to constitutions not only because they have a limited field of action but also because they are bound to conform to the national Constitution. Unlike the

Charters of the Special Regions, the ordinary Charters cannot derogate from any constitutional provisions and, by contrast, are bound by the totality of the framework established by the national Constitution. In fact, according to Article 123 the Regional Charters must be "in harmony with the Constitution," which the Constitutional Court understands as going beyond narrowly abiding by the specific constitutional provisions: "the reference to 'harmony' . . . is intended not only to avoid conflict with the individual provisions [of the Constitution]—such conflict certainly would undermine harmony—but also to prevent the danger that a Charter, albeit adhering to the letter of the Constitution, nevertheless violate its spirit." (Judgment 2/2004)

Therefore, says the Court in the same judgment:

> [T]he Regional Charters must not only scrupulously abide by "every provision of the Constitution", as all the legal rules of our system must do, but must also adhere to its spirit, in the name of the required "harmony with the Constitution" (Judgment 304/2002). This has been most recently confirmed in the holding that the Charters "must be in harmony with the precepts and principles derivable from the Constitution". (Judgment 196/2003)

In other words, Regional Charters cannot be compared to any extent to State constitutions in a federal State. They have a limited field of action and even within their jurisdiction they are not free to set whatever sort of regulation: the breadth of understanding of the requirement of "harmony with the Constitution" reveals that the Italian regional State is conceived as a unitary State with a unique Constitution granting some space for regional autonomy, rather than as a federal State. Although the Regional Charters are expressions of the Regions' autonomy, this autonomy cannot be confused with sovereignty (see Judgment 365/2007, quoted in section 1, above).

Within each Region, however, the Charters enjoy the highest authority:

> The relationship between Regional Charters and regional laws is delineated by the Constitution both in hierarchical terms—given the "fundamental character of the statutory source demonstrated by the special procedure provided by Art. 123, second and third paragraphs, of the Constitution" (Judgment 4/2010)—and in terms of authority, since Art. 123 also provides for the "existence of true and proper reservations of power to the Charters, rather than the regional legislature, within the regional system (Judgments 188/2007, 272/2004, 2/2004, and 196/2003)." (Judgment 188/2011)

Considering Regional Charters from a formal and procedural point of view, they constitute higher law within the regional legal system. Whereas regional laws are adopted by the Regional Council by a simple majority and then promulgated by the President of the Region, the procedure for the approval and the amendment of a Regional Charter is more elaborate and requires two deliberations of the Regional Council taken by the absolute majority; moreover, they are subject to the control of the Constitutional Court and they may be submitted to popular referendum. According to Article 123 of the Constitution, "Regional Charters are adopted and amended by the Regional Council with a law approved by an absolute majority of its members, with two subsequent deliberations at an interval of not less than two months." Although this law does not require the approval of the central State, the Government of the Republic may challenge the constitutional legitimacy of a Regional Charter in the Constitutional Court within 30 days of its publication.

The Charter is submitted to popular referendum if one-fiftieth of the electors of the Region or one-fifth of the members of the Regional Council so request within three months of its publication. The Charter that is submitted to referendum is not promulgated if it is not approved by the majority of valid votes.

4. Legislative Autonomy

As described earlier, the Italian regional system specifies three different categories of legislative powers: the State's *exclusive* powers, the Regions' *concurring* powers, and the Regions' *residual* powers. Article 117 of the Italian Constitution regulates all three categories. Paragraph 2 contains the exclusive State competences, a list of matters in which only the national Parliament has legislative authority; paragraph 3 enumerates the concurring competences, listing those matters remanded to regional legislative power (except for the fundamental principles of the Constitution, which are entrusted to exclusive state competence). Finally, we have the residual competences, which include all matters not expressly conferred by the other categories.

Obviously, such a complex distribution of legislative powers relies greatly on the clear-cut definition of each single matter. The more the definition is flexible or vague, the more the exact dividing line between State and regional lawmaking powers become uncertain and, therefore, results in potential conflict. As shown in Appendix III ("Basics Statistics on the Constitutional Court"), after the 2001 reform cases involving conflicts between the State and Regions increased considerably. This suggests both that the drafting of the 2001 reform was less than satisfactory and that today the Constitutional Court plays a key role in the concrete molding of the regional system by providing an authoritative interpretation of the meaning of the constitutional text through specific cases.

4.1 HOW TO DEFINE A MATTER? FROM THE LITERAL MEANING TO THE "PREVALENCE DOCTRINE"

The main problem for constitutional adjudication within a system founded on the separation of legislative powers based on enumerated "matters" within each authority's competence is how to define the real meaning and scope of the "matter" in question, in the event of a dispute.

The Constitutional Court in its case law during the last decade elaborated a remarkable quantity of jurisprudential doctrine on "matter design." The starting point can be called an *objective-literal interpretive canon*. The Court says:

> [T]he identification of a matter from among those found in Art. 117 of the Constitution, for the purpose of dividing the legislative powers between the State and the Regions, must be carried out with an eye to its object and to the regulation it establishes, taking into account its rationale, and ignoring its more marginal aspects and indirect impact.

But what if two or more different competences are (or, at least, seem to be) overlapping? Consider, for example, the exact border between "environmental protection" (exclusive) and "health care" (concurrent); between "local public transportation" (residual) and "antitrust" (exclusive); between "urban planning" (concurrent) and "public or social housing" (residual); between "agriculture" and "tourism" (both residual) and "promotion of environmental goods" (concurrent) and "environmental protection" (exclusive); and so on.

The older jurisprudence on this issue followed the so-called "prevalence doctrine":

> The use of this doctrine to settle the overlap between competing competences implies . . . on the one hand, a form of regulation that, by placing itself at the intersection of several matters, expresses the need for a unified regulatory scheme, and, on the other hand, that one of the matters may be considered dominant, insofar as it is possible to find out within the whole regulatory scheme an essential nucleus belonging only to one subject matter, or that the various regulations have the same purpose. (Judgment 226/2010)

To give an example, consider the case of a law adopted by the Autonomous Province of Trento to regulate "stray and potentially dangerous animals." Although the Province regarded the issue as falling within its regional authority over "hygiene and public health," the Constitutional Court held that the law was instead a matter of "public order and safety," which is within the exclusive powers of the State:

> The challenged regulations prove to be united by a single *ratio*: to better assure the safety of citizens against the risk of attack by dogs belonging to particularly aggressive breeds, as explained in the preamble to the law, which draws the urgent need for regulation from the frequent occurrence of episodes of animal aggression. (Judgment 226/2010)

Therefore, among different overlapping powers, the *prevalent* one (according to the aims of the regulation) is "public order and safety."

4.2 THE STRONG "CENTRIPETAL" PULL IN THE DISTRIBUTION OF POWERS BETWEEN STATE AND REGIONS

In many cases, the potential overlap between State and regional legislative powers is much more complicated than in the previous example, and in those cases the Constitutional Court's extremely wide margin of interpretive freedom in setting the border between them is decisive.

In a first and fairly short period after the 2001 reforms, the Court's jurisprudence in this area seemed to remain substantially in accord with the 2001 reform's general aim to strengthen the role of Regions and local authorities. Thereafter, however, it began a slow but gradually intensifying swing in the opposite direction. Most recently, the Constitutional Court is more likely to endorse the central legislation over the local, in cases of conflict between the State and Regions. Today one can observe a remarkable inclination of the Constitutional Court to uphold the legislative activism of the central State at the expense of the legislative powers of the regional system.

Several factors may help to account for this strong "centripetal" drift in State-Regions relationships. For instance, in Italy as in most "compound" States, whether formally federal or otherwise, the central authority retains all the powers over the public safety of the whole, as well as over the coordination of the various parts. Similarly, the Italian national institutions, including the Constitutional Court, have historically shown a cultural hostility toward regional and local authorities in general, while the latter have suffered from political weakness as they have often failed to demonstrate that they can govern more effectively than the national

Parliament or the Executive. The most undisputable reason for this strong change of direction of the Constitutional Court, however, has been the global financial and economic crisis that affected Italy from 2007 onward. The largest portion of all the regional legislative powers concern the welfare state; the healthcare sector alone accounts for approximately 70 percent of regional budget. The need to control and cut public expenditures as a strong countermeasure to the crisis greatly increased the interference of central State powers with regional legislative authority, especially in connection with spending policies.

4.2.1 "Cross-Cutting" Competences

A first example of the Court's conceptual tools in allocating authority between the State and Regions is what is referred to in the scholarly legal commentary as "cross-cutting" matters, meaning those exclusive State competences that are intrinsically capable of having an effect on and interfering with other powers accorded to the Regions. For example, with respect to authority over environmental protection—reserved exclusively to the State under Article 117(2)(s) of the Constitution—the Constitutional Court has said that:

> [It] cannot be described in the technical sense as a "matter" reserved to the power of the State, since it amounts to a constitutionally protected value, and, therefore, instantiates other powers that could very well be regional, entitling the State to establish a uniform standard of protection throughout the entire Nation. It follows that the exclusive power of the State is not incompatible with a regional legislature taking specific actions in accordance with its own. (Judgment 108/2005)

Similarly, regarding the exclusive State power on antitrust regulation (Art. 117(2)(e) of the Constitution), the Court affirmed that "the protection of competition has a cross-cutting character, which implies that, since its object is to regulate the market surrounding economic activities, it may also implicate matters, concurrent or residual, attributed to the regional legislatures." (Judgment 420/2007)

These areas may be compared to the judicial application of the Commerce Clause of the U.S. Constitution by the U.S. Supreme Court, where the specific power of the U.S. Congress to regulate commerce among the several states has been interpreted in a very extensive manner so as to allow federal legislation also to regulate "intrastate" activities that may have substantial effects on interstate relations.

Another cross-cutting exclusive State power is the regulation of private law, specified in Article 117(2)(l) of the Constitution. The constitutional prohibition on the

Regions to enact laws regulating private law issues, mentioned earlier, means that the central State can deeply affect—in a "cross-cutting" way—many regional powers. For example, with regard to the regulation of employment contracts between Regions and their managers, the Constitutional Court in Judgment 18/2013 says clearly: "The regulation of economic treatment of public managers in the field of operations must be considered to fall within the matter of 'private law regulation', a power exclusively belonging to the State, in accordance with Art. 117, second paragraph, point 1 of the Constitution."

Another example is the regulation of building activities. Generally speaking, the regulation of land use is a concurrent regional competence provided by Article 117(3) of the Constitution. However, according to the Constitutional Court in Judgment 6/2013, a Region that seeks to regulate the minimum standard distance between different buildings may exceed its authority over land-use planning and enters into the exclusive State power to regulate private law:

This Court has already held that regulating the distance between buildings is within the matter of "private law regulation", which belongs exclusively to the State legislative power. The regulation [before the Court] principally makes direct reference to relationships between owners of neighboring plots and is rooted first and foremost in the Civil Code. . . . Nevertheless, constitutional precedent has clarified that, since "the buildings are on land that may have—for natural and historical reasons—special characteristics their regulation . . . extends beyond the proper limits of private relationships and also touches public interests" (Judgment 232/2005), the responsibility for which has been entrusted to the Regions, on the basis of their concurrent competence in the matter of "land use regulation" according to Art. 117, third paragraph of the Constitution.

For these reasons, . . . if, on the one hand, we cannot entirely deny a regional legislative competence concerning the distance between buildings, on the other hand such a competence, overlapping with "private law regulation", is strictly limited in its scope—the administration of the land—and this also dictates the way the competence may be exercised. Therefore, regional legislation which regulates in this area is legitimate only insofar as its purpose is explicitly urban planning, leaving the execution of its provisions to "urbanistic tools that work toward a comprehensive and unitary plan concerning specific geographic areas" (Judgment 232/2005). The regional norms that go beyond this scope to regulate the distance between buildings illegitimately fall within the purview of "private law regulation", which is reserved to the exclusive legislative competence of the State.

4.2.2 "Catch-all" Competences

During the most recent times the Court has gone even further along this path toward the (re)centralization of legislative authority, moving from an emphasis on cross-cutting powers to a recognition of what we should call "catch-all" clauses. These are matters constitutionally allocated to the exclusive legislative authority of the State, and that in the interpretation of the Constitutional Court can be used as a tool for the national Parliament to intervene in every possible regional competence.

One of the clearest examples is the concurrent regional power over the coordination of public finances. In this area, according to the scheme of Article 117(3) of the Constitution, regulatory authority should be exercised at the regional level, except with respect to the general principles to be provided by State legislation. Judgment 22/2014 provides a paradigmatic case. In this dispute the Regions constitutionally challenged a State law regulating the union of small Municipalities. The law in question sought to attain economic efficiency in the exercise of public functions such as urban planning, infrastructure development, public transportation, utilities, and so forth, by unifying the structures of functions of Italy's many very small Municipalities. This kind of regulation in principle should be entirely reserved to the Regions, without any interference of the State, as a residual legislative power under Article 117(4) of the Constitution. According to the Constitutional Court, however:

> Nevertheless, . . . where the concurrent legislative power is exercised [by the Regions] to restrain public expenditure, a source of legitimacy for the State to intervene in this area is found in the fundamental principles of "public finance coordination", under Art. 117, third paragraph, of the Constitution.
>
> To these ends, this Court has stressed on multiple occasions that the State Legislature may, by providing a regulatory framework, legitimately impose budget limitations upon Regions and local entities, for reasons of financial coordination connected to national objectives and conditioned by supranational obligations, even if these inevitably translate into indirect limitations on the local authorities' spending autonomy . . .
>
> In the case under examination, the contested laws appear to be clearly geared toward the restraint of public spending, creating a system that is, by nature, beneficial for the associated management of functions (most importantly the fundamental ones) among Municipalities, which aims to cut expenses at both the organizational—"administrative" —"and organizational—"political" —"levels, leaving to the Regions the contiguous exercise of their constitutionally guaranteed power without any implications for the reservation found in the fourth paragraph of Art. 123 of the Constitution.

Ultimately, this involves a legitimate exercise of concurrent State power in the area of "public finance coordination", in the sense of the third clause of Art. 117 of the Constitution.

In short, here we have an extremely broad interpretation of the scope of "coordination of public finance" that encompasses the regulation of local authorities, which is otherwise a prototypically regional competence. The logical argument is that every kind of regulation that has a "substantial effect" (to borrow from U.S. Supreme Court jurisprudence) on the financial conditions must be included in the "coordination of public finance" category. Yet, it is clear that virtually any kind of regulation has such potential impact. In this way the State can intervene in practice in all of the regional powers.

4.2.3 "Detailed" Principles

Another relevant jurisprudential doctrine endowing the central State with a powerful instrument with which to encroach upon the regional competences is the peculiar interpretation of the role of the State legislation within the concurrent regional powers.

Article 117(3) of the Constitution, listing a series of matters over which legislative power is shared between the center and periphery, specifies: "In the subject matters covered by concurring legislation, legislative powers are vested in the Regions, except for the determination of the fundamental principles, which are laid down in State legislation." The literal meaning of this article would seem quite clear: with respect to all of the concurrent regional powers, the State can intervene only in order to set "fundamental principles." The original aims of this provision were to maintain a coherent national framework even in those matters in which regional legislation is permitted, and to avoid disproportionate differentiation among the Regions. Therefore, the Constitutional Court affirms:

in matters of concurrent legislation, the State only has power to establish fundamental principles; the power to issue rules concerning details is the purview of the Regions. The relationship between principle and detailed rules must be understood according to the formula that the former is entitled to prescribe criteria and objectives, while to the latter is reserved the specification of concrete tools to reach those objectives (Judgment 341/2010).

However, despite this plain meaning, drawn from both the text and original purpose of the provision, the Constitutional Court began to interpret this provision as allowing the State, under certain circumstances, to establish increasingly more "detailed principles." In this way the Court has permitted State laws to create very detailed rules in areas otherwise within the concurrent regional powers, whenever those rules are necessarily or essentially linked to the general principles. For example, the Court has upheld State laws in concurrent regional matters providing for technical norms and standards (Judgments 254/2010, 201/2012), for detailed authorization procedures (Judgment 336/2005), specifying the final deadline of those procedures (Judgment 364/2006), information and communication protocols (Judgments 190/2008, 121/2012), and sanctions and fines (Judgment 289/2008).

5. Administrative Autonomy: The Principle of Subsidiarity
5.1 "VERTICAL" VS. "HORIZONTAL" SUBSIDIARITY

As noted earlier, one of the main pillars upon which the new regional architecture was built is the new Article 118 of the Constitution, which regulates the administrative powers of the Regions. The main novelty introduced by the 2001 reform was the explicit reference to the principle of "subsidiarity," which has both a vertical and a horizontal dimension.

Vertical subsidiarity means that in principle all administrative functions are to be allocated to the level of public authority closest to the citizens (in the Italian case, Municipalities) unless those functions can be better performed by a higher-level authority (Provinces, Metropolitan Cities, Regions, and the State). The subsidiarity principle in its vertical dimension works as an elevator that, moving from the lower levels, ascends toward a level that is more appropriate in terms of either efficiency or territorial range.

Horizontal subsidiarity, as specified in Article 118, instead means that "the State, Regions, Metropolitan Cities, Provinces and Municipalities shall promote the autonomous initiatives of citizens, both as individuals and as members of associations, relating to activities of general interest, on the basis of the principle of subsidiarity." Here the notion of subsidiarity is quite different. It is not about the distribution of functions among the different levels of public authority forming the Republic but between public powers and private citizens or civil society associations. Here the principle is more connected to its original meaning—deriving from Catholic social thought—as a limitation on public power according to which the State and all public authorities should not substitute themselves unnecessarily for civil society in carrying out "activities of general interest." Article 118 recognizes that not all administrative functions need to be performed by the State or some other public authority of the Republic. On the contrary, there are "public" functions (that is, of general interest) that can be appropriately and effectively carried out directly by civil society, "as individuals and as members of associations."

In its horizontal dimension, subsidiarity is an expression of the very fundamental principle contained in the Article 2 of the Constitution, which (as discussed in Chapter 4) protects fundamental rights not only of individuals as such but also of persons within the "social groups" necessary for their flourishing. In this sense, subsidiarity can be understood not only as a right (of individuals and private associations to exercise their own social responsibility) but also as part of the "underogable duties of political, economic and social solidarity," that is, a duty on the part of the State and other public authorities to respect the autonomy of social actors.

5.2 THE "SUBSIDIARITY CALL" DOCTRINE

One of the most relevant legal conundrums deriving from the application of the principle of subsidiarity in its vertical dimension is its connection with the constitutional allocation of legislative powers.

A perception of the dilemma begins from a distinctly European civil law understanding of the rule of law, which requires that all administrative functions have to be established and regulated by a prior legislative act. Therefore, whenever the subsidiarity principle requires that a specific administrative function be moved up from the ordinary municipal level to a higher level (Province, Region, or State), that administrative power must be assigned through a specific legislative act. This generates a problem when an administrative function falling within a regional legislative power is subsequently "recalled" by the State, by virtue of applying the principle of subsidiarity. The logical consequence is that in this case the State also acquires the legislative power to legislatively establish and regulate that specific administrative function, even if such legislation would otherwise constitutionally fall within the scope of regional powers.

As the Court stated in its famous first precedent on this doctrine (Judgment 303/2003), Article 118(1) of the Constitution:

> explicitly refers to the administrative functions, but introduces a dynamic mechanism for these which renders the distribution of legislative powers . . . less rigid by providing that the administrative functions, generally attributed to the Municipalities, may be allocated to a different level of government on the basis of the principles of subsidiarity, differentiation, and adequacy, in order to assure their uniform exercise. After all, it is consistent with the theoretical matrix as well as the practical meaning of subsidiarity that the distribution should effect a *subsidium* when a particular level of Government is inadequate

to achieve the intended purpose. However, given this affirmation of the potential to ascend to a higher level, it follows that when a uniform exercise surpasses even the regional level, the State may exercise that administrative function.

This cannot but have consequences for the exercise of the legislative function, since the principle of legality, which dictates that functions assumed under the subsidiarity principle must also be organized and regulated by law, logically results in preventing the individual Regions, with different regulations, from organizing and regulating administrative functions drawn up to the national level and confirming that only the State may do so.

Therefore, the State, through this "subsidiarity call," can assume a lower authority's administrative functions on the basis of "subsidiarity, differentiation and adequacy" and to that extent can consequently legislate on this issue as well.

This legislative power must, however, comply with some restrictive standards: proportionality, reasonableness, and loyal cooperation.

As this Court has repeatedly held concerning the principle of substantive legality—since the legislative organ that evaluates whether there is a need to bestow a particular administrative function upon a territorial authority higher than a Municipality must be at least at the level of the territorial Region in question—the evaluation must be justified under the principles of subsidiarity, differentiation and adequacy.

Therefore, ... an exception to the distribution called for in Art. 117 of the Constitution can only be justified if the evaluation of the shared interest underlying the State's assumption of regional functions is proportionate, is not unreasonable, and was the object of an agreement with the affected Region.

Thus, in order for a State law to legitimately attribute administrative functions to the central Government in the areas covered by Article 117, third and fourth paragraphs, of the Constitution, and at the same time regulate their exercise, it must articulate a logically pertinent regulation (therefore suitable to regulate the aforementioned functions), which is limited to measures that are strictly indispensable to the purpose and is enacted following procedures that assure the participation of the levels of Government through instruments of loyal cooperation, or, in any case, through adequate mechanisms of cooperation for the concrete exercise of administrative functions allocated chiefly to the central Government organs. Only when these prerequisites are met, similarly to a constitutional analysis under strict scrutiny, is the State justified in its choice of a uniform exercise of functions, when the need for a uniform exercise of those functions becomes clear.

5.3 HORIZONTAL SUBSIDIARITY: THE "SOCIAL LIBERTY" DOCTRINE

Although the Constitutional Court has been much more careful so far in the implementation of Article 118's new paragraph on horizontal subsidiarity, it has issued some very interesting decisions in this area as well.

The first relevant case is Judgment 300/2003, in which the Court had to rule on a constitutional claim by some Regions requesting the power to regulate the internal organization of "banking foundations" (foundations involved in banking and grant-making activities), which are defined by law as "private legal persons." The Court argued that:

> Their definition as private legal persons, endowed with full statutory and administrative autonomy [and] the recognition of the kind of social utility that characterizes the goals they pursue, . . . —*also in consideration of what Art. 118, fourth paragraph of the Constitution prescribes*—places the "banking foundations" among the subjects of the organization of "social liberty" (Judgment 50/1998), rather than public functions, although still falling within the limits and controls compatible with their character. [Emphasis added.]

In other words, those foundations are expressions of citizens' "social liberty" and, as such, cannot be considered as equivalent to "public functions" subjected to public regulation.

Another interesting example can be found in Judgment 203/2013, in which the Court heard a reference from an Administrative Tribunal questioning the constitutionality of a legal provision regarding maternity and paternity, insofar as it did not entitle a public employee to take a family medical leave to assist an uncle with a serious health condition (dependent from employee's family).[9] The Court considered that the extension of family medical leave to all the members of the family represents an indirect protection for severely disabled persons. In particular, the Court found that the full protection of vulnerable subjects requires, in addition to necessary health care and rehabilitation, also social inclusion and, above all, the continuity of those relationships that are constitutive of the human personality. The Court therefore read the legislation as providing the entitlement also to a cohabiting nephew, as a requirement not only of solidarity (Art. 2) and the right to health care (Art. 32) but also of subsidiarity (Art. 118).

---

[9] This case was discussed in greater detail in Chapter 4.

6. Financial Autonomy

The third dimension of regional autonomy (in addition to the legislative and administrative dimensions addressed in the preceding sections) is financial autonomy. It is obvious that the autonomy of a public authority that can freely legislate and administer but that is completely dependent on the central State with regard to its financial resources is illusory.

This is at present one of the most controversial issues in Italian regionalism because, since its very beginning, the taxation and budgetary powers given to the Regions and local authorities by the Constitution were extremely weak. Article 119 of the Constitution says that:

> Municipalities, Provinces, Metropolitan Cities and Regions shall have independent financial resources. They set and levy taxes and collect revenues of their own, in compliance with the Constitution and according to the principles of co-ordination of State finances and the tax system. They share in the tax revenues related to their respective territories.

This language in effect means that Ordinary Regions do not really have an independent power to levy and collect new taxes, but that they are only entrusted with a derivative financial power: they not only have to respect constitutional principles (obviously)—but also have to abide by the State legislative competence on "public finance coordination" that was examined previously. Moreover, in 2012 Article 119 of the Italian Constitution was reformed (Constitutional Law 1/2012) to introduce another general limitation to regional and local budgetary autonomy, "the observance of economic and financial limitations deriving from the European Union."

The Constitutional Court's jurisprudence has mainly confirmed this general picture, affirming in Judgment 37/2004 that Article 119:

> considers the Municipalities, the Provinces, the Metropolitan Cities, and the Regions to be on the same plane in principle, establishing that all these entities "have revenue and expenditure autonomy" (first paragraph), have "independent financial resources", and "set and levy taxes and collect revenues of their own", both "in compliance with the Constitution and according to the principles of co-ordination of State finances and the tax system". Moreover, "they may have shares of the State tax revenues related to their respective territories" (second paragraph). The resources derived from these sources and from the equal distribution fund established by State law, allow—that is to say, they

must allow—these entities to "fully finance the public functions attributed to them" (fourth paragraph), except for the possibility that the State allocate additional resources to carry out special interventions in favor of specific Municipalities, Provinces, Metropolitan Cities, and Regions, for purposes of providing the development and guarantees described in the same rule, or "to achieve goals other than those pursued in the ordinary implementation" of the functions of autonomous entities (fifth paragraph).

However, the actualization of this constitutional design requires, as a necessary premise, the intervention of the State Legislature, which, in order to coordinate the entire public fiscal system, must not only establish the principles by which the regional Legislatures must abide, but must also set the general framework for the entire tax system and delineate the spaces and limits within which the intrusive power of the State, Regions, and local entities, respectively, may act.

Thus, the Court substantially upholds the idea of regional financial autonomy as a weak system, giving a strong role to the central State.

At the same time, in other case law the Justices have tried to set forth some core principles limiting State legislative power over regional finance:

We must conclude that, from now on, Art. 119 of the Constitution places precise limits on the State Legislature concerning its regulation of the financing procedures for functions reserved to the system of local authorities. First of all, conditional State funding in areas and functions that fall within the regional purview is not permitted, whether they fall within the exclusive competence of the Regions or in the concurrent one when, in the case of the latter, the Region abides by the fundamental principles fixed by State law. . . . Furthermore, as the precedent of this Court makes clear, the introduction of Art. 119 of the Constitution enacted an additional limit on the State Legislature, a prohibition against taking action in a way contrary to that described in Art. 119: that is, to simply suppress, without making any substitution, the spaces of autonomy granted to Regions or local entities that are already recognized by valid State law, or to establish a general fiscal system that violates the principles established by Art. 119. (Judgment 320/2004)

7 National Constitutional Adjudication in the European Space

1. The European Clauses of the Italian Constitution

As a matter of principle, in a centralized system like the Italian one, the Constitutional Court is endowed with the exclusive power of reviewing legislation. As a matter of fact, however, the Italian Constitutional Court shares its authority with other judicial bodies, whose importance has grown over time. In particular, important roles have been assigned to the Court of Justice of the European Union (CJEU)—based in Luxembourg—and to the European Court of Human Rights (ECtHR), operating within the context of the Council of Europe and of the European Convention on Human Rights (ECHR), based in Strasbourg. To be sure, the missions of the three Courts do not overlap, and neither of the two European Courts has jurisdiction over constitutional judicial review of national legislation, which is in the domain of the Constitutional Court. Nevertheless, taken together, the three legal orders—EU, ECHR, and national constitutions—have developed into a "composite" constitutional system, and a number of interactions occur among their respective judicial bodies, especially when they act as human rights adjudicators.

In order to understand relationships among the highest judicial authorities in Europe, it is first useful to recall concisely the main principles regulating the relationship between the Italian legal order and European and international law in general.

Italy is a country characterized by a dualist tradition in which the international and national legal systems are each conceived as autonomous. There are two fundamental provisions in the Italian Constitution regarding the relationship between international and domestic law: Articles 10 and 11. These articles draw an important distinction between general rules of international law and international treaties. According to Article 10, the former—which correspond to customary international law—are directly incorporated into the Italian system and enjoy the same rank as constitutional provisions—although they are required to abide by the supreme fundamental principles of the Constitution, as stated in Judgment 238/2014. As for international treaties, they must be incorporated into national law, in order to be binding within the domestic system. According to Articles 80 and 87, ratification is provided by the President of the Republic, but in some enumerated cases—which cover a wide spectrum of treaties—a previous act of Parliament is required. In practice, most international treaties become part of the Italian system through a legislative act of Parliament, which confers on the treaty provisions the same legal binding force of every ordinary legislative act. Consequently, international treaties are usually considered of lesser authority than constitutional law in the hierarchy of sources of law.

Originally, both the Founding Treaties of the European Union and the European Convention on Human Rights were assimilated into every other international treaty. Eventually their position was differentiated. Since the 1970s, EU legislation was considered to fall within the scope of Article 11: "Italy agrees on conditions of equality with other States, to the limitation of sovereignty that may be necessary to a world order ensuring peace and justice among the Nations." Consequently, EU legislation now enjoys a higher rank, superseding domestic ordinary law in case of conflict. Moreover, Article 117, paragraph 1, which was introduced by a constitutional amendment in 2001, today governs the position of international treaties—including the ECHR—within the domestic system: "Legislative powers shall be vested in the State and the Regions in compliance with the Constitution and with the constraints deriving from EU legislation and international obligations." As we will see, since its approval, this provision has triggered an interesting evolution in the Constitutional Court's case law. As a consequence, at present both EU legislation and ECHR judgments, although distinct from each other, enjoy a special status.

2. The Constitutional Court and the European Union

Italy's membership in the European Union has, over time, reshaped some major principles of the Italian constitutional system and deeply affected the model of constitutional adjudication as originally designed by the Italian Constitution of 1948.

Two important principles of European law are most responsible for such a dramatic transformation: the principles of supremacy and of direct effect of European law. Neither is explicitly stated in the European treaties. In particular, there is no "supremacy clause" in the Founding Treaties comparable to Article VI, clause 2 of the U.S. Constitution; nevertheless the CJEU concluded that the supremacy principle was implied in the new legal system, in order for European legislation to be binding on all Member States.[1] Similarly, the principle of direct effect was derived by the CJEU,[2] establishing that some European norms are capable of creating individual rights that can be enforced before national judges of the Member States. Following the case law of the CJEU, we can provisionally define those two principles as follows: supremacy denotes the capacity of a norm of European law to overrule inconsistent norms of national law; direct effect is the capacity of that norm to be applied in domestic court proceedings, setting aside and replacing competing national norms.

The principle of supremacy has in fact introduced a new source of higher law, which competes with national constitutions as a benchmark for judicial review of national legislation. Direct effect entrusts all lower courts, rather than only the Constitutional Court, with the power of performing judicial review of legislation in relation to European law. Put another way, one could say participation in the European Union has introduced a "second judicial review of legislation," parallel to the original one. The second review potentially competes with the original, constitutional review. First, whereas the constitutional judicial review of legislation was and still is conducted in relation to the principles inscribed in the national Constitution, the judicial review required by the European Union is meant to ensure that Member States abide by European legislation. Consequently it uses all sorts of European legislation—treaties, regulations, directives, and so forth—as yardsticks to appraise the applicability of national legislation. Second, whereas the constitutional model is a centralized one, based on a specialized court vested with the exclusive power of reviewing legislation, the European one is highly decentralized and diffused, empowering all ordinary courts to review legislation.

---

[1] CJEU Judgment 15 July 1964, case 6/64, *Costa v. ENEL.*
[2] CJEU Judgment 5 February 1963, case 26/62, *Van Gend & Loos.*

It is no surprise, then, that the Italian Constitutional Court—like higher courts in other Member States—firmly resisted the principles of supremacy and direct effect of European law, since those principles implied a veritable revolution of the role of the Judiciary and required national constitutional courts to hand over an important portion of their most crucial function to other nonspecialized lower courts. Indeed, the Constitutional Court was fully aware of the consequences of dealing with cases that involved the effects of European law.

For this reason, the Constitutional Court had a long way to go before fully complying with the European requirements. The great distance between the Italian understanding of judicial review of legislation and the model adopted by the European Union required the Court to undertake a "European journey."[3] The journey can be divided into four stages: (1) constitutional resistance to the supremacy of European legislation; (2) limitations of sovereignty; (3) constitutional surrender to the supremacy of EU legislation; and (4) the last citadel: the doctrine of "counter-limits."

2.1 CONSTITUTIONAL RESISTANCE TO THE SUPREMACY OF EUROPEAN LEGISLATION

If direct effect and supremacy are universally considered to be essential characteristics of European law today, that was certainly not the case in the years prior to the two landmark Court of Justice Judgments, *Van Gend & Loos* of 1963 and *Costa/ENEL* of 1964. The treaties were silent about these principles while the constitutional principles of most Member States did not favor them.

As previously acknowledged, Italy's constitutional system follows the dualist principle, maintaining a distinction between the national legal order and international law. In Italy, therefore, international norms are not enforceable as such, but they may become enforceable by courts as national law after their transformation into domestic legislation. Moreover, before the already mentioned constitutional amendment of 2011, when treaties were incorporated into domestic law by an act of Parliament, they were endowed with the same rank as any other piece of ordinary legislation. The result was that they took precedence over earlier legislative acts, but could be overturned by later ordinary legislative acts according to the rule *lex posterior derogat priori*. In other words, due to its dualistic tradition, Italy was neither prepared to accept direct effect, nor to recognize the supremacy of European law.

Predictably, then, in the first stage of its European journey the Italian Constitutional Court was at odds with the doctrine of the Court of Justice. In fact, the contrast could not have been more explicit, because the two Courts were

---

[3] P. Barile, *Il cammino comunitario della Corte*, in *Giurisprudenza costituzionale*, 1973, pp. 2406–2419.

required to intervene in the same proceedings, concerning the Italian law nationalizing the electricity industry. The Italian judge in Milan, arguing that the nationalization law was invalid, referred both a preliminary ruling to the Court of Justice in order to verify whether the laws conflicted with the European treaty and a preliminary ruling to the Italian Constitutional Court for judicial review of legislation. Within the context of the same judicial controversy, the Courts reached two opposite conclusions. For the Court of Justice, that was the very occasion to affirm the supremacy of European Law:

> By contrast with ordinary international treaties, the [Treaty Establishing the European Economic Community (EEC Treaty)] has created its own legal system which, on the entry into force of the Treaty, became an integral part of the legal systems of the Member States and which their courts are bound to apply.
>
> By creating a Community of unlimited duration, having its own institutions, its own personality, its own legal capacity and capacity of representation on the international plane and, more particularly, real powers stemming from a limitation of sovereignty or a transfer of powers from the States to the Community, the Member States have limited their sovereign rights, albeit within limited fields, and have thus created a body of law which binds both their nationals and themselves.
>
> The integration into the laws of each Member State of provisions which derive from the Community, and more generally the terms and the spirit of the Treaty, make it impossible for the States, as a corollary, to accord precedence to a unilateral and subsequent measure over a legal system accepted by them on a basis of reciprocity. Such a measure cannot therefore be inconsistent with that legal system. The executive force of Community law cannot vary from one State to another in deference to subsequent domestic laws, without jeopardizing the attainment of the objectives of the Treaty. . . .
>
> The obligations undertaken under the Treaty establishing the Community would not be unconditional, but merely contingent, if they could be called into question by subsequent legislative acts of the signatories. . . .
>
> It follows from all these observations that the law stemming from the Treaty, an independent source of law, could not, because of its special and original nature, be overridden by domestic legal provisions, however framed, without being deprived of its character as Community law and without the legal basis of the Community itself being called into question.
>
> The transfer by the States from their domestic legal system to the Community legal system of the rights and obligations arising under the Treaty carries with it a permanent limitation of their sovereign rights, against which a subsequent

unilateral act incompatible with the concept of the Community cannot prevail. Consequently Article 177 is to be applied regardless of any domestic law, whenever questions relating to the interpretation of the Treaty arise.[4]

Dealing with the same legal question, the Italian Constitutional Court, in Judgment 14/1964, answered:

> The violation of the [European] Treaty, although it does entail the responsibility of the State on the international plane, does not deprive the law that contradicts it of its full efficacy.
>
> There is no doubt that the State must honor the commitments it assumes and no doubt that the Treaty has the legal force that the executing laws grant to it. But because it is necessary to maintain the supremacy of the laws subsequent to it, according to the principles of the temporal succession of laws, it follows that any possible conflict between one and the others cannot give rise to questions of constitutionality.

In the Constitutional Court's reasoning at that time, the European treaties have to be treated as any other international treaty. They are given the same value as ordinary laws of the Italian Parliament, and therefore cannot prevail over more recent pieces of legislation. The disagreement with the Court of Justice was complete.

It might be interesting to note that, similarly, the supremacy of Community law also was not initially welcomed in other Member States, like France and the United Kingdom, because it did not fit with the traditional constitutional principle of the sovereignty of the Parliament.

2.2 LIMITATIONS OF SOVEREIGNTY

In the following years, however, the Italian Constitutional Court incrementally smoothed out its attitude of opposition to the supremacy of European law, and distinguished the status of European treaties from all other international norms. Whereas the dualistic framework continued to be confirmed in general, the Italian Court tried to accommodate the European requirements within those principles by establishing new rules specific to the European norms. The pivot of this new line of

---

[4] CJEU Judgment 15 July 1964, case 6/64, *Costa v. ENEL*. Article 177 of the original version of the EEC Treaty—now Article 267 of the TFEU—provides for the "preliminary ruling" process, through which every national judge can refer to the CJEU a question relating to the interpretation of European legislation or relating to its validity. *See infra*, section 2.5.

reasoning was the idea of "limitations of sovereignty," mentioned in Article 11 of the Italian Constitution.

This new trend in the case law of the Constitutional Court appeared for the first time in Judgment 183/1973. The Court was asked to decide whether a crucial provision of the European treaties—Article 189 of the EEC Treaty, now Article 288 of the Treaty on the Functioning of the European Union (TFEU)—which confers on European institutions the power to issue normative acts, such as regulations and directives—was at all compatible with the Italian Constitution. It is in this context that the idea of limitations of sovereignty plays a decisive role:

> This formula (limitations of sovereignty) legitimates the limitation of the powers of the State with respect to its legislative, executive, and judicial functions, which was necessary for the institution of a Community among the European States—that is, a new, supranational, interstate organization having a permanent character, legal personality, and the capacity for international representation. Italy and the other sponsoring States conferred upon and recognized in the Economic Community—open to all the other European States (Art. 237 of the Treaty)[5] and conceived as an instrument of integration among the participating States, for the purposes of economic and social development, and thus also for the purposes of the defense of peace and liberty—certain sovereign powers, constituting it as an institution characterized by an autonomous and independent legal order.
>
> In particular, with Art. 189 of the Founding Treaty,[6] the Council and the Commission of the Community were given the power to issue rules with general application—that is, according to the interpretation given in Community jurisprudence and in the now harmonious jurisprudence of various Member States as well as in the dominant scholarly commentary, acts having a general normative content equal to State laws, having obligatory efficacy in all their parts, and directly applicable in each of the Member States, or in other words immediately binding on the States and their citizens, without the need for internal measures of adaptation of reception.
>
> The organs of the Community have this normative authority "for the fulfillment of their tasks and under the conditions contemplated by the Treaties." In this way, each of the Member States has effected a partial transfer of its legislative functions to the Community organs, on the basis of a precise criterion of the division of competences over the subjects analytically indicated in the

---

[5] *See* now Art. 49 Treaty on the European Union (TEU).
[6] *See* now Art. 288 Treaty on the Functioning of the European Union (TFEU).

second and third parts of the Treaty, and as necessarily correlated to the goals of general interest to the economic and social policy of the Community that have been established by the same Treaty.

Here the Constitutional Court abandoned the framework of classical international law, because European integration has special features and cannot be adequately understood through the lens of the general principles of international law. This decision is grounded on the idea of the "limitations of sovereignty" established under Article 11 of the Italian Constitution. With membership in the European Communities (now the European Union), the Italian institutions—Parliament, Government, Judiciary, Regions, and even the Constitutional Court—have limited their sovereign powers and surrendered some of them to the European institutions. Insofar as the European institutions perform their activities within the boundaries of competences established by the Founding Treaties, their acts—regulations and directives—enjoy a special status, since they can be directly relevant within the domestic legal order, with no need to be "transplanted" into domestic legislation:

> Fundamental requirements of equality and of legal certainty suggest that the Community norms—which cannot be characterized either as sources of international law, nor of foreign law, nor of the internal law of single States—should have full obligatory effect and direct application in all of the Member States, without the need for laws of incorporation and adaptation, as acts having the force of law in every country of the Community so that they enter into force everywhere simultaneously and have equal and uniform application with respect to all of their subjects. (Judgment 183/73)

The Court thus paved the way for the principle of supremacy and direct effect of European legislation, within the limit of competences established by the treaties. The German Constitutional Court followed a similar set of arguments. However, even after this important step, some hidden ambiguities still remained unresolved and were bound to come to light, sooner or later, in the subsequent case law of the Italian Constitutional Court.

2.3 CONSTITUTIONAL SURRENDER TO THE SUPREMACY OF EU LEGISLATION

Once the Constitutional Court accepted the supremacy of European Law on the basis of Article 11 of the Italian Constitution with Judgment 183/1973, a new problem arose, and possibly the most crucial one. The question the Constitutional Court had to confront now considered the jurisdictional issue: Who is the guardian of the supremacy of European Law within the national legal systems?

On this point, the Court of Justice and the Constitutional Court once again took opposite positions at the outset. The European Court required the power of guardianship be granted to lower courts, establishing a diffuse judicial review of national legislation in relation to European law. This did not match the Italian tradition of centralized judicial review, where only the Constitutional Court is vested with the exclusive power of judging the laws.

In fact, in the *Simmenthal* Judgment of 1978, the Court of Justice stated that:

> Every national court must, in a case within its jurisdiction, apply Community law in its entirety and protect rights which the latter confers on individuals and must accordingly set aside any provision of national law which may conflict with it, whether prior or subsequent to the Community rule.[7]

This conferral of powers on "every national court" to set aside national legislation was a shock for the Italian system, and it brought about a true innovation, both from a theoretical point of view and from a practical one. Within the doctrinal framework of the Constitutional Court, each national provision conflicting with European legislation was to be considered contrary to Article 11 of the Constitution. Consequently, each conflict between national and European norms fell within the jurisdiction of the Constitutional Court. In contrast, the Court of Justice dealt with conflicts between European laws and national legislation with a different perspective, as if the two sets of rules were part of the same legal system with the national courts—every national court—acting as European judges and guardians of European legislation.

It is no wonder, then, that it took a number of years for Italian legal scholarship and the Constitutional Court to accept the "silent revolution" brought about by the Court of Justice in *Simmenthal*. Only in 1984 with Judgment 170 (*Granital*) did the Constitutional Court overrule its previous case law, affirming that European Community law "must always be applied, whether it precedes or follows the ordinary laws incompatible with it: and the national judge, vested with the respective application may benefit from the assistance offered by the preliminary question of interpretation, in the sense of Article 177 [now Article 267 of the TFEU] of the Treaty."

To be more precise, despite remaining faithful to its original dualistic doctrine, the Italian Constitutional Court takes a very subtle position on the consequences

---

[7] CJEU Judgment 9 March 1978, case 106/77, *Simmenthal*, par. 21.

of the direct effect of European legislation for the national legislation with which it conflicts. As the Constitutional Court explained in Judgment 170/1984:

> The effect of the [European legislation] is not that of annulling, in the proper meaning of the term, the incompatible internal norm, but of preventing that norm from being applied for the resolution of the controversy before the national judge . . . For the very reason of the distinction between the two legal orders, the priority of the regulation adopted by the [European Community] means . . . that the [national] law does not interfere in the sphere which the [European] act occupies, which is completely preempted by the Community law. . . . Outside of the material domain and the temporal limits in which the Community discipline is in force, the national rule preserves, intact, its proper legal authority and keeps its legal efficacy.

After this decision, the task of directly applying European law was shifted to the lower courts, with the Constitutional Court preserving some jurisdiction only in residual and marginal cases.

By the mid 1980s the Constitutional Court had come to adapt the principles of national constitutional law to the new European context in which the Court was called to perform its functions. The Constitutional Court has now therefore reached a "practical concordance" with the CJEU, even though important differences still remain at the theoretical level, insofar as the CJEU case law is still based on a monist principle, whereas the Italian Constitutional Court still adheres to a dualist doctrine.

2.4 THE LAST CITADEL: THE DOCTRINE OF "COUNTER-LIMITS"

The supremacy of European law is not without limits within the Italian legal system. The Italian Constitutional Court, like many other national constitutional courts—starting with the German *Bundesverfassungsgeright*—has accepted the supremacy of European law "subject to conditions." While European legislation in general prevails over national legislation (including the national Constitution, as required by the Court of Justice[8]), European norms are not allowed to override the core principles of the Italian Constitution, in particular the constitutional guarantees of fundamental rights. The core principles of the national Constitution are considered "counter-limits" to the limitations of sovereignty. It is on the basis of this understanding that the national powers agreed to reduce their functions in order to enter the European Communities. As a result, European legislation and other

---

[8] CJEU Judgment 17 December 1970, case 11/70, *Internationale Handelsgesellshaft*.

European acts prevail over all national legislation, and can even derogate from the national Constitution, but only within the boundaries of these counter-limits.

In order to understand this peculiar notion of counter-limits, one should consider that when the supremacy of European law was established, during the late 1960s and 70s, there was no bill of rights in any European Treaty and the Court of Justice had declined[9] any competence to rule on the protection of fundamental rights. As a result, national constitutional courts were concerned about the lack of protection afforded human rights, especially in cases of human rights violations produced by European acts. In particular, the German Constitutional Court firmly expressed this concern in the "*Solange*" Judgments of 1974 and 1986. The Italian Constitutional Court did so as well in Judgments 183/1973 (*Frontini*) and 170/1984 (*Granital*).

Later, when the Court of Justice filled the gap in the protection of fundamental rights,[10] allaying the fear that citizens might be deprived of their rights without judicial remedy, a number of national constitutional courts reiterated the counter-limits doctrine as a means of protecting national constitutional identities, especially at the time of the debate over the proposed European Constitution (2000–2004). The pluralistic feature of the European legal order depended upon a balanced mix of developing common constitutional principles while preserving the diversity of the 28 constitutional traditions. The counter-limits doctrine was thus a legal device whose function was to protect this European constitutional pluralism. At present, most European countries, such as Germany, have developed similar safeguard clauses designed to protect the core values of their national constitutional identity from all sorts of interference from foreign or European law, including France, Italy, Spain, and many of the Central and Eastern European countries that entered the Union in 2004.

As to Italy, the doctrine of counter-limits was clearly established in Judgment 183/1973:

On the basis of Art. 11, limitations of sovereignty have been allowed solely for the attainment of the goals indicated there; and it must therefore be ruled out that those limitations concretely delineated in the Treaty of Rome—adopted by Nations with legal systems that are inspired by the rule

---

[9] CJEU Judgment 4 February 1959, case 1/58, *Stork*.

[10] Starting with Judgment 12 November 1969, case 29/69, *Stauder*, Judgment 14 May 1974, case 4/73, *Nold*, and Judgment 13 December 1979, case 44/79, *Hauer*, the CJEU affirmed: "Fundamental rights form an integral part of the general principles of the law, the observance of which is ensured by the Court. In safeguarding those rights, the latter is bound to draw inspiration from constitutional traditions common to the Member States, so that measures which are incompatible with the fundamental rights recognized by the Constitutions of those States are unacceptable in the Community. International treaties for the protection of human rights on which the Member States have collaborated or of which they are signatories, can also supply guidelines which should be followed within framework of Community law."

of law and that guarantee the essential liberties of their citizens –may in any case entail for the organs of the Community an inadmissible power to violate the fundamental principles of our constitutional order or the inalienable rights of the human person. And it is obvious that in the event that Art. 189 should ever be given such an aberrant interpretation, the guarantee of the jurisdiction of this Court to decide the enduring compatibility of the Treaty with the aforesaid fundamental principles will always be assured.

In sum, European legislation must respect the core principles of the Italian Constitution from a substantive point of view, and in case of a violation of those principles, the Constitutional Court claims jurisdiction.

What might be the consequences of the European Union's violation of the core principles of the national Constitution? Here the answer is only speculative, because, for the time being, there has been no practical application to EU legislation of this doctrine in the case law of the Italian Court.

However, there has been a shift in the doctrine, which should be pointed out. In Judgment 183/1973 the Constitutional Court asserted that in case of infringements on the counter-limits, the membership of Italy in the European Union would be in question. In fact, the Court warns of "the guarantee of the jurisdiction of this Court to decide the enduring compatibility of the treaty with the aforesaid fundamental principles." Later, however, the Court tempered its position. In Judgment 232/1989, it redefined the doctrine of counter-limits as an ability to:

verify, through the constitutional control of the executing laws, that any norm of the Treaty, in the manner in which it is interpreted and applied by the institutions and by the Community organs, is not in conflict with the fundamental principles of our constitutional order or not mindful of the inalienable rights of the human person.

Consequently, any act or provision of European law is theoretically submitted to the authority of the Constitutional Court to make sure there is compliance with the fundamental core of the Constitution, in which the national constitutional identity is encompassed.

Even though the counter-limits doctrine has not yet been applied in any case of EU legislation brought before the Constitutional Court,[11] the concerns of the

---

[11] However, the Council of State, Section V, applied this doctrine in Judgment 8 August 2005, case 4207/2005, related to the regulation of municipal pharmacies in order to justify the decision of not referring to the Court of Justice for preliminary ruling. In Judgment 238/2014 the Constitutional Court applied the counter-limits doctrine to delimit the international customary rule of State immunity in a case concerning the damages claimed by the victims of the Nazi regime, involving gross violation of humanitarian international law.

Member States' supreme courts regarding their constitutional identities prompted the inclusion of the national identity clause in the Treaty of Lisbon (2009), Article 4: "The Union shall respect the equality of Member States before the treaties as well as their national identities, inherent in their fundamental structures, political and constitutional, inclusive of regional and local self-government."

2.5 THE CONSTITUTIONAL COURT AND THE PRELIMINARY RULING TO THE COURT OF JUSTICE OF THE EUROPEAN UNION

The preliminary ruling procedure, under Article 267 of the TFEU, has been of seminal importance for the development of EU law and for its relationship with the national legal systems:

> The Court of Justice of the European Union shall have jurisdiction to give preliminary rulings concerning:
>
> (a) the interpretation of the Treaties;
> (b) the validity and interpretation of acts of the institutions, bodies, offices or agencies of the Union;
>
> Where such a question is raised before any court or tribunal of a Member State, that court or tribunal may, if it considers that a decision on the question is necessary to enable it to give judgment, request the Court to give a ruling thereon.
>
> Where any such question is raised in a case pending before a court or tribunal of a Member State against whose decisions there is no judicial remedy under national law, that court or tribunal shall bring the matter before the Court. . . .

This procedure echoes the Italian Constitutional Court's indirect method of judicial review. Other constitutional courts, like the German one, for example, also have similar indirect procedures, and they likely served as models for the Founding Fathers when they drafted the original Article 177 of the EEC Treaty (now Article 267 TFEU). The preliminary ruling is the most important instrument of dialogue and cooperation between national courts and the CJEU. It is not an appellate process, but is rather based on the decision by national courts to refer a question to the CJEU.

Unlike similar procedures before national constitutional courts, whose main goal is to assess the validity of legislation, the preliminary rulings have played and still play a major role in establishing the uniform interpretation of EU law in all Member States. Through its preliminary rulings regarding the appropriate interpretation of the European law, originally requested by national courts, the CJEU has developed principles such as the direct effect and supremacy of EU law. National courts seek a ruling from the CJEU in order to settle the meaning of a specific provision, to clarify whether a particular provision has direct effect, or to determine the reach of EU law when it comes into conflict with national legal norms.

The preliminary ruling is one of the most successful mechanisms of the EU legal system, and it has generously contributed to the strength of legal integration in Europe. Lower national judges have always used this procedure enthusiastically. For a long time, however, supreme courts and constitutional courts were less open to embracing it. Despite the wording of Article 267, which uses mandatory language for courts and tribunals against whose decisions there is no judicial remedy, the highest courts have been very reluctant to petition the CJEU on questions of the interpretation or validity of EU law. With the remarkable exception of the Austrian and the Belgian Constitutional Courts, they avoided engaging in formal contacts with their European counterpart.

In the last few years, however, things have quickly changed. Since the entry into force of the Lisbon Treaty, a number of relevant cases have been brought to the Court in Luxembourg by national constitutional tribunals: Spain, France, and Germany. The attitude of the Italian Constitutional Court also reflects this development, having been very reluctant for a long time and more open in recent years.

2.5.1 The Constitutional Court as a "Sovereign" Judge

For many decades, the Italian Constitutional Court avoided taking a position on the preliminary ruling and simply ignored the option of its use. In Judgment 536/1995, however, the Court gave the theoretical reasons for its reluctance to employ the preliminary ruling procedure:

> [T]he Community [EU] judge may not be resorted to, as hypothesized in a preceding ruling by the Constitutional Court, which (itself) "essentially functions as a constitutional control [and] as the supreme guarantor of the observance of the Constitution of the Republic by the constitutional bodies of the State and those of the Regions;"
>
> [F]urthermore, that "national jurisdiction" to which Art. 177 of the Founding Treaty of the European Economic Community [now Art. 267 TFEU] refers is not apparent in the Constitutional Court, since the Court cannot "be included among the judicial organs, whether they be ordinary or exceptional, given that the differences are so many and so profound between the tasks entrusted to the former—which is without precedent in the Italian

legal system—and the well-known and historically consolidated ones proper to judicial ["jurisdictional"] organs.

[I]t is instead the judge referring the question . . . who must take it upon himself, in the absence of precise legal precedents by the [European] Court of Justice, to legally address the latter in order to elicit that certain and reliable interpretation . . . of the Community disposition."

In a previous Judgment (168/1991) the Court had left open the possibility of referring a question to the CJEU, as a legal option although not as a duty. This position was not in conformity with the language of the European Treaty, which imposes a duty on supreme courts to address the CJEU with preliminary rulings. At the same time, the position was also criticized by a number of Italian scholars, who considered it both inappropriate for the Constitutional Court, as a "sovereign" court, to show deference to any other judge, and also incoherent with the dualist theory that the Italian Court endorses with respect to European law. Opening the door to the preliminary ruling was perceived as an assent to the primacy of the European Court. For this reason, in Judgment 536/1995, the Italian Court reevaluated and excluded any possibility of submitting preliminary rulings to the CJEU.

The argument used by the Constitutional Court is very debatable. It relies on the specific nature of the Constitutional Court, which is not a common judge, in order to escape the obligation to interact with the CJEU. Yet, although the Court is a special judge, the exact nature of which has long been debated, there is no doubt at all that the Court performs a jurisdictional function. There is something preposterous in the idea that the Court is not qualified as a "jurisdiction" within the meaning of Article 267 TFEU, given that its function is to control the constitutionality of legislation. In fact, some years later the situation evolved yet again.

2.5.2 A One-Way Conversation: Lower Courts as the Official "Speakers" of the National Legal System

While it excluded itself from the preliminary ruling mechanism, the Italian Constitutional Court did not absolutely deny every form of dialogue with the CJEU. On the contrary, the Italian Court has always been very attentive to the developments of CJEU case law. For example, over the years it has pursued alternative, indirect, and even hidden forms of dialogue with the Luxembourg Court, in order to combine a respect for EU obligations with the preservation of its own constitutional supremacy as a judicial body. Instead of directly asking the CJEU for an interpretation of European law, the Constitutional Court prefers to "send someone else": it encourages lower courts to clarify all interpretative doubts regarding European law with the aid of the CJEU before addressing any question of constitutionality to the Constitutional Court. Consider, for example, Judgment 108/1998: "It is up to the referring judge, who invokes a Community norm as a condition or standard of the question of constitutionality, to elicit the 'certain and reliable' interpretation [of EU law] by referring himself to the Court of Justice."

It is worth noting that the Constitutional Court not only allows but requires lower judges to refer any problem of interpretation of European law to the CJEU, otherwise the question of constitutionality will be declared inadmissible in the Constitutional Court.

Consider those cases in which the lower court has doubts about the constitutionality of a piece of legislation and where, at the same time, the legislation appears to be in conflict with European law. In such instances, the judge needs both a decision from the Constitutional Court as well as an interpretation from the CJEU to settle a dispute. These are known as cases of "dual preliminarity" (*doppia pregiudizialità*), because the lower courts must address the question to the Constitutional Court through indirect procedure and to the CJEU through preliminary ruling. In those cases, the Italian Constitutional Court asks the judge *a quo* first to solve all problems of interpretation of European law and then to ask the question of constitutionality. Moreover, when the question of constitutionality is raised contemporaneously to a request for a preliminary ruling, the Constitutional Court usually waits for the CJEU to pronounce itself before settling the constitutionality issue. In this way, the Constitutional Court accords an interpretive priority to the questions pending before the CJEU and de facto suspends its own proceedings, without itself using the preliminary ruling mechanism, which is instead triggered by the lower courts. It is a sort of indirect dialogue with the CJEU, which allows the Constitutional Court to take the interpretive decisions of the CJEU into consideration, while escaping direct confrontation with the opinions of the European Court. In this way, in case of dissent, the Constitutional Court still retains control of a "security exit" that avoids open conflicts with the CJEU.

2.5.3 The First Preliminary Ruling of the Italian Constitutional Court to the Court of Justice of the European Union

While the "indirect dialogues" remain the Constitutional Court's preferred avenue of communication with the CJEU, in 2008 the Court sent its first preliminary ruling to the CJEU. The Court followed the example of other European constitutional and supreme courts, like the *Cour d'arbitrage* in Belgium and the Austrian Constitutional Tribunal that had previously pioneered the preliminary rulings to the CJEU in 2001 and 2003. Other national high courts followed later.

Judgment 103/2008 overruled the previous statements of the Constitutional Court regarding the European preliminary ruling. However, the scope of this judgment should not be overstated. The Court limited its referral decision to direct proceedings, stressing the different structure that characterizes the indirect form of constitutional review of legislation. The Court was also careful to prevent any extension of this reversal to indirect procedures, where the main actors of the judicial dialogue remain the lower courts:

[T]he Constitutional Court, even in its unique position as the supreme body of constitutional guarantees in the internal legal order, constitutes a national jurisdiction within the meaning of Art. 234 [now Art. 267 TFEU], third paragraph, of the European Community (EC) Treaty and, in particular, [it constitutes] a jurisdiction of only resort (inasmuch as no challenge is permitted against its decisions, as set forth in Art. 137, third clause, of the Constitution): the Court, in its judgments on constitutionality submitted by the direct method of review, is authorized to propose preliminary questions to the Court of Justice; ...

[I]n these judgments of constitutional legitimacy, in contrast to those submitted in the incidental way, this Court is the only judge called to rule on the controversy; ...

[C]onsequently, in judgments of constitutional legitimacy submitted by the direct method where it is not possible to obtain a preliminary ruling under Art. 234 [now 267 TFEU] of the EC Treaty, the general interests of a uniform application of Community law, as interpreted by the Court of Justice, would be harmed.

After this first preliminary ruling sent by the Italian Court in a minor case concerning a regional measure on tax law allegedly in contrast with the freedom of establishment and freedom to provide services (2008),[12] in July 2013 the Court sent a further preliminary ruling with Judgment 207/2013. It was about the interpretation of Directive 1999/70/EC on fixed-term employment and its applicability to teachers and other personnel working in public schools.

Unlike the previous one, this preliminary ruling was sent by the Italian Constitutional Court in the context of an incidental procedure. The Court thus took an important step because the previous case law suggested that only cases arising under the direct procedure were appropriate for the Court to raise a preliminary

---

[12] The reply of the European Court came with decision 17 November 2009, C-169/08, acknowledging that the Regional Legislation was not compatible with Articles 49 and 87 of the EC Treaty.

ruling. The last procedural barrier to full cooperation between the two courts was removed. The European Court issued its decision on November 2014.[13] It is worth remarking that a similar question was already pending before the European Court, sent by a lower Italian court. The Constitutional Court was fully aware of it, but decided to add its own request, bringing its own arguments to the bench of the judges in Luxembourg. The result was a very richly reasoned decision of the European Court of Justice that examines and discusses in detail the Italian legislation under review, providing the Constitutional Court with a thorough assessment of the Italian system of recruitment of teachers in the State school from the point of view of the European principles of labor law.

Although limited in its scope, the path to a direct dialogue has nonetheless been cleared between the Constitutional Court and the Court of Justice. This is to the benefit of the coherence of the legal orders, of the correct interpretation of European law, of constitutional pluralism, and, more important, of citizens' rights.

3. The Constitutional Court and the European Convention on Human Rights

3.1 THE EUROPEAN CONVENTION ON HUMAN RIGHTS: A GENERAL OVERVIEW

Alongside the European Union, the human rights system of the Council of Europe (COE) is becoming increasingly relevant in the Italian constitutional system. This is mainly based on the 1950 European Convention on Human Rights (ECHR), as it is interpreted and applied by the European Court of Human Rights. The Council of Europe's human rights system and the European Court of Human Rights (based in Strasbourg) should not be confused with the European Union and the CJEU (based in Luxembourg). Each originated from different treaties and was established for different purposes. The Treaty of Lisbon, which amended the European Union Treaties in 2009, envisions the accession of the European Union to the ECHR (see Art. 6 of the Treaty on European Union), so that in the future the development of a stricter interaction between the two forms of European integration may be possible. So far, however, the two systems are separate. It is worth noticing that each encompasses a different number of components: whereas the European Union has 28 Member States, the COE has 47.

---

[13] CJEU decision 26 November 2014, C-22/13, C-61/13 to C-418/13, *Muscolo, Forni, Racca*, ruling that the Italian legislation is required to comply to some conditions spelled out by the Court in order to fulfill the obligation imposed by European law.

The ECHR was approved just after World War II in order to add a further possibility of protection of the fundamental rights of European citizens, in cases where the national States failed to guarantee adequate protection. Therefore, the ECHR system of protection is conceived as "subsidiary" to the protection accorded by the national Constitutions. According to Articles 34 and 35 of the ECHR, "the Court may receive applications from any person, non-governmental organization or group of individuals claiming to be the victim of a violation by one of the High Contracting Parties of the rights set forth in the Convention," but at the same time "the Court may only deal with the matter after all domestic remedies have been exhausted." The core idea is that individuals should first try to have their rights recognized by national judges, and then bring the case as a last resort to the European Court of Human Rights. However, in recent years, application to the Strasbourg Court has come to be regarded as an ordinary remedy: the European Court has become the place of final review for many national cases involving human rights issues. The European Court has thus become a sort of European Supreme Court, with a special jurisdiction focused only on human rights.[14]

Unlike the law of the European Communities, which claimed a privileged position since the very beginning of European integration and demanded a uniform legal status in all Member States, the ECHR has always been understood to be an "ordinary" international treaty. Its legal status within the national legal order therefore follows the regime of international law generally or the special regime that each national constitutional system may grant to it. The Contracting States thus have discretion with regard to the legal status of the Convention in their domestic legal orders. In particular, it is up to each State to decide what its national courts should do when confronted with a statute that conflicts with the ECHR. This means that there is a rich variety of solutions throughout the 47 Member States.

As a sample of this variety, consider for example that until the enactment of the 1998 Human Rights Act, in the United Kingdom the ECHR was not part of the domestic legal system at all. Even after the Human Rights Act, British judges are not allowed to set aside statutes as being contrary to any right protected by the Convention. They can seek an interpretation that harmonizes the statute with the Convention, but if the conflict persists, the only thing that the highest courts can do is to issue a declaration of incompatibility, which the political branches are expected to take into serious consideration when deciding whether to amend or repeal the statute in question. At the opposite extreme, in some countries the European Convention is vested with the same legal status as the Constitution (e.g., Austria), while, and in certain countries,

---

[14] One consequence has been an extraordinary overload of cases before the European Court of Human Rights. As of September 2014, there were approximately 85,000 pending cases.

the judiciary enjoys greater authority to control legislation when Convention rights are invoked than when the national Constitution is at issue (e.g., Netherlands). In still other countries the Convention enjoys a supralegislative rank (e.g., France, Spain, and Belgium), and the judicial review of legislation according to the European Convention is decentralized, since it falls within the jurisdiction of ordinary judges, whereas the review of constitutionality belongs to the exclusive domain of a central-ized special tribunal like a constitutional court. Many other countries, such as the Scandinavian states, give the Convention a simple rank of ordinary legislation.

With this background in mind, we can now better appreciate the evolution of the Italian constitutional system in relation to the European Convention on Human Rights.

3.2 FROM "CONSTITUTIONAL PATRIOTISM" TO "INTEGRATION THROUGH INTERPRETATION"

In accordance with the dualist tradition discussed earlier, the Constitutional Court for decades regarded the European Convention on Human Rights as a typical inter-national treaty not endowed with any distinctive position. In the hierarchy of sources of law, the ECHR had the same rank as an ordinary legislative act. From this posi-tion, the ECHR could not serve as a standard for the Constitutional Court's judi-cial review of legislation: the protection of fundamental rights by the Constitutional Court referred only to the rights included in the Constitution. This period, which lasted until the second half of the 1990s, can be defined—borrowing from the famous words by Habermas—as "constitutional patriotism," because it implicitly regarded fundamental rights as entrenched in a specific cultural background, which varied from country to country, and led the Constitutional Court to resist opening the door to international instruments as sources of norms for judicial review of legislation.

However, the growing importance throughout Europe of the ECHR and of the jurisprudence of the Strasbourg Court, and the particular relevance of the Convention to prototypically constitutional issues, especially given its concern for the protection of individual rights, exerted pressure on the Constitutional Court to elevate the status of the Convention to a higher level of legal authority.

The Constitutional Court's first, though isolated, attempt to distinguish the ECHR from other international treaties was in Judgment 10/1993, concerning the right of defendants in criminal procedures to be assisted by an interpreter.

> The [ECHR] establishes that "everyone charged with a criminal offense has the right ... to be informed promptly, in a language which he understands and in detail, of the nature and cause of the accusation against him. ..."

The international norms just cited were introduced into the Italian legal order with the force of law proper to the acts containing the respective orders of execution ... and they are still in force today. They certainly cannot be considered abrogated by subsequent provisions of the Code of Criminal Procedure, ... because they are norms deriving from an atypical competence and, as such, are not susceptible to abrogation or modification by provisions of ordinary laws.

The Court's pronouncement that the law implementing the ECHR is an expression of an "atypical competence" is rather obscure; its most probable meaning is that although the law is contained in a statutory act of Parliament, it cannot be abrogated or derogated by Parliament, first, due to its specific content relating to human rights, and second, because it enforces an international agreement. In any case, the Court only timidly hinted at the necessity of distinguishing the ECHR (and other international conventions for the protection of human rights) from other international treaties.

The modest development suggested in Judgment 10/1993 was dropped by subsequent decisions of the Constitutional Court, and for many years the ECHR continued to consider it an ordinary international treaty, deprived of any special rank and unable to provide a benchmark for judicial review of legislation before the Court.

3.3 INTERPRETING DOMESTIC LAW "ACCORDING TO" THE EUROPEAN CONVENTION

However, in the late 1990s, ordinary courts and in particular the Supreme Court of Cassation took a different attitude toward the European Convention, giving it an ever greater importance, especially in criminal cases, in order to enhance the procedural guarantees of defendants. Pressed by this "de facto" transformation occurring in the Judiciary, the Constitutional Court reviewed and revamped its doctrine. Although the formal rank of the ECHR had not changed and still corresponded to that of any other legislative act, in Judgment 388/1999 and many others of that period, the Constitutional Court assigned more legal weight to the provisions of the ECHR and to the decisions of the European Court of Human Rights, at least at the interpretive level. The ECHR thus began to be a relevant, if not the most relevant, tool of interpretation of fundamental rights for the Constitutional Court:

Independently of the value to be attributed to the Treaty norms, which are not in and of themselves situated at the constitutional level but depend on the legislator to give them effect, it is noteworthy that human rights, guaranteed also by universal or regional conventions ratified by Italy, find expression and no less intense guarantee in the Constitution—not only because of the value given to the general recognition of the inviolable rights of man in Art. 2 of the Constitution, and always increasingly felt in the contemporary conscience to be coessential to the dignity of the person, but also because, beyond any convergence in the catalogues of rights, the diverse formulas for expressing them are integrated into one another, mutually completing each other in their interpretation.

In the field of human rights, the margins of interpretation are very broad, because in general the provisions in charters of rights are loosely worded and allow for the discretionary power of the judges. This hermeneutic openness of fundamental rights principles makes it reasonable, in consequence, for the Constitutional Court to state that the national Constitution and other instruments for the protection of fundamental rights—in particular the ECHR—"are integrated into one another, mutually completing each other in their interpretation." This means that, regardless of the formal status of the European Convention, the Constitutional Court has begun to take it very seriously in its constitutional adjudication.

3.4 THE TURNING POINT: THE EUROPEAN CONVENTION ON HUMAN RIGHTS' SPECIAL RANK

In Italy today, the legal status of the ECHR has been raised to an intermediate level, between ordinary legislation and constitutional provisions. The Constitutional Court sanctioned the new ranking of the ECHR within the Italian legal system with the "twin Judgments" 348/2007 and 349/2007.

A number of factors led the Court to overrule its previous doctrine. First, legal scholars were uneasy with the traditional doctrine, which, assuming the traditionally dualistic Italian position, considered that the ECHR and all other international treaties possessed the same status as the national legislative acts through which they had became part of the internal legal order. Many pointed out the sharp discrepancy between the "constitutional content" of the ECHR and the "ordinary legislative form" of the act that incorporated it. These scholars tried to find a constitutional basis for the ECHR in order to justify a higher position for the Convention in the hierarchy of law. The Constitutional Court, however, has not shown any great enthusiasm for these attempts to give the ECHR special constitutional consideration.

However, some ordinary judges took a different position at the beginning of the new millennium, in an era of enthusiasm for the "Europe of rights" that followed the approval of the Charter of Fundamental Rights of the European Union in

December 2000. Some of them, including the highest ordinary and administrative courts, introduced a new judicial approach to the ECHR, one that extended the principles of supremacy and direct effect of EU law to the ECHR.[15] Subsequent constitutional jurisprudence would eventually prove this judicial approach to be incorrect, nevertheless it spread among a number of judges in different courts and in different parts of Italy. It was a clear sign that the old doctrine, which considered the ECHR in the same way as it would any other legislative act, was ripe for an update.

Even more relevant, the constitutional revision adopted in 2001 (mentioned above in this chapter) introduced a new provision that triggered a new development in the legal status of international treaties. On the one hand, the dualistic framework remains intact and international treaties still do not enjoy constitutional status. On the other hand, however, since the new constitutional provision requires all legislative powers to be exercised in compliance with international obligations, no legislative acts of the national and regional legislatures are allowed to derogate from or abrogate any international treaty without breaching the Constitution. The Italian State remains free to denounce its international treaties subject to the ordinary rules of international law, but so long as Italy remains a party to a treaty in international law, subsequent national legislation in breach of that treaty's obligations can be constitutionally challenged and declared invalid by the Constitutional Court.

After a few years, the Italian Constitutional Court followed this interpretation of Article 117, paragraph 1 in Judgments 348/2007 and 349/2007 in relation to the ECHR. As stated in the latter of these two judgments:

> Article 117, paragraph 1 of the Constitution requires the exercise of the legislative power of the State and the Regions to comply with international law obligations, which undoubtedly include the European Convention on Human Rights. Prior to its introduction, the inclusion of international treaty rules into the Italian legal system was, in accordance with the previous reasoning of the Constitutional Court, traditionally dependent on an act of ratification, which normally had the status of an ordinary law which could hence potentially be modified by other subsequent ordinary laws. . . . Significant margins of uncertainty remained. . . . This situation of uncertainty has led several judgments of the ordinary courts to directly set aside legislative provisions which contrast with the ECHR, as interpreted by the Strasbourg Court. . . . Today this court

---

[15] This trend has been so widespread and persistent that the CJEU in Judgment 24 April 2012, C-case 571/10, *Kamberaj*, had to make clear that "Article 6, paragraph 3 TEU does not govern the relationship between the ECHR and the legal systems of the Member States and nor does it lay down the consequences to be drawn by a national court in case of conflict between the rights guaranteed by that Convention and a provision of national law."

is called upon to clarify this normative and institutional problem, which has significant practical implications for the everyday practice of legal practitioners. [W]hilst the new version of Article 117, paragraph 1 of the Constitution on the one hand places beyond doubt the greater resilience of the ECHR to subsequent ordinary legislation, on the other hand it brings the Convention within the jurisdiction of this Court, since eventual contrasts will not generate problems of the temporal succession of laws or assessments of the respective hierarchical arrangement of the provisions in contrast, but questions of constitutional legitimacy. The ordinary courts do not therefore have the power to set aside ordinary legislation in contrast with the ECHR, since the alleged incompatibility between the two takes the form of a question of constitutional legitimacy due to an eventual violation of Article 117, paragraph 1 of the Constitution, falling under the exclusive jurisdiction of the Constitutional Court. . . .

On the one hand, the Court recognized that the ECHR possesses a higher position than any other ordinary legislation. At the same time, it acknowledged that the Constitutional Court itself exercises jurisdiction over any conflicts between national legislation and the ECHR, as interpreted by the European Court of Human Rights. The Court specified that:

> Compared to other international law treaties, the ECHR has the particular characteristic of having provided for the jurisdiction of a court, the European Court of Human Rights, which is charged with the role of interpreting the provisions of the Convention. . . . Since legal norms live through the interpretation which is given to them by legal practitioners, and in the first place the courts, the natural consequence . . . is that the international law obligations undertaken by Italy in signing and ratifying the ECHR include the duty to bring its own legislation into line with the Convention, in line with the meaning attributed by the Court specifically charged with its interpretation and application.

According to the Court, Article 117, paragraph 1 has given the ECHR a particular status. It is still an ordinary law, but it is accorded recognition through Article 117 of the Constitution and therefore can become an intermediate standard (*parametro interposto*) for judicial review of legislation:

> the principle contained in Article 117, paragraph 1 of the Constitution becomes operative *in concreto* only if the "international law obligations" which restrict

the legislative power of the State and the Regions are specified. In the particular case before this Court, the principle is supplemented and made operative by the provisions of the ECHR, the role of which in this case is therefore to give substance to the State's international law obligations.

However, the ECHR is still subject to the Italian Constitution and can be used by the Italian Constitutional Court as a standard of judicial review of national legislation only insofar as its provisions, as interpreted by the European Court of Human Rights, conform with the Constitution:

> The arguments set out above do not imply that the ECHR, as interpreted by the Strasbourg Court, acquires the force of constitutional law and is therefore immune to assessments by this Court of its constitutional legitimacy. It is precisely because the provisions in question supplement a constitutional principle, whilst always retaining a lower status, that it is necessary that they respect the Constitution. [T]he complete effectiveness of interposed rules is conditional on their compatibility with the Italian constitutional order, which cannot be modified by external sources.

To summarize, the current doctrine of the Constitutional Court in relation to the ECHR is based on one principle and three corollaries:

- The ECHR has an intermediate position between ordinary laws and the Constitution;
- As a consequence, the ECHR is used by the Constitutional Court in judicial review of legislation as an "intermediate standard" (*parametro interposto*);
- The ECHR and the interpretations given to it by the European Court of Human Rights are required to conform with the Italian Constitution; and
- Ordinary judges are not allowed to set aside Italian legislation in conflict with the ECHR and the European Court's judgments: in such cases they are required to send the question to the Constitutional Court; however, ordinary judges are allowed to seek interpretations of Italian laws that are most respectful of the ECHR. In other words, they can apply a method of interpretation "according to the ECHR."

As a result, the Italian legal order has incrementally opened up to the influence of European legislation, and even more to the judge-made law of the two European Courts, which is becoming more and more relevant, in particular in human rights cases. In some areas, the impact of European case law has produced a beneficial effect and has induced the Constitutional Court to revise its previous jurisprudence. The influence can be seen, for instance, in cases concerning criminal procedure and retroactive legislation. Under the influence of European standards, the Constitutional Court has endorsed a higher level of protection of rights in its cases regarding, for example, trial *in absentia* (Judgment 317/2009) and the right to a public hearing in criminal proceedings (Judgments 93/2010 and 80/2011), and the limits of retroactive legislation (Judgments 191/2014, 170/2013, 78/2012, and 209/2010). The Constitutional Court even foresaw a new revision of criminal procedure in order to comply with a decision of ECtHR finding a violation of fair trial (Judgment 113/2011).

Yet, in the European context, the Italian national legal system is still not conceived as subordinate to the transnational ones. The Italian system still retains a distinctive constitutional dimension and substantive peculiarities, which are of great importance in and of themselves. That is why, occasionally, the Italian Constitutional Court has adopted a divergent opinion from the ECtHR,[16] as in Judgment 264/2012 touching upon the retroactive legislative repeal of a privileged treatment of some class of retired people, and in Judgment 263/2011 concerning the scope of the *lex mitior* principle in criminal law.[17]

How can we define, in a word, the attitude of the Italian Constitutional Court, vis-à-vis the European actors? Cooperation, reluctance, defense, challenge? All these reactions can be recorded in the history of the Constitutional Court. At present, the Italian Court looks engaged in the European constitutional space, both seeking its own voice and listening to different traditions. By means of judicial conversations with the European Courts as well as other national constitutional tribunals in the European region, the Italian Court contributes to the shaping of a European constitutional *koiné*—a sort of European common law—without dismissing the national constitutional peculiarities, according to what Joseph Weiler has called the principle of "constitutional tolerance."[18]

---

[16] ECtHR, Grand Chamber, 31 May 2011, *Maggio c. Italia*.

[17] A broader scope of the same principle is recognized in ECtHR, Grand Chamber, 17 September 2009, *Scoppola c. Italia*.

[18] J. H. H. Weiler, *The Constitution of Europe*, Cambridge University Press, 1999.

Conclusion

THE "ITALIAN STYLE" IN GLOBAL CONSTITUTIONAL ADJUDICATION

1. The Globalization of Constitutional Adjudication

Constitutional adjudication in the twenty-first century has acquired an undeniably global dimension. Although already in the closing decades of the last century both comparative constitutional law and cross-jurisdictional judicial exchange had grown dramatically in scope and sophistication, today the global character of constitutional justice has become a structural component of globalization itself. It has been internalized quickly by judiciaries in all parts of the world, with both national high courts and supranational courts participating substantially in a common community of discourse about norms and principles of constitutional law. As some scholars have put it, the "cosmopolitan turn in constitutional sources"[1] is a documented worldwide phenomenon, and judicial openness to looking beyond national borders and using comparative law arguments has become "inevitable."[2]

The fact that constitutional courts have taken a place among the main actors of globalization represents a remarkable reversal from their historic role, which was

---

[1] P. Glenn, *The Cosmopolitan State*, 2013, p. 207.

[2] M. Tushnet, *The Inevitable Globalization of Constitutional Law*, 49 *Vand. J. Int'l L.* (2009).

traditionally seen as intrinsically "national" or "domestic." Where in the recent past constitutional courts were perceived to be the custodians of national cultural values, or at most the standard-bearers of a postnationalist, Habermasian "constitutional patriotism," today they are instead at the forefront of globalization—often even more so than other branches of Government.

Much has been written to try to account for and understand the dynamics of judicial globalization, and it is beyond the scope of this book to enter substantially into that debate. But identifying a few of the key factors that contribute to the active role that courts play in these developments can help us situate the significance of Italian Constitutional adjudication in a global context.

From a methodological point of view, courts enjoy a number of qualities that make them well suited to the dynamics of globalization. They resolve issues case by case, therefore judicial lawmaking is interstitial and smoothly percolates between gaps. Judicial lawmaking is also incremental, proceeding on a trial-and-error basis from one case to the next, and therefore leaves room for changes and adjustments. Courts generally adhere to very similar rules of natural justice: for instance, they hear the parties and give reasoned explanations of their decisions. The relation between constitutional courts, when they communicate and borrow principles and practices, is more horizontal than hierarchical, and courts thus tend to form a sort of network. Courts can also recognize and establish general principles, standards of decisions, doctrines, and tests that are very broadly applicable and easily transferrable, but also flexible enough to be adjusted according to different contexts and thus adaptable to local realities. Judicial lawmaking can thereby link the local and the global dimensions of justice, both appealing to universal principles and giving plural and differentiated answers to different situations and demands.

Viewing the phenomenon instead from the point of view of the substantive contents of constitutional adjudication, the globalization of constitutional adjudication is also driven by an increasing number of problems brought to the bench that can no longer be contained merely within the limited horizons of the nation-state. Some issues draw constitutional justice into a transnational space for what might be called "external" characteristics. That is, international or foreign law is implicated because the empirical reality of the problem before the courts necessarily crosses national borders: to name just a few examples, people's mobility and migration, financial flows and foreign investments, or transnational standards in the fields of environmental protection.

Other disputes deal with questions that tend toward the global dimension because of their internal characteristics—norms and principles that intrinsically claim a certain universality that transcends borders. Here, human rights claims are paradigmatic. The role of courts as human rights adjudicators has evolved rapidly, along with the amplification of "rights talk" generally, since the final decades of the twentieth century, and today the language of rights is often the primary mode for reasoning about new challenging social and legal problems (e.g., nondiscrimination issues, or questions arising out of the development of new technologies). This evolution greatly affects the role of judges, not only because it asks courts to become protagonists of social change but also because a rights-saturated culture inevitably fuels transnational judicial interactions. Human rights, by virtue of their appeal to a transcendent dignity that all persons have by virtue of being human, have a natural vocation to trespass beyond the border of any single country. Moreover, as subjective rights belong to individual persons, the rights claims move as their holders themselves move, bringing together the external and the internal factors impelling judicial globalization. It is no surprise, therefore, that human rights are one of the most fertile grounds for transnational judicial dialogue and exchange.

For these and other reasons, constitutional courts have also maintained a certain advantage over parliaments in their capacity to adapt to the demands of globalization. In the volatile conditions of the present era "reactive" institutions, such as courts, appear better suited than "active" institutions such as parliaments (to use Mirjan Damaska's well-known distinction) to giving prompt answers to complex problems and to mediating between global and local interests, between equality and diversity. Courts are in a good position to take up these challenges and work as a transmission belt between the local and global, the particular and the universal, the national and the supranational, since they are still deeply entrenched in the domestic legal system, but they also belong to the global space, establishing links with other national, international, and supranational, legal orders and with their respective courts.

This richly cosmopolitan scenario is particularly pronounced on the European continent, which has become a special space of constitutional interdependence. National constitutional courts are now embedded in a constitutional fabric made of national constitutions, EU law, European treaties, and international conventions. This is all the more evident in the domain of fundamental rights, where the European Convention on Human Rights and its Court play a key role. On the European stage the interplay between the domestic and the supranational is even more active, both because legal relations develop in a horizontal dimension among peers and on a voluntary basis, and because under some conditions national courts are bound by European legislation and by the decisions of the supranational courts (see Chapter 7).

Some courts are more reluctant than others to adjust their traditional competences and methods to a wider and more complex legal order, and instead seem inclined to keep the use of transnational law to a minimum level in their own decisions, to decide cases on domestic grounds rather than on European ones, to avoid formal references to supranational law, and to resist engagement with other foreign or supranational courts. Occasionally certain courts have even challenged directly the applicability of a decision of a European or an international court, opening a phase of silent conflict. In most cases, however, national courts (at least in Europe) proactively cooperate with other judges and willingly take part in the global judicial conversation. In recent years an increasing number of national constitutional courts have contributed to the development of common legal principles, taking an active role on the European and global stage through their interpretation and enforcement of common transnational standards.

This is the general context in which we can ask where the Italian Constitutional Court fits. How does it reflect and contribute to global constitutional adjudication? As the preceding chapters have already shown, the attitude of the Court toward the supranational legal order has changed over time, and at present, the Italian Constitutional Court has definitely assumed a posture of active participation in the European and global arena. It is very open to adopt transnational principles as constitutional principles, and to take seriously the relationship of the Italian constitutional system to foreign and international law. At the same time, the Italian Court is also very intent on remaining true to the Italian constitutional tradition. Its distinctive voice is clear and very present, exemplifying exactly that dialectic between global and local that lies at the heart of global constitutional dynamics.

Even more interestingly, that distinctive voice has its own contributions to make to the broader conversation among courts and constitutional systems. Fifty years after John Henry Merryman introduced the idea of an "Italian style" to comparative law in general, we can see in the Italian Constitutional Court today an "Italian style" of constitutional justice.

2. The "Italian Style" in Constitutional Adjudication

No single idea can capture the essence of any institution as rich in history, complexity, and even contradiction as the Italian Constitutional Court. But many of the interesting aspects of the Court and its jurisprudence that stand out when viewed in the context of global constitutional models may be expressed in the term *relationality*. Whether in its historical development, its internal workings and methods, its institutional relations with other political organs or courts, or its substantive jurisprudence on a number of issues of global concerns, the Court at its best operates with a notable attentiveness to the relations between persons, institutions, powers, associations, and nations. Like any judge in well-functioning systems of justice generally, the Constitutional Court is indeed independent from other branches of Government; however, it never sings "solo," but always acts as a member of a choir, within which many other institutional actors have their part as well. Although granted the *final* word by the Constitution, it does not speak the *only* word in constitutional matters. Instead it is embedded in a fabric of relations that affect its agenda, its deliberative process, its method of interpretation, the typology of its decisions, and even its vision of the persons, society, and state subject to its judgments.

This is not to imply that the Italian Court is always perfectly consistent and successful in maintaining this distinctive identity or that its relational approach is always an unambiguous asset (its thick give-and-take with Parliament, for instance, can sometimes be as much a negative as a positive aspect of a relational mindset). Nor do we mean to suggest that the Italian Court is absolutely singular in this effort at relationality; any successful constitutional tribunal needs to attend to some degree to the political realities of its place in the constitutional order, and undoubtedly the Italian Court still has much to learn from other systems in this regard. Nevertheless, when seeking to identify what constructive contribution the Italian Court could make in the context of a global dialogue and interchange, it is helpful to adopt a hermeneutic of positivity—to tease out of a complex jumble of data that which is of particular value, and to offer it as a narrative that calls forth the best version of the Court both for itself and for its global interlocutors.

This relational approach to constitutional adjudication can be documented in a variety of aspects of the Italian Constitutional Court's activities that have already been described in the preceding chapters.

2.1 INSTITUTIONAL RELATIONALITY

As emphasized in Chapter 1, since the beginning the Court has tried to combine its responsibility and authority as guarantor of the Constitution with effective relations with other constitutional actors. This relation-building capacity of the Constitutional Court was one of the main reasons for its unexpected and swift success in establishing and consolidating its constitutional role, despite the widespread distrust of all forms of judicial review of legislation within the prevailing juridical culture and within the main political bodies of the epoch. That initial genetic imprint carried forward into the ensuing decades as the Court's relationships with other institutional actors developed.

One of the major challenges for a Constitutional Court taking its first steps, in a constitutional culture dominated by a rigid idea of parliamentary sovereignty and a conception of separation of powers as a subordination of the Judiciary rather than as checks and balances, was to be both self-assertive and yet cooperative with Parliament. Although any court required to review acts of legislation is in a certain sense in opposition per se to the Legislative Branch, after its inauguration in 1956 the Italian Constitutional Court was not seen to be a true antagonist of the representative bodies. This was mainly because it spent its initial energies, beginning with its very first decision, on eliminating all the Fascist vestiges from the new constitutional legal order. In the beginning, the natural target of judicial review was the old Fascist legislation contained, for example, in the civil code and in the criminal code and patently incompatible with the republican constitution. The activity of the new republican legislature only came under the Court's scrutiny years later. This made for a vital and constructive alliance between the new republican Parliament and the Constitutional Court against the fascist legacy, which politically strengthened the legitimacy of the Constitutional Court vis-à-vis the political institutions and the society as a whole.

Over time, other doctrines elaborated by the Court (and more fully described in Chapter 3) have helped to maintain smooth relations with Parliament. For example, the fundamental "interpretive judgments" doctrine, separating the *norme* from the *disposizioni*, allowed the Court to strike "interpretations" down, while keeping the parliamentary "texts" alive. From this seminal doctrine derived a number of important techniques seen in the *sentenze interpretative*, all aimed at upholding constitutional norms and principles while minimizing the substitution of the Court for the lawmaking power of Parliament. In many ways even the judgments that add, substitute, or remove something from a statute can be understood as attempts at cooperation with the legislature, given that in those cases the court preserves the parliamentary act, introducing only the revisions strictly necessary to make that act consistent with the Constitution. Similarly, the Court's adjustment of the temporal effects of its judgments (e.g., Judgment 10/2015, in Chapter 3), represents a Court actively searching for a mutual relationship with Parliament by modulating the applicability of its decisions. All of these techniques contribute to the remarkable absence (especially from an American perspective) of concern over the counter-majoritarian difficulty in Italian constitutional and political debate ever since the Court began its activity in 1956.

Cooperative relations with other national judicial bodies have been equally crucial for the Italian Constitutional Court. The incidental method of review (Chapter 2), which remains the main pathway for access to the Constitutional Court, establishes the ordinary judiciary as gatekeepers of the Constitutional Court, deciding which case will enter and which won't. If ordinary courts do not activate the procedure, the Constitutional Court cannot play its part. That is why the Constitutional Court at the outset of its activity encouraged lower courts to bring cases through a loose interpretation of the procedural requirements for referral. Only when the court began to be overwhelmed by thousands of cases, did the Court begin to tighten its scrutiny. Moreover, the Constitutional Court has shown a great deal of trust in the ordinary judiciary, preserving the primary competence of the latter as interpreter of the legislation, for example, through the doctrine of the "living law" and also by favoring creative methods of interpretation *conforme a costituzione*. Most decisions of the Constitutional Court, in fact, presuppose a healthy cooperation with the ordinary judiciary, both with lower courts and with the highest courts (the *Corte di Cassazione* and the *Consiglio di Stato*). Without this interjudicial relationality the pronouncements of the Constitutional Court would remain ineffective.

As to the relations with the European Courts—the Court of Justice of the European Union and the European Court of Human Rights—and with foreign constitutional courts, the Italian Constitutional Court has dramatically changed its attitude over time (Chapter 7). Indifference and formal segregation of jurisdictional authority were the Cartesian coordinates that described the starting position of the Court vis-à-vis its supranational and foreign counterparts. Then, a period of informal reciprocal influence followed, during which the Italian Constitutional Court avoided all formal reference to the jurisprudence of the two European Courts but was in fact well aware of the case law developed in Luxembourg and in Strasbourg. Long before opening up to a direct dialogue with the European Courts, the Italian Constitutional Court maintained an implicit, silent, though influential, attention to their decisions. A similarly implicit and silent but influential consideration is paid by the Constitutional Court to foreign law and to comparative sources: whereas in recent years occasionally the Italian Constitutional Court openly refers to the case law of other constitutional courts, the influence of the latter is much deeper than is apparent on the surface. In sum, Italian constitutional justice has incrementally entered into an active relationship with European, international, and comparative law, and especially with the judge-made law of the two European supranational courts, in particular in human rights cases. While in some areas the impact of these external sources has induced the Constitutional Court to revise its previous jurisprudence and to develop new principles and standards, in some other cases the Italian Constitutional Court intentionally takes a position distinct from European or foreign courts, especially when the core values of the constitutional identity are at stake. In short, the Court engages now in open and direct relations with external judicial bodies, but those relations are not oriented to an unreasoned importation of judicial solutions from outside; it is rather a two-way relation among peers, a dialogue that triggers constructive convergence but also leaves room for difference and distinctiveness.

2.2 INTERPRETIVE RELATIONALITY

The *institutional relationality* of the Italian Constitutional Court described above—its ability to establish sound and vital two-way relations with other institutional actors, both political and judicial, national and supranational—is in significant ways mirrored in its internal activity. As a matter of fact, an analogous relational mindset can also be identified in the methods of constitutional interpretation that distinguish the Italian Constitutional Court—what could be called *interpretive relationality*.

In its legal reasoning, the constitutional court follows a comprehensive methodology, one that does not shy away from complexity. As detailed in Chapter 3, a simultaneous multiplicity of approaches to constitutional interpretation can often be found in the decisions of the Italian Constitutional Court. Moreover, and even more relevant, the Court interprets the Constitution as a whole, as a system, avoiding the fragmented interpretation of a single provision detached from its contextual relationship with other principles, rules, and rights inscribed in the Constitution. The Court's methods of interpretation and of legal reasoning are broadly inclusive, and the tools for realizing that constant interrelationship among an integrated set of constitutional provisions are the three doctrines that increasingly provide structure to the constitutional reasoning of the Court: balancing, reasonableness, and proportionality.

This relational approach to the interpretation of Constitution is most evident in the field of fundamental rights (Chapter 4), which for the reasons noted earlier is the gravitational center of global constitutional exchange, and thus in which the distinctive voice of the Italian Court has much to contribute to interjudicial dialogues. In recent years the Italian Constitutional Court has worked out a consistent jurisprudence in the area. The Court has insisted first of all on the fact that no individual right is absolute; all rights protected by the Constitution are to be balanced with other rights and relevant public interests. Therefore it insists on a holistic, rather than piecemeal, interpretation of the Constitution. That is, rather than regarding the Constitution as an assemblage of fragmented and unconnected propositions, all the rights and values proclaimed in it are considered to be components of a unified mosaic, so much so that each element reveals its full meaning only in the context of a broader design.

Underlying this relational interpretation of the Constitution is the notion that although rights belong indeed to the individual, they pertain ineradicably to her relational nature. Article 2 of the Constitution insists from the outset on this relational understanding of the human being, putting the "person" as opposed to the "individual" at the center, since human experience is always taken into consideration in its practical and historical, relational aspects. *L'homme situé*, that is, the person in context, is the principal subject of the constitutional design, and therefore the fundamental rights are grouped under different headings, capturing the diverse relations of the human and social experience (civil, ethical, social, economic, political). This relational understanding of the human person can sometimes result in juridical approaches that diverge both from those of constitutional courts in other jurisdictions and from those of the European supranational courts, in which a decidedly more individualistic understanding prevails.

3. The Sources of the Italian Constitutional Court's Distinctive Voice

Where does the relational mindset of the Italian Constitutional Court originate? This pervasive feature of the Italian Constitutional Court and its jurisprudence is deeply rooted in an ideologically diverse society that adopted a pluralistic constitution in 1948, created a hybrid model of judicial review of legislation, and mandated a differentiated composition of the Constitutional Court itself.

Beginning with the third of these factors, the initial thing to be stressed is that this institutional and interpretative relational leaning of the Italian Constitutional Court emerges to a significant degree from the very particular intra-institutional relation-building capacity internal to the Court itself. The interpretative relational approach that can be discerned in the case law reflects the Court's internal pluralism and collegiality.

To begin with, the Justices are diverse because of their different appointment sources—some selected by highest courts of the ordinary judiciary, others by Parliament, and still others by the President—and because of their different backgrounds, with career judges working alongside university professors and practicing lawyers. They are all united broadly by a common legal education, but differ completely in their professional trajectories and in their personal cultural formation. This pluralism has always been a great asset for the Court, and it has to a degree compensated for the otherwise deficient diversity of the Court along certain other sociological lines such as age, geography, or—most pointedly—gender (see Chapter 2).

Notwithstanding these differences, the Justices are nevertheless prompted to dialogue and agreement because of the principle of collegiality that governs the work of the Court. The internal organization and working procedures of the Court (see Chapter 2) are designed to spur the justices to work intensely in common with one another; they are obliged to dialogue with one another. This fosters reciprocal cross-fertilization among the members of the Court and their respective ideas, political and social backgrounds, cultures, and mentalities, and serves as the principal growth factor in the Court's capacity for building relations. The absence of separate opinions and the requirement that texts be read together in chambers and approved collectively, for instance, fosters compromise and encourages the Justices to incorporate broadly the particular views of their individual colleagues into the final text. The comprehensive and integrative approach to the Constitution that can be found in the reasoning of the Court is in some measure attributable to these methods that catalyze sustained efforts to reconcile and unify divergent views into a composite that is not reducible to the perspective of a judge or politician or scholar alone.

A second factor that helps to explain the discernably relational approach of the Constitutional Court described above is the procedural model of access to judicial review of legislation. As has already been said, the incidental method has over time encouraged the Constitutional Court to maintain good relations with other national judges. Even more profoundly, however, it is an instrument that has helped to develop the Court's approach to balancing and integrating fundamental rights described earlier. The incidental review process situates the Court at the intersection of the specific demands of a concrete case, and the general concern for the overall legal order, understood in such a way as to favor the systematic protection of the rights of all persons. This procedure thus has a composite nature. It is concrete insofar as the constitutional questions arise in the application of the laws and in the context of a specific controversy. Yet, the Court in these cases is never the judge merely of the concrete case alone. Insofar as the question before the Court arises through the incidental method, it poses all of the particular problems of that single situation. Insofar as it is aimed at yielding a general judgment of broad applicability and with *erga omnes* effects, the Court decides the question in view also of the implications that it can have for the overall constitutional order and for the entire complex of fundamental rights. The incidental method in Italy provides protection for fundamental rights in a way that is similar both to models of constitutional adjudication offering direct individual recourse to a high court, and to those authorizing diffuse review, as in the United States. But by not assuming the concrete case in its entirety and instead abstracting from the case for the purposes of its judgment, the Italian Court also heightens its special concern for the systemic and political (in the broad sense of pertaining to the *polis*) dimensions of the question before it.

In these ways, the incidental method is versatile and at the same time has the virtue of uniting symmetrically the protection of a person's individual interests with concern for overarching constitutional values and for the legitimacy and coherence of the legal order as a whole. In this way it may be especially suited as a model for responding to some of the common demands of contemporary constitutionalism in general, which is based on pluralistic constitutions and interconnected systems of review and protection.

The third and perhaps most fundamental factor to be taken into consideration in order to understand the distinctive voice of the Constitutional Court is the Constitution itself, which the Court is required to expound. The Italian Court is called to be the custodian of a long and complex Constitution, with more than 130 articles, which is the fruit of difficult compromises among sharply divergent and opposed political cultures (see Chapter 1). This Constitution arises out of the second wave of constitutionalism, after the Second World War, when the new constitutional orders no longer reflect the political homogeneity of the eighteenth- and nineteenth-century Liberal constitutions and instead have a decidedly pluralistic political content. The Italian constitutional text is marked by compromise and even contradictions, and contains a language quite different from its constitutional forebears of prior centuries (such as that of the United States). Among its most salient departures from the earlier mold is the Italian Constitution's lengthy and interconnected catalogue of rights, in which many are framed as relationally oriented "positive freedoms" and not only as classically individualistic "negative liberties." All this has contributed to a great breadth and variety of constitutional principles and values, such that any constitutional question framed in terms of a specific right almost never has to do *solely* with that single constitutional provision. Moreover, that internal complexity has increased over the life of the Constitution, as the constitutional text has opened up to the transnational horizon described earlier.

In addition to the normative pluralism of the Constitution, the peculiar constitutional architecture in which the Court finds itself gives it another push toward honing its relational capacities. As described more fully in Chapter 5, the Italian constitutional design is more oriented toward a cooperative structure among the separate powers of the State than toward an American-style checks-and-balances approach toward the separation of powers. Accordingly, in its function as a mediator of constitutional conflicts, the Constitutional Court is not so much a sentinel patrolling the boundaries between different functions or powers, as it is a connector, a networking facilitator, aiming to maintain constitutionally sound relations among powers. The political core of the Italian constitutional regime, its parliamentary system, is only regulated within the Constitution by a few broad constitutional principles, because the Framers preferred to leave the definition of Legislative-Executive relations to the concrete political patterns emerging from the electoral process. Consequently, the Court had to be able to follow and adapt to those changing scenarios over time, without ever surrendering its function as constitutional mediator.

Generally speaking, this adaptation has been one of the Constitutional Court's assets (even if it has occasionally subjected the Court to accusations that it bends too uncritically to the prevailing political orientations of the time). For example, the Court has adjusted dynamically first to the (relative) regionalization of the Italian constitutional system, and then more recently to the strong centripetal pull toward the center, the State, rather than the peripheries, the Regions (see Chapter 6).

4. An "Italian Style" for a Pluralistic Global Constitutionalism?

In sum, in many ways the Italian Constitutional Court finds itself operating in a context of strongly pluralistic constitutionalism. Judicial review in these conditions is not so much a process of assessing the compatibility of a single statute with a determinate constitutional provision, but instead calls for a judgment of the appropriate (i.e., reasonable and proportionate) balance among multiple and competing interests, rights, and principles. To be the faithful guardian of the Constitution in this multicultural context requires the ability to listen to a number of subjects speaking with different voices and to develop a mindset oriented toward the search for harmony among them through the integration of the multiple factors in play.

The globalization of constitutionalism frequently poses similar challenges. It is not uncommon to find attitudes that tend to conceive of judicial review in a binary, "all-or-nothing" fashion, as a contest over validity between rival powers, whether legislative and judicial or national and supranational. Where high degrees of normative and institutional pluralism prevail, however—as is certainly and increasingly the case in all regions of the world—such a mindset is incapable of encompassing the complexity of the juridical reality. What is needed instead is a mindset able to undertake an inclusive approach, embracing relationship over fragmentation, reasonableness over rationalism, integration over hierarchy, complexity over reduction. We live today in a world where Walt Whitman's famous words describing the contemporary democratic "self" are applicable to any number of societies and constitutional systems:

> The past and present wilt—I have fill'd them, emptied them.
> And proceed to fill my next fold of the future. . . .
> Do I contradict myself?
> Very well then, I contradict myself,
> (I am large. I contain multitudes.)[3]

Perhaps the Italian style can make a contribution to the emergence of a global constitutionalism that is up to the task of governing such a world.

---

[3] Walt Whitman, *Song of Myself*, in *Leaves of Grass*, 1855.

The Constitution of the Republic of Italy

Fundamental Principles

Art. 1

Italy is a democratic Republic founded on labor.

Sovereignty belongs to the people and is exercised by the people in the forms and within the limits of the Constitution.

Art. 2

The Republic recognizes and guarantees the inviolable rights of the man, both as an individual and in the social groups where his personality is developed, and requires fulfillment of the underogable duties of political, economic, and social solidarity.

Art. 3

All citizens have equal social dignity and are equal before the law, without distinction of sex, race, language, religion, political beliefs, or personal and social conditions.

It is the task of the Republic to remove those obstacles of an economic or social nature which, by limiting in fact the freedom and equality of citizens, prevent the full development of the human person and the effective participation of all workers in the political, economic and social organization of the country.

Art. 4

The Republic recognizes the right of all citizens to work and promotes the conditions, which render this right effective.

Every citizen has the duty, according to personal potential and individual choice, to perform an activity or a function that contributes to the material or spiritual progress of society.

Art. 5

The Republic, one and indivisible, recognizes and promotes local autonomies; it implements the fullest measure of administrative decentralization in those services which depend from the State; it adapts the principles and methods of its legislation to the requirements of autonomy and decentralization.

Art. 6

The Republic safeguards linguistic minorities by means of appropriate norms.

Art. 7

The State and the Catholic Church are independent and sovereign, each within its own sphere.

Their relations are regulated by the Lateran Pacts. Amendments to such Pacts accepted by both parties shall not require the procedure of constitutional amendments.

Art. 8

All religious denominations are equally free before the law.

Denominations other than Catholicism have the right to self-organization according to their own statutes, provided these do not conflict with the Italian legal order.

Their relations with the State are regulated by laws based on agreements with their respective representatives.

Art. 9

The Republic promotes the development of culture and of scientific and technical research.

It safeguards natural landscape and the historical and artistic patrimony of the Nation.

Art. 10

The Italian legal order conforms to the generally recognized principles of international law.

The legal status of foreigners is regulated by law in conformity with international norms and treaties.

A foreigner who, in his home country, is denied the actual exercise of the democratic freedoms guaranteed by the Italian Constitution, shall be entitled to the right of asylum in the territory of the Italian Republic under the conditions established by law.

A foreigner may not be extradited for a political offence.

Art. 11

Italy rejects war as an instrument of aggression against the freedom of other peoples and as a means for the settlement of international disputes; it agrees, on conditions of equality with other States, to the limitations of sovereignty that may be necessary to a world order ensuring peace and justice among the Nations; Italy promotes and encourages international organizations furthering such ends.

Art. 12

The flag of the Republic is the Italian tricolor: green, white and red, in three vertical bands of equal size.

Part I Rights and Duties of Citizens

TITLE I CIVIL RELATIONS

Art. 13

Personal liberty is inviolable.

No form of personal detention, inspection, or search is permitted, nor any other restriction on personal liberty except by an order of a judicial authority stating a reason, and only in such cases and manner as provided by law.

In exceptional cases of necessity and urgency, strictly defined by law, the police may take provisional measures that shall be referred within 48 hours to the Judiciary for validation and which, in default of such validation in the following 48 hours, shall be revoked and considered null and void.

Any act of physical and moral violence against a person subjected to restriction of personal liberty shall be punished.

The law shall establish the maximum duration of preventive detention.

Art. 14

Personal domicile is inviolable.

Home inspections, searches, or seizures may not be carried out save in the cases and manners complying with measures to safeguard personal liberty.

Controls and inspections for reason of public health and safety, or for economic and fiscal purposes, shall be regulated by appropriate laws.

Art. 15

Freedom and confidentiality of correspondence and of every other form of communication is inviolable. Limitations may only be imposed by judicial decision stating the reasons and in accordance with the guarantees provided by the law.

Art. 16

Every citizen has the right to reside and travel freely in any part of the country, except for such general limitations as may be established by law for reasons of health or security. No restriction may be imposed for political reasons.

Every citizen is free to leave the territory of the Republic and return to it, notwithstanding any legal obligations.

Art. 17

Citizens have the right to assemble peaceably and unarmed.

No previous notice is required for meetings, including those held in places open to the public.

In case of meetings held in public places, previous notice shall be given to the authorities, who may prohibit them only for proven reason of security or public safety.

Art. 18

Citizens have the right to form associations freely and without authorization for those ends that are not forbidden by criminal law.

Secret associations and associations that, even indirectly, pursue political aims by means of organizations having a military character shall be forbidden.

Art. 19

Everyone is entitled to freely profess their religious belief in any form, individually or with others, and to promote them and celebrate rites in public or in private, provided they are not offensive to public morality.

Art. 20

No special legislative limitation or tax burden may be imposed on the establishment, legal capacity or activities of any organization on the ground of its ecclesiastical nature or its religious or worship aims.

Art. 21

Everyone has the right to freely express their thoughts in speech, writing, or any other form of communication.

The press may not be subjected to any authorization or censorship.

Seizure may be permitted only by judicial order stating the reason and only for offences expressly determined by the law of the press or in case of violation of the obligation to identify the persons responsible for such offences.

In such cases, when there is absolute urgency and timely intervention of the Judiciary is not possible, a periodical may be confiscated by the criminal investigation police, which shall immediately and in no case later than 24 hours refer the matter to the Judiciary for validation. In default of such validation in the following 24 hours, the measure shall be revoked and considered null and void.

The law may introduce general provisions for the disclosure of financial sources of periodical publications. Publications, performances, and other exhibits offensive to public morality shall be prohibited. The law shall establish preventive and repressive measure against such violations.

Art. 22

No one may be deprived of his legal capacity, citizenship, or name for political reasons.

Art. 23

No obligation of a personal or financial nature may be imposed on any person except by law.

Art. 24

Everyone may bring cases before a court of law in order to protect their rights under civil and administrative law.

Defense is an inviolable right at every stage and instance of legal proceedings.

The poor are entitled by law to proper means for action or defense in all courts.

The law shall define the conditions and forms of reparation in case of judicial errors.

Art. 25

No one may be removed from the natural jurisdiction of the court previously established by law.

No one will be punished except by virtue of a law in force at the time the offence was committed. No restriction may be placed on a person's liberty save for as provided by law.

Art. 26

Extradition of a citizen may be granted only if it is expressly envisaged by international conventions. In any case, extradition may not be permitted for political offences.

Art. 27

Criminal responsibility is personal.

A defendant shall be considered not guilty until a final sentence has been passed.

Punishments may not be inhumane and shall aim at re-educating the convicted.

The death penalty is prohibited.

Art. 28

Officials of the State or public agencies shall be directly responsible under criminal, civil, and administrative law for acts committed in violation of rights. In such cases, civil liability shall extend to the State and to such public agency.

TITLE II ETHICAL AND SOCIAL RELATIONS

Art. 29

The Republic recognizes the rights of the family as a natural society founded on marriage.

Marriage is based on the moral and legal equality of the spouses within the limits laid down by law to guarantee the unity of the family.

Art. 30

It is the duty and right of parents to support, raise, and educate their children, even if born out of wedlock. In the case of incapacity of the parents, the law provides that their tasks be discharged.

The law ensures to any children born out of wedlock every legal and social protection measures as are compatible with the rights of the members of the legitimate family.

The law shall establish rules and constraints for the determination of paternity.

Art. 31

The Republic assists the formation of the family and the fulfillment of its duties, with particular consideration for large families, through economic measures and other benefits.

The Republic protects motherhood, childhood and youth encouraging the institutions necessary for that purpose.

Art. 32

The Republic safeguards health as a fundamental right of the individual and as a collective interest, and guarantees free medical care to the indigent.

No one may be obliged to undergo any health treatment except under the provisions of the law. The law may not under any circumstances violate the limits imposed by respect for the human person.

Art. 33

The Republic guarantees the freedom of the arts and sciences, which may be freely taught.

The Republic lays down general rules for education and establishes state schools of all branches and grades.

Entities and private persons have the right to establish schools and institutions of education, at no cost to the State.

The law, in setting out the rights and obligations for the non-state schools which request parity, shall ensure that these schools enjoy full liberty and offer their pupils an educational treatment equal to pupils in State schools.

State examinations are prescribed for admission to and graduation from the various branches and grades of schools and for qualification to exercise a profession.

Higher cultural institutions, universities and academies, have the right to establish their own autonomous regulations within the limits laid down by the law.

Art. 34

Schools are open to everyone.

Primary education, given for at least eight years, is compulsory and free of tuition.

Capable and deserving pupils, even if lacking financial resources, have the right to attain the highest levels of education.

The Republic renders this right effective through scholarships, allowances to families and other benefits, which shall be assigned through competitive examinations.

TITLE III ECONOMIC RELATIONS

Art. 35

The Republic protects work in all its forms and practices.

It provides for the training and professional advancement of workers.

It promotes and encourages international agreements and organizations with the aim of establishing and regulating labor rights.

It recognizes the freedom to emigrate, subject to the obligations set out by law in the general interest, and protects Italian workers abroad.

Art. 36

Workers have the right to a remuneration commensurate to the quantity and quality of their work and in any case such as to ensure them and their families a free and dignified existence.

Maximum daily working hours are established by law.

Workers have the right to a weekly rest day and paid annual holidays, and cannot waive this right.

Art. 37

Working women are entitled to equal rights and, for comparable jobs, equal pay as men. Working conditions must allow women to fulfill their essential role in the family and ensure appropriate protection for the mother and child.

The law establishes the minimum age for paid labor.

The Republic protects the work of minors by means of special provisions and guarantees to them the right to equal pay for equal work.

Art. 38

Every citizen unable to work and without the necessary means of subsistence is entitled to support and social assistance.

Workers have the right to be assured adequate means for their needs and necessities in the case of accidents, illness, disability, old age and involuntary unemployment.

Disabled and handicapped persons are entitled to receive education and vocational training. Responsibilities under this article are entrusted to entities and institutions established by or supported by the State.

Private-sector assistance may be freely provided.

Art. 39

Trade unions may be freely established.

No obligations may be imposed on trade unions other than registration at local or central offices, according to the provisions of the law.

A condition for registration is that the statutes of the trade unions establish their internal organization on a democratic basis.

Registered trade unions are legal persons. They may, through a unified representation that is proportional to their membership, enter into collective labor agreements that have a mandatory effect for all persons belonging to the categories referred to in the agreement.

Art. 40

The right to strike shall be exercised in harmony with the law.

Art. 41

Private economic enterprise is free.

It may not be carried out against the common good or in such a manner that could damage safety, liberty and human dignity.

The law shall provide for appropriate programs and controls so that public and private sector economic activity may be oriented and coordinated for social purposes.

Art. 42

Property is public or private. Economic assets may belong to the State, to entities or to private persons.

Private property is recognized and guaranteed by the law, which prescribes the ways it is acquired, enjoyed and its limitations so as to ensure its social function and make it accessible to all.

In the cases provided for by the law and with provisions for compensation, private property may be expropriated for reasons of general interest.

The law establishes the regulations and limits of legitimate and testamentary inheritance and the rights of the State in matters of inheritance.

Art. 43

For the purposes of the common good, the law may establish that an enterprise or a category thereof be, through a pre-emptive decision or compulsory purchase authority with provision of compensation, reserved to the Government, a public agency, a workers' or users' association, provided that such enterprise operates in the field of essential public services, energy sources or monopolies and are of general public interest.

Art. 44

For the purpose of ensuring the rational use of land and equitable social relationships, the law imposes obligations and constraints on private ownership of land; it sets limitations to the size of property according to the region and the agricultural area; encourages and imposes land reclamation, the conversion of latifundia and the reorganization of farm units; and assists small and medium-sized properties.

The law makes provisions for mountain areas.

Art. 45

The Republic recognizes the social function of co-operation of a mutually supportive, non-speculative nature. The law promotes and encourages cooperation through appropriate means and ensures its character and purposes through appropriate checks.

The law safeguards and promotes the artisanal work.

Art. 46

For the economic and social betterment of labor and in harmony with the needs of production, the Republic recognizes the rights of workers to collaborate in the management of enterprises, in the ways and within the limits established by law.

Art. 47

The Republic encourages and safeguards savings in all forms. It regulates, co-ordinates and oversees the operation of credit.

The Republic promotes house and farm ownership and direct and indirect shareholding in the main national enterprises through the use of private savings.

TITLE IV POLITICAL RELATIONS

Art. 48

All citizens, male or female, who have attained majority, are entitled to vote.

The vote is personal and equal, free and secret. The exercise thereof is a civic duty.

The law establishes the requirements and modalities for citizens residing abroad to exercise their right to vote and guarantees that this right is effective. A constituency of Italians abroad shall be established for elections to the Houses of Parliament; the number of seats of such constituency is set forth in a constitutional provision according to criteria established by law.

The right to vote cannot be restricted except for civil incapacity or as a consequence of an irrevocable penal sentence or in cases of moral unworthiness as indicated by the law.

Art. 49

All citizens have the right to freely associate in parties to contribute to determining national policies through democratic processes.

Art. 50

All citizens may present petitions to Parliament to request legislative measures or to express collective needs.

Art. 51

All citizens of either sex are eligible for public offices and elected positions on equal terms, according to the conditions established by law. To this end, the Republic shall adopt specific measures to promote equal opportunities between women and men.

The law may equalize Italians who do not belong to the Republic with citizens for the purposes of access to public offices and elected positions.

Whoever is elected to a public function is entitled to the time needed to perform that function and to retain a previously held job.

Art. 52

The defense of the country is a sacred duty for every citizen.

Military service is obligatory within the limits and in the manner set by law. Its fulfillment shall not prejudice a citizen's job, nor the exercise of political rights.

The organization of the armed forces shall be based on the democratic spirit of the Republic.

Art. 53

Every person shall contribute to public expenses in accordance with his capacities.

The tax system shall be progressive.

Art. 54

All citizens have the duty to be loyal to the Republic and to uphold its Constitution and laws.

Those citizens to whom public functions are entrusted have the duty to fulfill such functions with discipline and honor, taking an oath in those cases established by law.

Part II Organization of the Republic

TITLE I THE PARLIAMENT

Section I The Houses

Art. 55

Parliament consists of the Chamber of Deputies and the Senate of the Republic.

Parliaments shall meet in joint session only in cases established by this Constitution.

Art. 56

The Chamber of Deputies is elected by direct and universal suffrage.

The number of deputies is six hundred and thirty, twelve of which are elected in the overseas constituency. All voters who have attained the age of twenty-five on the day of elections are eligible to be deputies.

The division of seats among the electoral districts, with the exception of the number of seats assigned to the overseas constituency, is obtained by dividing the number of inhabitants of the Republic, as shown by the latest general census of the population, by six hundred eighteen and by distributing the seats in proportion to the population in every electoral district, on the basis of whole shares and highest remainders.

Art. 57 -

The Senate of the Republic is elected on a regional basis, with the exception of the seats assigned to the overseas constituency.

The number of senators to be elected is three hundred and fifteen, six of whom are elected in the overseas constituency.

No Region may have fewer than seven senators; Molise shall have two, Valle d'Aosta one.

The division of seats among the Regions, with the exception of the number of seats assigned to the overseas constituency and in accordance with the provisions of Article 56 above, is made in proportion to the population of the Regions as per the latest general census, on the basis of whole shares and highest remainders.

Art. 58

Senators are elected by universal and direct suffrage by voters who are twenty-five years of age.

Voters who have attained the age of forty are eligible to be elected to the Senate.

Art. 59

Former Presidents of the Republic are senators by right and for life unless they renounce the office.

The President of the Republic may appoint as life senators five citizens who have honored the Nation through their outstanding achievements in the social, scientific, artistic and literary fields.

Art. 60

The Chamber of Deputies and the Senate of the Republic are elected for five years.

The term for each House may not be extended, except by law and only in the case of war.

Art. 61

Elections for a new Parliament shall take place within seventy days from the end of the term of the previous Houses. The first meeting is convened no later than twenty days after the elections.

Until such time as the new Houses meet, the powers of the previous Houses are extended.

Art. 62

In default of any other provisions, Parliament shall be convened on the first working day of February and October.

Each House may be convened in special session on the initiative of its President, the President of the Republic or a third of its members.

When one House is convened in special session, the other House is convened as a matter of course.

Art. 63

Each House shall elect a President and a Bureau from among its members.

When Parliament meets in joint session, the President and the Bureau are those of the Chamber of Deputies.

Art. 64

Each House adopts its own Rules by an absolute majority of its members.

The sittings are public; however, each of the Houses and Parliament in joint session may decide to convene a closed session.

The decisions of each House and of Parliament are not valid if the majority of the members are not present, and if they are not passed by a majority of those present, save for those instances where the Constitution prescribes a special majority.

Members of the Government, even when not members of Parliament, have the right, and, when requested, the obligation, to attend the sittings. They shall be heard every time they so request.

Art. 65

The law determines the cases of disqualification with the office of deputy or senator.

No one may be a member of both Houses at the same time.

Art. 66

Each House verifies the credentials of its members and the causes of disqualification that may arise at a later stage.

Art. 67

Each member of Parliament represents the Nation and carries out his duties without a binding mandate.

Art. 68

Members of Parliament cannot be held accountable for the opinions expressed or votes cast in the performance of their function.

In default of the authorization of his House, no member of Parliament may be submitted to personal or home search, nor may he be arrested or otherwise deprived of his personal freedom, nor held in detention, except when a final court sentence is enforced, or when the member is apprehended in the act of committing an offence for which arrest flagrante delicto is mandatory.

An analogous authorization shall also be required in order to monitor a member of Parliament's conversations or communications, or to seize such member's mail.

Art. 69

Members of Parliament shall receive an allowance established by law.

Section II The Legislative Process

Art. 70

The legislative function is exercised collectively by both Houses.

Art. 71

Legislation may be introduced by the Government, by a member of Parliament and by those entities and bodies so empowered by constitutional law.

The people may initiate legislation by proposing a bill drawn up in sections and signed by at least fifty-thousand voters.

Art. 72

A Bill introduced in either House of Parliament shall, under the Rules of procedure of such House, be scrutinized by a Committee and then by the whole House, which shall consider it section by section and then put it to the final vote.

The Rules shall establish shorter procedures to consider a Bill that has been declared urgent.

They may also establish when and how the consideration and approval of bills may be referred to Committees, including Standing Committees, composed so as to reflect the proportion of the Parliamentary Groups. Even in such cases, until the moment of its final approval, a Bill may be referred back to the whole House, if the Government or one-tenth of the members of the House or one-fifth of the Committee request that it be debated and voted on by the House itself or that it be submitted to the House for final approval, following explanations of vote. The Rules shall establish the ways in which the proceedings of Committees are made public.

The ordinary procedure for consideration and direct approval by the House is always adopted according to the bills on constitutional and electoral matters, delegating legislation, ratification of international treaties and the approval of budgets and accounts.

Art. 73

Laws are promulgated by the President of the Republic within one month of their approval.

If the Houses, each by an absolute majority of its members, declare a law to be urgent, the law is promulgated within the deadline established therein.

The laws are published immediately after promulgation and enter into force on the fifteenth day following publication, unless such law establishes a different deadline.

Art. 74

The President of the Republic, prior to a law's promulgation, may send Parliament a reasoned opinion to request that a law be considered anew. If such law is passed again, it shall be promulgated.

Art. 75

A popular referendum may be held to repeal, in whole or in part, a law or a measure having the force of law, when so requested by five hundred thousand voters or five Regional Councils.

No referendum may be held on a law regulating taxes, the budget, an amnesty or pardon, or a law ratifying an international treaty.

Any citizen entitled to vote for the Chamber of Deputies has the right to vote in a referendum.

The referendum shall be considered carried out if the majority of those eligible have voted and a majority of valid votes has been achieved.

The manner of carrying out the referendum shall be determined by law.

Art. 76

The exercise of the legislative function may not be delegated to the Government unless principles and criteria have been determined and then only for a limited time and for specified purposes.

Art. 77

The Government may not, without an enabling act from the Houses, issue decrees having force of law. When the Government, in extraordinary cases of necessity and urgency, adopts under its own authority a temporary measure having the force of law, it shall introduce such measure on the same day to Parliament for conversion into law. If dissolved, Parliament shall be convened for this purpose within five days of such introduction.

Such a measure loses effect from the beginning if it is not converted into law by Parliament within sixty days of its publication. Parliament may regulate the legal relations arisen from the non-converted measure.

Art. 78

Parliament has the authority to declare a state of war and vest the necessary powers into the Government.

Art. 79

Amnesty and pardon may be granted by a law, which has received a two thirds majority in both Houses of Parliament, on each section and on the final vote.

Such law shall set the deadline for the implementation of amnesty or pardon.

In any case, amnesty and pardon thus introduced may not be granted in the cases of a crime committed after the introduction of such bill.

Art. 80

Parliament shall authorize by law the ratification of such international treaties as have a political nature, require arbitration or a legal settlement, entail change of borders, spending or new legislation.

Art. 81

The State shall ensure the balance between revenue and expenditure in its budget, taking into account the adverse and favorable phases of the economic cycle.

No recourse shall be made to borrowing except for the purpose of taking into account the effects of an economic cycle or, subject to authorization by the two Houses approved by an absolute majority vote of their members, in exceptional circumstances.

Any law involving new or increased expenditures shall provide for the resources to cover such expenditures.

Each year the Houses shall pass a law approving the budget and the accounts submitted by the Government.

Provisional implementation of the budget shall not be allowed except by specific legislation and only for periods not exceeding four months in total.

The content of the budget law, and the fundamental rules and the criteria adopted to ensure a balance between revenue and expenditure and the sustainability of general government debt shall be established by legislation approved by an absolute majority of the members of each House in harmony with the principles established with a constitutional law.

Art. 82

Each House of Parliament may conduct enquiries on matters of public interest.

For this purpose, it shall detail from among its members a Committee formed in such a way so as to represent the proportionality of existing Parliamentary Groups. A Committee of Enquiry may conduct investigations and examination with the same powers and limitations as the Judiciary.

TITLE II THE PRESIDENT OF THE REPUBLIC

Art. 83

The President of the Republic is elected by Parliament in joint session.

Three delegates from every Region elected by the Regional Council so as to ensure that minorities are represented shall participate in the election. Valle d'Aosta has one delegate only.

The election of the President of the Republic is by secret ballot with a majority of two thirds of the assembly. After the third ballot an absolute majority shall suffice.

Art. 84

Any citizen who has attained fifty years of age and enjoys civil and political rights can be elected President of the Republic.

The office of President of the Republic is incompatible with any other office.

The remuneration and entitlements of the President are established by law.

Art. 85

The President of the Republic is elected for seven years.

Thirty days before the expiration of the term, the President of the Chamber of Deputies shall summon a joint session of Parliament and the regional delegates to elect the new President of the Republic.

If the Parliament is dissolved or in the three months preceding dissolution, the election shall be held within the first fifteen days of the first sitting of a new Parliament. In the intervening time, the powers of the incumbent President are extended.

Art. 86

The functions of the President of the Republic, in all cases in which the President cannot perform them, shall be performed by the President of the Senate.

In case of permanent incapacity or death or resignation of the President of the Republic, the President of the Chamber of Deputies shall call an election of a new President of the Republic within fifteen days, notwithstanding the longer term envisaged if Parliament is dissolved or in the three months preceding dissolution.

Art. 87

The President of the Republic is the Head of the State and represents national unity.

The President may send messages to Parliament.

The President shall:

- call for elections of the new Chambers and establish the date for the first assembly;
- authorize the introduction to Parliament of bills initiated by the Government;
- promulgate laws and issue decrees having the force of law, and regulations;

- call a general referendum in the cases provided for by the Constitution;
- appoint State officials in the cases provided for by the law;
- accredit and receive diplomatic representatives, and ratify international treaties which have, where required, been authorized by Parliament.

The President is the commander-in-chief of the armed forces, shall preside over the Supreme Council of Defense established by law, and shall make declarations of war as have been agreed by Parliament.

The President shall preside over the High Council of the Judiciary.

The President may grant pardons and commute punishments.

The President shall confer the honorary distinctions of the Republic.

Art. 88

In consultation with the presiding officers of Parliament, the President may dissolve one or both Houses of Parliament.

The President of the Republic may not exercise such right during the final six months of the presidential term, unless said period coincides in full or in part with the final six months of the Parliamentary session.

Art. 89

A writ of the President of the Republic shall not be valid unless countersigned by the proposing Ministers, who shall be accountable for it.

A writ having force of law and other writs issued by virtue of a law shall also be countersigned by the President of the Council of Ministers.

Art. 90

The President of the Republic is not responsible for acts performed in the exercise of his functions, except in the case of high treason or violation of the Constitution.

In such cases, the President may be impeached by Parliament in joint session, with an absolute majority of its members.

Art. 91

Before taking office, the President of the Republic shall take an oath of allegiance to the Republic and pledge to uphold the Constitution before Parliament in joint session.

TITLE III THE GOVERNMENT

Section I The Council of Ministers

Art. 92

The Government of the Republic is made up of the President of the Council and the Ministers who together form the Council of Ministers.

The President of the Republic appoints the President of the Council of Ministers and, on his proposal, the Ministers.

Art. 93

Before taking office, the President of the Council of Ministers and the Ministers shall be sworn in by the President of the Republic.

Art. 94

The Government must receive the confidence of both Houses of Parliament.

Each House grants or withdraws its confidence through a reasoned motion voted on by roll-call.

Within ten days of its formation the Government shall come before Parliament to obtain confidence.

An opposing vote by one or both the Houses against a Government proposal does not entail the obligation to resign.

A motion of no confidence must be signed by at least one-tenth of the members of the House and cannot be debated more than three days before its presentation.

Art. 95

The President of the Council conducts and holds responsibility for the general policy of the Government.

The President of the Council ensures the coherence of political and administrative policies, by promoting and coordinating the activity of the Ministers.

The Ministers are collectively responsible for the acts of the Council of Ministers; they are individually responsible for the acts of their own ministries.

The law establishes the organization of the Presidency of the Council, as well as the number, competence and organization of the ministries.

Art. 96

The President of the Council of Ministers and the Ministers, even if they resign from office, are subject to ordinary courts for crimes committed in the exercise of their duties, provided authorization is given by the Senate of the Republic or the Chamber of Deputies, in accordance with the norms established by Constitutional Law.

Section II Public Administration

Art. 97

Public administration, in accordance with European Union law, shall ensure balanced budgets and the sustainability of public debt.

Public offices are organized according to the provisions of law, so as to ensure the efficiency and impartiality of administration.

The regulations of the offices lay down the areas of competence, the duties and the responsibilities of the officials.

Employment in public administration is accessed through competitive examinations, except in the cases established by law.

Art. 98

Civil servants are exclusively at the service of the Nation.

If they are members of Parliament, they may not be promoted in their services, except through seniority. The law may set limitations on the right to become members of political parties in the case of magistrates, career military staff in active service, law enforcement officers, and overseas diplomatic and consular representatives.

Section III Auxiliary Bodies

Art. 99

The National Council for Economics and Labor is composed, as set out by law, of experts and representatives of the economic categories, in such a proportion as to take account of their numerical and qualitative importance.

It serves as a consultative body for Parliament and the Government on those matters and those functions attributed to it by law.

It can initiate legislation and may contribute to drafting economic and social legislation according to the principles and within the limitations laid out by law.

Art. 100

The Council of State is a legal-administrative consultative body and it oversees the administration of justice.

The Court of Accounts exercises preventive control over the legitimacy of Government measures, and also ex-post auditing of the administration of the State Budget. It participates, in the cases and ways established by law, in auditing the financial management of the entities receiving regular budgetary support from the State. It reports directly to Parliament on the results of audits performed.

The law ensures the independence from the Government of the two bodies and of their members.

TITLE IV THE JUDICIARY

Section I The Organization of the Judiciary

Art. 101

Justice is administered in the name of the people.

Judges are subject only to the law.

Art. 102

Judicial proceedings are exercised by ordinary magistrates empowered and regulated by the provisions concerning the Judiciary.

Extraordinary or special judges may not be established. Only specialized sections for specific matters within the ordinary judicial bodies may be established, and these sections may include the participation of qualified citizens who are not members of the Judiciary.

The law regulates the cases and forms of the direct participation of the people in the administration of justice.

Art. 103

The Council of State and the other bodies of administrative justice have jurisdiction over the protection of legitimate interests against the public administration and, in particular matters laid out by law, also of subjective rights.

The Court of Accounts has jurisdiction in matters of public accounts and in other matters laid out by law. Military tribunals in times of war have the jurisdiction established by law. In times of peace they have jurisdiction only for military crimes committed by members of the armed forces.

Art. 104

The Judiciary is a branch that is autonomous and independent of all other powers.

The High Council of the Judiciary is presided over by the President of the Republic.

The first president and the general prosecutor of the Court of Cassation are members by right.

Two thirds of the members are elected by all the ordinary judges belonging to the various categories, and one third are elected by Parliament in joint session from among university professors of law and lawyers with fifteen years of practice.

The Council elects a vice-president from among those members designated by Parliament.

Elected members of the Council remain in office for four years and cannot be immediately re-elected.

They may not, while in office, be registered in professional rolls, nor serve in Parliament or on a Regional Council.

Art. 105

The High Council of the Judiciary, in accordance with the regulations of the Judiciary, has jurisdiction for employment, assignments and transfers, promotions and disciplinary measures of judges.

Art. 106

Judges are appointed through competitive examinations.

The law on the regulations of the Judiciary allows the appointment, also by election, of honorary judges for all the functions performed by single judges.

Following a proposal by the High Council of the Judiciary, university professors of law and lawyers with fifteen years of practice and registered in the special professional rolls for the higher courts may be appointed for their outstanding merits as Cassation councilors.

Art. 107

Judges may not be removed from office. They may not be dismissed or suspended from office or assigned to other courts or functions unless by a decision of the High Council of the Judiciary, taken either for the reasons and with the guarantees of defense established by the provisions concerning the organization of Judiciary or with the consent of the judges themselves.

The Minister of Justice has the power to originate disciplinary action.

Judges are distinguished only by their different functions.

The state prosecutor enjoys the guarantees established in the prosecutor's favor by the provisions concerning the organization of the Judiciary.

Art. 108

The provisions concerning the organization of the Judiciary and of every judge are laid out by law.

The law ensures the independence of judges of special courts, of state prosecutors of those courts, and of other persons participating in the administration of justice.

Art. 109

The legal authorities have direct use of the judicial police.

Art. 110

Without prejudice to the authority of the High Council of the Judiciary, the Minister of Justice has responsibility for the organization and functioning of those services involved with justice.

Section II Rules on Jurisdiction

Art. 111

Jurisdiction is implemented through due process regulated by law.

All court trials are conducted with adversary proceedings and the parties are entitled to equal conditions before an impartial judge in third party position. The law provides for the reasonable duration of trials.

In criminal law trials, the law provides that the alleged offender shall be promptly informed confidentially of the nature and reasons for the charges that are brought and shall have adequate time and conditions to prepare a defense; that he shall have the right to cross-examine or to have cross-examined before a judge the persons making accusations and to summon and examine persons for the defense in the same conditions as the prosecution, as well as the right to produce all other evidence in favor of the defense. The defendant is entitled to the assistance of an interpreter in the case that he or she does not speak or understand the language in which the court proceedings are conducted.

In criminal law proceedings, the formation of evidence is based on the principle of adversary hearings. The guilt of the defendant cannot be established on the basis of statements by persons who, out of their own free choice, have always voluntarily avoided undergoing cross-examination by the defendant or the defense counsel.

The law regulates the cases in which the formation of evidence does not occur in an adversary proceeding with the consent of the defendant or owing to reasons of ascertained objective impossibility or proven illicit conduct.

All judicial decisions shall include a statement of reasons.

Appeals to the Court of Cassation in cases of violations of the law are always allowed against sentences and against measures affecting personal freedom pronounced by ordinary and special courts. This rule can only be waived in cases of sentences by military tribunals in time of war.

Appeals to the Court of Cassation against decisions of the Council of State and the Court of Accounts are permitted only for reasons of jurisdiction.

Art. 112

The public prosecutor has the obligation to exercise criminal proceedings.

Art. 113

The judicial safeguarding of rights and legitimate interests before the bodies of ordinary or administrative justice is always permitted against acts of the public administration.

Such judicial protection may not be excluded or limited to particular kinds of appeal or for particular categories of acts.

The law determines which judicial bodies are empowered to annul acts of public administration in the cases and with the consequences provided for by the law itself.

TITLE V REGIONS, PROVINCES, MUNICIPALITIES

Art. 114

The Republic is composed of the Municipalities, the Provinces, the Metropolitan Cities, the Regions and the State.

Municipalities, Provinces, Metropolitan Cities and Regions are autonomous entities having their own statutes, powers and functions in accordance with the principles laid down in the Constitution.

Rome is the capital of the Republic. Its status is regulated by State Law.

Art. 115

(Repealed)

Art. 116

Friuli-Venezia Giulia, Sardinia, Sicily, Trentino-Alto Adige/Südtirol and Valle d'Aosta/Vallée d'Aoste have special forms and conditions of autonomy pursuant to the special charters adopted by Constitutional Law.

The Trentino-Alto Adige/Südtirol Region is composed of the Autonomous Provinces of Trento and Bolzano. Additional special forms and conditions of autonomy, related to the areas specified in art. 117, paragraph three and paragraph two, letter l)—limited to the organizational requirements of the Justice of the Peace—and letters n) and s), may be attributed to other Regions by State Law, upon the initiative of the Region concerned, after consultation with the local authorities, in harmony with the principles set forth in art. 119. Said Law is approved by both Houses of Parliament with the absolute majority of their members, on the basis of an agreement between the State and the Region concerned.

Art. 117

Legislative powers shall be vested in the State and the Regions in harmony with the Constitution and with the constraints deriving from EU legislation and international obligations.

The State has exclusive legislative powers in the following matters:

a. foreign policy and international relations of the State; relations between the State and the European Union; right of asylum and legal status of non-EU citizens;
b. immigration;
c. relations between the Republic and religious denominations;
d. defense and armed forces; State security; armaments, ammunition and explosives;
e. the currency, savings protection and financial markets; competition protection; foreign exchange system; state taxation and accounting systems; harmonization of public accounts; equalization of financial resources;
f. State bodies and relevant electoral laws; State referenda; elections to the European Parliament;
g. legal and administrative organization of the State and of national public agencies;
h. public order and security, with the exception of local administrative police;
i. citizenship, civil status and register offices;
l. jurisdiction and procedural law; civil and criminal law; administrative justice;
m. determination of the essential level of benefits relating to civil rights and social entitlements to be guaranteed throughout the national territory;
n. general provisions on education;
o. social security;
p. electoral legislation, governing bodies and fundamental functions of the Municipalities, Provinces and Metropolitan Cities;
q. customs, protection of national borders and international prophylaxis;
r. weights and measures; standard time; statistical and computerized coordination of data of State, regional and local administrations; copyright;
s. protection of the environment, the ecosystem and cultural heritage.

Concurring legislation applies to the following subject matters: international and EU relations of the Regions; foreign trade; job protection and safety; education, subject to the autonomy of educational institutions and with the exception of vocational education and training; professions; scientific and technological research and innovation support for productive sectors; health protection; nutrition; sports; disaster relief; land-use planning; civil ports and airports; large transport and navigation networks; communications; national production, transport and distribution of energy; complementary and supplementary social security; co-ordination of public finance and taxation system; enhancement of cultural and environmental properties, including the promotion and organization of cultural activities; savings banks, rural banks, regional credit institutions; regional land and agricultural credit institutions. In the subject matters covered by concurring legislation legislative powers are vested in the Regions, except for the determination of the fundamental principles, which are laid down in State legislation.

The Regions have legislative powers in all subject matters that are not expressly covered by State legislation.

The Regions and the Autonomous Provinces of Trento and Bolzano take part in preparatory decision-making process of EU legislative acts in the areas that fall within their responsibilities. They are also responsible for the implementation of international agreements and

EU measures, subject to the rules set out in State law which regulate the exercise of subsidiary powers by the State in the case of non-performance by the Regions and Autonomous Provinces.

Regulatory powers shall be vested in the State with respect to the subject matters of exclusive legislation, subject to any delegations of such powers to the Regions. Regulatory powers shall be vested in the Regions in all other subject matters. Municipalities, Provinces and Metropolitan Cities have regulatory powers as to the organization and implementation of the functions attributed to them.

Regional laws shall remove any hindrances to the full equality of men and women in social, cultural and economic life and promote equal access to elected offices for men and women.

Agreements between a Region and other Regions that aim at improving the performance of regional functions and that may also envisage the establishment of joint bodies shall be ratified by regional law.

In the areas falling within their responsibilities, Regions may enter into agreements with foreign States and local authorities of other States in the cases and according to the forms laid down by State legislation.

Art. 118

Administrative functions are attributed to the Municipalities, unless they are attributed to the Provinces, Metropolitan Cities and Regions or to the State, pursuant to the principles of subsidiarity, differentiation and proportionality, to ensure their uniform implementation.

Municipalities, Provinces and Metropolitan Cities carry out administrative functions of their own as well as the functions assigned to them by State or by regional legislation, according to their respective competences.

State legislation shall provide for co-ordinated action between the State and the Regions in the subject matters as per Article 117, paragraph two, letters b) and h), and also provide for agreements and coordinated action in the field of cultural heritage preservation.

The State, Regions, Metropolitan Cities, Provinces and Municipalities shall promote the autonomous initiatives of citizens, both as individuals and as members of associations, relating to activities of general interest, on the basis of the principle of subsidiarity.

Art. 119

Municipalities, Provinces, Metropolitan Cities and Regions shall have autonomy regarding revenues and expenditures, subject to the obligation to balance their budgets, and shall contribute to ensuring compliance with the economic and financial constraints deriving from European Union law.

Municipalities, Provinces, Metropolitan Cities and Regions shall have independent financial resources. They set and levy taxes and collect revenues of their own, in harmony with the Constitution and according to the principles of co-ordination of State finances and the tax system. They share in the tax revenues related to their respective territories.

State legislation shall provide for an equalization fund—with no allocation constraints—for the territories having lower per-capita taxable capacity.

Revenues raised from the above-mentioned sources shall enable Municipalities, Provinces, Metropolitan Cities and Regions to fully finance the public functions attributed to them.

The State shall allocate supplementary resources and adopt special measures in favor of specific Municipalities, Provinces, Metropolitan Cities and Regions to promote economic development along with social cohesion and solidarity, to reduce economic and social imbalances, to foster the exercise of the rights of the person or to achieve goals other than those pursued in the ordinary implementation of their functions.

Municipalities, Provinces, Metropolitan Cities and Regions have their own assets, which are allocated to them pursuant to general principles laid down in State legislation. They may have recourse to borrowing only as a means of financing investment expenditure, with the concomitant adoption of amortization plans and subject to the condition that a balanced budget is ensured for all Regional authorities taken as a whole. State guarantees on loans contracted by such authorities are prohibited.

Art. 120

Regions may not levy import or export or transit duties between Regions or adopt measures that in any way obstruct the freedom of movement of persons or goods between Regions. Regions may not limit the right of citizens to work in any part whatsoever of the national territory.

The Government can act for bodies of the Regions, Metropolitan Cities, Provinces and Municipalities if the latter fail to comply with international rules and treaties or EU legislation, or in the case of grave danger for public safety and security, or whenever such action is necessary to preserve legal or economic unity and in particular to guarantee the essential level of benefits relating to civil rights and social entitlements, regardless of the geographic borders of local authorities. The law shall lay down the procedures to ensure that subsidiary powers are exercised in harmony with the principles of subsidiarity and loyal co-operation.

Art. 121

The bodies of the Region are: the Regional Council, the Regional Executive and its President.

The Regional Council shall exercise the legislative powers attributed to the Region as well as the other functions conferred by the Constitution and the laws. It may submit bills to Parliament.

The Regional Executive is the executive body of the Region.

The President of the Executive represents the Region, directs the policymaking of the Executive and is responsible for it, promulgates laws and regional statutes, directs the administrative functions delegated to the Region by the State, in conformity with the instructions of the Government of the Republic.

Art. 122

The electoral system and the cases of ineligibility and incompatibility of the President, the other members of the Regional Executive and the Regional councilors shall be established by a regional law in accordance with the fundamental principles established by a law of the Republic, which also establishes the term of elective offices.

No one may belong at the same time to a Regional Council or to a Regional Executive and to either House of Parliament, another Regional Council, or the European Parliament.

The Council shall elect a President and a Bureau from amongst its members.

Regional councilors are unaccountable for the opinions expressed and votes cast in the exercise of their functions.

The President of the Regional Executive shall be elected by universal and direct suffrage, unless the Regional Charter provides otherwise. The elected President shall appoint and dismiss the members of the Executive.

Art. 123

Each Region shall have a Charter, which, in harmony with the Constitution, shall lay down the form of government and basic principles for the organization of the Region and the conduct of its business. The Charter shall regulate the right to initiate legislation and promote referenda on the laws and administrative measures of the Region as well as the publication of laws and of regional regulations.

Regional Charters are adopted and amended by the Regional Council with a law approved by an absolute majority of its members, with two subsequent deliberations at an interval of not less than two months. This law does not require the approval of the Government commissioner. The Government of the Republic may challenge the constitutionality of a Regional Charter before the Constitutional Court within thirty days of its publication.

The Charter is submitted to popular referendum if one-fiftieth of the electors of the Region or one-fifth of the members of the Regional Council so request within three months from its publication. The Charter that is submitted to referendum is not promulgated if it is not approved by the majority of valid votes.

In each Region, Charters regulate the activity of the Council of local authorities as a consultative body on relations between the Regions and local authorities.

Art. 124

(Repealed)

Art. 125

Administrative tribunals of first instance shall be established in the Region, in accordance with the rules established by the law of the Republic. Sections may be established in places other than the regional capital.

Art. 126

The Regional Council may be dissolved and the President of the Executive may be removed with a reasoned decree of the President of the Republic in the case of acts in contrast with the Constitution or grave violations of the law. The dissolution or removal may also be decided for reasons of national security. Such decree is adopted after consultation with a Committee of deputies and senators for regional affairs which is set up in the manner established by a law of the Republic.

The Regional Council may adopt a reasoned motion of no confidence against the President of the Executive that is undersigned by at least one-fifth of its members and adopted by roll call vote with an absolute majority of members. The motion may not be debated before three days have elapsed since its introduction. The adoption of a no confidence motion against a President of the Executive elected by universal and direct suffrage, and the removal, permanent inability, death or voluntary resignation of the President of the Executive entail the resignation of the Executive and the dissolution of the Council. In every case, the same effects are produced by the simultaneous resignation of the majority of the Council members.

Art. 127

The Government may question the constitutional legitimacy of a regional law before the Constitutional Court within sixty days from its publication, when it deems that the regional law exceeds the competence of the Region.

A Region may raise a constitutional challenge to a State or regional law or measure having the force of law before the Constitutional Court within sixty days of its publication, when it deems that said law or measure infringes upon its authority.

Art. 128

(Repealed)

Art. 129

(Repealed)

Art. 130

(Repealed)

Art. 131

The following Regions shall be established:
Piedmont;
Valle d'Aosta;
Lombardy;
Trentino-Alto Adige;
Veneto;
Friuli-Venezia Giulia;
Liguria;
Emilia-Romagna;
Tuscany;
Umbria;
The Marches;
Latium;
Abruzzi;
Molise;
Campania;
Apulia;
Basilicata;
Calabria;
Sicily;
Sardinia.

Art. 132

By a Constitutional Law, after consultation with the Regional Councils, a merger between existing Regions or the creation of new Regions having a minimum of one million inhabitants may be agreed, when such request has been made by a number of Municipal Councils representing not less than one-third of the populations involved, and the request has been approved by referendum by a majority of said populations.

The Provinces and Municipalities which request to be detached from a Region and incorporated in another may be allowed to do so, following a referendum and a law of the Republic, which obtains the majority of the populations of the Province or Provinces and of the Municipality or Municipalities concerned, and after having heard the Regional Councils.

Art. 133

Changes in provincial boundaries and the institution of new Provinces within a Region are regulated by the laws of the Republic, on the initiative of the Municipalities, after consultation with the Region.

The Region, after consultation with the populations involved, may establish through its laws new Municipalities within its own territory and modify their districts and names.

TITLE VI CONSTITUTIONAL GUARANTEES

Section I The Constitutional Court

Art. 134

The Constitutional Court shall pass judgment on:

- controversies on the constitutional legitimacy of laws and enactments having force of law issued by the State and Regions;
- conflicts over allocation of the powers of the State, and between those powers allocated to the State and Regions or between Regions;
- charges brought against the President of the Republic, according to the provisions of the Constitution.

Art. 135

The Constitutional Court shall be composed of fifteen judges, a third nominated by the President of the Republic, a third by Parliament in joint session and a third by the ordinary and administrative supreme courts.

The judges of the Constitutional Court shall be chosen from among judges, including those retired, of the ordinary and administrative higher courts, university professors of law and lawyers with at least twenty years practice.

Judges of the Constitutional Court shall be appointed for nine years, beginning in each case from the day of their swearing in, and they may not be re-appointed.

At the expiry of their term, the constitutional judges shall leave office and the exercise of the functions thereof.

The Court shall elect from among its members, in accordance with the rules established by law, a President, who shall remain in office for three years and may be re-elected, respecting in all cases the expiry term for constitutional judges.

The office of constitutional judge shall be incompatible with membership of Parliament, of a Regional Council, the practice of the legal profession, and with every appointment and office indicated by law.

In impeachment procedures against the President of the Republic, in addition to the ordinary judges of the Court, there shall also be sixteen members chosen by lot from among a list of citizens having the qualification necessary for election to the Senate, which the Parliament prepares every nine years through election using the same procedures as those followed in appointing ordinary judges.

Art. 136

When the Court declares the constitutional illegitimacy of a law or enactment having force of law, the law ceases to have effect on the day following the publication of the decision.

The decision of the Court shall be published and communicated to Parliament and the Regional Councils concerned, so that, wherever they deem it necessary, they shall act in conformity with constitutional procedures.

Art. 137

A constitutional law shall establish the conditions, forms, terms for proposing judgments on constitutional legitimacy, and guarantees on the independence of constitutional judges.

Ordinary laws shall establish the other provisions necessary for the constitution and the functioning of the Court.

No appeals are allowed against the decision of the Constitutional Court.

Section II Amendments to the Constitution. Constitutional Laws

Art. 138

Laws amending the Constitution and other constitutional laws shall be adopted by each House after two successive debates at intervals of not less than three months, and shall be approved by an absolute majority of the members of each House in the second voting.

Said laws are submitted to a popular referendum when, within three months of their publication, such request is made by one-fifth of the members of a House or five hundred thousand voters or five Regional Councils. The law submitted to referendum shall not be promulgated if not approved by a majority of valid votes.

A referendum shall not be held if the law has been approved in the second voting by each of the Houses by a majority of two-thirds of the members.

Art. 139

The republican form of government shall not be a matter for constitutional amendment.

Transitional and Final Provisions

I

With the entry into force of the Constitution the provisional Head of the State shall exercise the functions of President of the Republic and assume that title.

II

If, at the date of the election of the President of the Republic, all the Regional Councils have not been set up, only members of the two Houses shall participate in the election.

III

For the first composition of the Senate of the Republic are nominated senators, with a decree of the President of the Republic, deputies to the Constituent Assembly who possess all the requisites by law to be senators and who:

- had been Presidents of the Council of Ministers or of legislative Assemblies;
- had been members of the dissolved Senate;
- had been elected at least three times including to the Constituent Assembly;
- had been dismissed at the sitting of the Chamber of Deputies of 9 November 1926;
- had been imprisoned for not less than five years by a sentence of the special Fascist tribunal for the defense of the State;

Those also shall be appointed senators, by decree of the President of the Republic, who had been members of the dissolved Senate and who had been members of the *Consulta Nazionale*.

The right to be appointed senator may be renounced before signing of the decree of appointment. Acceptance of candidacy in political elections shall constitute renunciation of the right to be appointed senator.

IV

For the first election of the Senate Molise shall be considered a Region in itself, having the due number of senators on the basis of its population.

V

The provisions of Article 80 of the Constitution on the question of international treaties, which involve budget expenditures or changes in the law, shall become effective as from the date of convocation of Parliament.

VI

Within five years after the Constitution has come into effect the special jurisdictional bodies still in existence shall be revised, except for the jurisdiction of the Council of State, the Court of Accounts, and the military tribunals.

Within a year of the same date, a law shall provide for the re-organization of the Supreme Military Tribunal according to Article 111.

VII

Until such time as the new law on the Judiciary in accordance with the Constitution has been issued, the provisions in force shall continue to be observed.

Until such time as the Constitutional Court begins its functions, the decision on controversies indicated in Article 134 shall be conducted in the forms and within the limits of the provisions already in existence before the implementation of the Constitution.

VIII

Elections of the Regional Councils and the elected bodies of provincial administration shall be called within one year of the implementation of the Constitution.

The laws of the Republic shall regulate for every branch of public administration the passage of the state functions attributed to the Regions. Until such time as the re-organization and re-distribution of the administrative functions among the local bodies has been accomplished, the Provinces and the Municipalities shall retain those functions they presently exercise and those others, which the Regions may delegate to them.

Laws of the Republic shall regulate the transfer to the Regions of officials and employees of the State, including those from central administrations, which shall be made necessary by the new provisions. In setting up their offices the Regions shall, except in cases of necessity, draw their personnel from among the employees of State local bodies.

IX

The Republic, within three years of the implementation of the Constitution, shall adjust its laws to the needs of local autonomies and the legislative jurisdiction attributed to the Regions.

X

The general provisions of Title V of the Second Part of this Constitution shall temporarily apply to the Region of Friuli-Venezia Giulia, as per Article 116, without prejudice to the protection of linguistic minorities in accordance with Article 6.

XI

Up to five years after the implementation of the Constitution other Regions may be established by constitutional laws, thus amending the list in Article 131, and without the conditions required under the first paragraph of Article 132, without prejudice, however, to the obligation to consult the peoples concerned.

XII

It shall be forbidden to reorganize, under any form whatsoever, the dissolved Fascist party. Notwithstanding Article 48, the law has established, for not more than five years from the implementation of the Constitution, temporary limitations to the right to vote and eligibility for the leaders responsible for the Fascist regime.

XIII

The members and descendants of the House of Savoy shall not be voters and may not hold public office or elected offices. Access and sojourn in the national territory shall be forbidden to the ex-kings of the House of Savoy, their spouses and their male descendants. The assets, existing on national territory, of the former kings of the House of Savoy, their spouses and their male descendants shall be transferred to the State. Transfers and the establishment of royal rights on said properties, which took place after 2 June 1946, shall be null and void.

XIV

Titles of nobility shall not be recognized.

The place-names included in those existing before 28 October 1922 shall serve as part of the name.

The Order of Saint Mauritius shall be preserved as a hospital corporation and shall function in the ways established by law.

The law shall regulate the suppression of the Heraldic Council.

XV

With the entry into force of the Constitution, the legislative decree of the Lieutenant of the Realm no. 151 of 25 June 1944 on the provisional organization of the State shall become law.

XVI

Within one year of the entry into force of the Constitution, the revision and co-ordination therewith of previous constitutional laws, which had not at that moment been explicitly or implicitly abrogated shall begin.

XVII

The Constituent Assembly shall be called by its President to decide, before 31 January 1948, on the law for the election of the Senate of the Republic, special regional statues and the law governing the press.

Until the day of the election of the new Parliament, the Constituent Assembly may be convened, when it is necessary to decide on matters attributed to its jurisdiction by Article 2, paragraphs one and two, and Article 3, paragraphs one and two, of legislative decree no. 98 of 16 March 1946.

At that time the Standing Committees shall maintain their functions. Legislative Committees shall send back to the Government those bills, submitted to them, with their observations and proposals for amendments.

Deputies may present questions to the Government with request for written answers.

In accordance with the second paragraph of this Article, the Constituent Assembly shall be called by its President following reasoned request of the Government or at least two hundred deputies.

XVIII

This Constitution shall be promulgated by the provisional Head of State within five days of its approval by the Constituent Assembly and shall come into force on 1 January 1948.

The text of the Constitution shall be deposited in the Town Hall of every Municipality of the Republic and there made public, for the whole of 1948, so as to allow every citizen to know of it.

The Constitution, bearing the seal of the State, shall be included in the Official Records of the laws and decrees of the Republic.

The Constitution must be faithfully observed as the fundamental law of the Republic by all citizens and bodies of the State.

Amendments of the Italian Constitution

Since the entry into force of the Italian Constitution on January 1948 up to the present, the special legislative procedure of Article 138 has been used 38 times.

Twenty-three were Constitutional Laws approved to regulate matters "outside" the Constitution but requiring the constitutional legislative procedure: they concerned the Charters of 5 Special Autonomy Regions (Sicily; Sardinia; Valle d'Aosta; Trentino-Alto Adige and Friuli-Venezia Giulia) and the functioning of the Constitutional Court.

Fifteen were Constitutional Amendments.

Constitutional Amendments

Amendments have affected the following articles of the Constitution: 27 (Abolition of the death penalty); 48 (Right to vote of Italian citizens resident abroad); 51 (Gender equality); 56, 57 and 60 (Composition and length of term of the Chamber of Deputies and Senate of the Republic); 68 (Indemnity and immunity of members of Parliament); 79 (Amnesty and Pardon); 81 (Budget); 88 (Dissolution of the Houses of Parliament); 96 (Crimes of Ministers); 97 (Public administration); 114 to 132 (Regions, Provinces and Municipalities in its entirety); 134 and 135 (Composition, competences, and length of term of the Constitutional Court).

1. Constitutional Law no. 2/1963 "Amendments of Articles 56, 57 and 60 of the Constitution" (GU no. 40/1963)
2. Constitutional Law no. 3/1963 "Amendments of Articles 131 and 57 of the Constitution and Institution of the Molise Region" (GU no. 3/1964)
3. Constitutional Law no. 2/1967 "Amendment of Article 135 of the Constitution and Provisions on the Constitutional Court" (GU no. 294/1967)
4. Constitutional Law no. 1/1989 "Amendment of Articles 96, 134 and 135 of the Constitution and of Constitutional Law of 11 March 1953, no. 1, and provisions on crimes provided by Article 96 of the Constitution" (GU no. 111/1986)
5. Constitutional Law no. 1/1991 "Amendment of Article 88, par. 2 of the Constitution" (GU no. 262/1991)
6. Constitutional Law no. 1/1992 "Revision of Article 79 of the Constitution on the Granting of Amnesty and Pardon" (GU no. 57/1992)
7. Constitutional Law no. 3/1993 "Amendment of Article 68 of the Constitution" (GU no. 256/1993)
8. Constitutional Law no. 1/1999 "Provisions Regarding the Direct Election of the President of the Region and the Regional Statutory Autonomy" (GU no. 299/1999)

9. Constitutional Law no. 2/1999 "Inclusion of Fair Trial Principles in Article 111 of the Constitution" (GU no. 300/1999)

10. Constitutional Law no. 1/2000 "Amendment of Article 48 of the Constitution Regarding the Institution of the 'Abroad' District for the Exercise of the Right to Vote of Italian Citizens Resident Abroad" (GU no. 15/2000)

11. Constitutional Law no. 1/2001 "Amendment to Articles 56 and 57 of the Constitution on the Number of Deputies and Senators Representing Italian Citizens Abroad" (GU no. 19/2001)

12. Constitutional Law no. 3/2001 "Amendment to Title V of Part II of the Constitution" (GU no. 248/2001)

13. Constitutional Law no. 1/2003 "Amendment of Article 51 of the Constitution" (GU no. 134/2003)

14. Constitutional Law no. 1/2007 "Amendment of Article 27 of the Constitution, Concerning Abolition of the Death Penalty" (GU no. 236/2007)

15. Constitutional Law no. 1/2012 "Introduction of the Balanced Budget in the Constitution" (GU no. 95/2012)

Justices 1955 to Present

Justices

Judge	Activity Before the Appointment	Appointed By	Year Appointed	President	Vice President
Ernesto Battaglini	Magistrate	Court of Cassation	1955		
Antonino Papaldo	Magistrate	Council of State	1955		1966–1967
Giuseppe Lampis	Magistrate	Court of Cassation	1955		
Mario Cosatti	Magistrate	Court of Accounts	1955		1962–1963
Francesco Pantaleo Gabrieli	Magistrate	Court of Cassation	1955		
Gaspare Ambrosini	Magistrate; Professor of Constitutional Law; Member of the Constituent Assembly	Parliament in Joint Session	1955	1962–1967	1961–1962
Mario Bracci	Professor of Administrative Law	Parliament in Joint Session	1955		
Giuseppe Cappi	Attorney; Member of the Constituent Assembly; Member of Parliament (1948–1950, 1953–1955, Christian Democratic Party)	Parliament in Joint Session	1955	1961–1962	1961
Nicola Jaeger	Professor of Civil Law and Civil Procedure	Parliament in Joint Session	1955		
Giovanni Cassandro	Attorney; Professor of History of Italian Law	Parliament in Joint Session	1955		
Enrico De Nicola	Attorney; President of the Republic (1948)	President of the Republic	1955	1956–1957	
Gaetano Azzariti	Magistrate	President of the Republic	1955	1957–1961	1956–1957

(Continued)

Judge	Activity Before the Appointment	Appointed By	Year Appointed	President	Vice President
Tomaso Perassi	Professor of International Law; Member of the Constituent Assembly	President of the Republic	1955		1957–1960
Giuseppe Capograssi	Professor of Philosophy of Law	President of the Republic	1955		
Giuseppe Castelli Avolio	Magistrate; Member of the Constituent Assembly; Member of Parliament (1948–1955, Christian Democratic Party)	President of the Republic	1955		1963–1966
Biagio Petrocelli	Magistrate; Professor of Criminal Law	President of the Republic	1956		1967–1968
Antonio Manca	Magistrate	Court of Cassation	1956		
Aldo Sandulli	Attorney; Professor of Administrative Law	President of the Republic	1957	1968–1969	
Giuseppe Branca	Attorney; Professor of Roman Law	Parliament in Joint Session	1959	1969–1971	1968–1969
Michele Fragali	Magistrate	Court of Cassation	1960		1969–1972
Costantino Mortati	Professor of Constitutional Law; Member of the Constituent Assembly	President of the Republic	1960		1972
Giuseppe Chiarelli	Professor of Institutions of Public Law	President of the Republic	1961	1971–1973	
Giuseppe Verzì	Magistrate	Court of Cassation	1962		1972–1974
Giovanni Battista Benedetti	Magistrate	Court of Accounts	1963		1974–1975
Francesco Paolo Bonifacio	Professor of Roman Law	Parliament in Joint Session	1963	1973–1975	

(Continued)

Judge	Activity Before the Appointment	Appointed By	Year Appointed	President	Vice President
Luigi Oggioni	Magistrate	President of the Republic	1966		1975–1978
Angelo De Marco	Magistrate	Council of State	1968		
Ercole Rocchetti	Attorney; Member of Parliament (1948–1963, Christian Democratic Party)	Parliament in Joint Session	1968		
Enzo Capalozza	Attorney	Parliament in Joint Session	1968		
Vincenzo Michele Trimarchi	Professor of Institutions of Private Law; Member of Parliament (1963–1967, Liberal Party)	Parliament in Joint Session	1968		
Vezio Crisafulli	Magistrate; Professor of Constitutional Law	President of the Republic	1968		
Nicola Reale	Magistrate	Court of Cassation	1968		
Paolo Rossi	Professor of Criminal Law; Member of the Constituent Assembly; Member of Parliament (1948–1968, Democratic Socialist Party)	President of the Republic	1969	1975–1978	
Leonetto Amadei	Attorney; Member of the Constituent Assembly; Member of Parliament (1946–1972, Democratic Socialist Party)	Parliament in Joint Session	1972	1979–1981	1978–1979
Giulio Gionfrida	Magistrate	Court of Cassation	1972		1979–1981
Edoardo Volterra	Professor of Institutions of Roman Law	President of the Republic	1973		1981–1982

(*Continued*)

Judge	Activity Before the Appointment	Appointed By	Year Appointed	President	Vice President
Guido Astuti	Professor of History of Italian Law	President of the Republic	1973		
Michele Rossano	Magistrate	Court of Cassation	1974		
Antonino De Stefano	Magistrate	Court of Accounts	1975		1982–1984
Leopoldo Elia	Professor of Constitutional Law; Member of Parliament (1987–1992, 1996–2001, Christian Democratic Party)	Parliament in Joint Session	1976	1981–1985	
Guglielmo Roehrssen	Magistrate	Council of State	1977		1984–1986
Oronzo Reale	Attorney; Member of Parliament (1963–1976, Republican Party)	Parliament in Joint Session	1977		
Brunetto Bucciarelli Ducci	Magistrate; Member of Parliament (1948–1976, Christian Democratic Party)	Parliament	1977		
Alberto Malagugini	Member of Parliament (1968–1976, Communist Party)	Parliament in Joint Session	1977		
Livio Paladin	Professor of Constitutional Law	President of the Republic	1977	1985–1986	
Arnaldo Maccarone	Magistrate	Court of Cassation	1977		
Antonio La Pergola	Professor of Public Law	President of the Republic	1978	1986–1987	1986
Virgilio Andrioli	Professor of Civil Procedure	President of the Republic	1978		1986–1987
Giuseppe Ferrari	Magistrate; Professor of Public Law	President of the Republic	1980		
Francesco Saja	Magistrate	Court of Cassation	1981	1987–1990	

(Continued)

Judge	Activity Before the Appointment	Appointed By	Year Appointed	President	Vice President
Giovanni Conso	Magistrate; Professor of Criminal Procedure	President of the Republic	1982	1990–1991	1987–1990
Ettore Gallo	Magistrate; Professor of Criminal Law	Parliament in Joint Session	1982	1991	
Aldo Corasaniti	Magistrate	Court of Cassation	1983	1991–1992	1991
Giuseppe Borzellino	Magistrate	Court of Accounts	1984		1991–1993
Francesco Greco	Magistrate	Court of Cassation	1984		1993
Renato Dell'Andro	Magistrate; Professor of Criminal Law and Criminal Procedure; Member of Parliament (1963–1985, Christian Democratic Party)	Parliament in Joint Session	1985		
Gabriele Pescatore	Magistrate	Council of State	1986		1993–1995
Ugo Spagnoli	Attorney	Parliament in Joint Session	1986		1995
Francesco Paolo Casavola	Professor of History of Roman Law	Parliament in Joint Session	1986	1992–1995	
Antonio Baldassarre	Professor of Constitutional Law	President of the Republic	1986	1995	
Vincenzo Caianiello	Magistrate	Parliament in Joint Session	1986	1995	1995
Mauro Ferri	Attorney; Member of Parliament (1953–1968, Democratic Socialist Party)	President of the Republic	1987	1995–1996	1995
Luigi Mengoni	Professor of Civil Law	President of the Republic	1987		1995–1996
Enzo Cheli	Professor of Constitutional Law	President of the Republic	1987		1996

(Continued)

Judge	Activity Before the Appointment	Appointed By	Year Appointed	President	Vice President
Renato Granata	Magistrate	Court of Cassation	1990	1996–1999	1999
Giuliano Vassalli	Attorney; Professor of Criminal Law	President of the Republic	1991	1999–2000	1996–1999
Francesco Guizzi	Magistrate; Professor of Roman Law; Member of Parliament (1987–1991, National Socialist Party)	Parliament in Joint Session	1991		1999–2000
Cesare Mirabelli	Magistrate; Professor of Ecclesiastic Law	Parliament in Joint Session	1991	2000	1999–2000
Fernando Santosuosso	Magistrate	Court of Cassation	1992		2001
Massimo Vari	Magistrate	Court of Accounts	1993		2001–2001
Cesare Ruperto	Magistrate	Court of Cassation	1993	2001–2002	
Riccardo Chieppa	Magistrate	Council of State	1995	2002–2004	2002
Gustavo Zagrebelsky	Professor of Constitutional Law	President of the Republic	1995	2004	2002–2004
Valerio Onida	Professor of Constitutional Law	Parliament in Joint Session	1996	2004–2005	2004
Carlo Mezzanotte	Attorney; Professor of Constitutional Law	Parliament in Joint Session	1996		2004–2005
Fernanda Contri	Magistrate	President of the Republic	1996		2005
Guido Neppi Modona	Magistrate; Professor of Institutions of Criminal Law and Criminal Procedure	President of the Republic	1996		2005
Annibale Marini	Attorney; Professor of Civil Law	Parliament in Joint Session	1997	2005–2006	2005
Franco Bile	Magistrate	Court of Cassation	1999	2006–2008	2005–2006
Giovanni Maria Flick	Magistrate; Professor of Institutions of Criminal Law	President of the Republic	2000	2008–2009	2005–2008

(*Continued*)

Judge	Activity Before the Appointment	Appointed By	Year Appointed	President	Vice President
Francesco Amirante	Magistrate	Court of Cassation	2001	2009–2010	2008–2009
Ugo De Siervo	Professor of Constitutional Law	Parliament in Joint Session	2002	2010–2011	2009–2010
Romano Vaccarella	Professor of Civil Procedure	Parliament in Joint Session	2002		
Paolo Maddalena	Magistrate	Court of Accounts	2002		2010–2011
Alfio Finocchiaro	Magistrate	Court of Cassation	2002		2011
Alfonso Quaranta	Magistrate	Council of State	2004	2011–2013	
Franco Gallo	Professor of Tax Law	President of the Republic	2004	2013	2011–2013
Luigi Mazzella	Attorney	Parliament in Joint Session	2005		2013–2014
Gaetano Silvestri	Magistrate; Professor of Constitutional Law	Parliament in Joint Session	2005	2013–2014	
Sabino Cassese	Professor of Administrative Law	President of the Republic	2005		
Maria Rita Saulle	Professor of International Law	President of the Republic	2005		
Giuseppe Tesauro	Professor of International Law	President of the Republic	2005	2014	
Paolo Maria Napolitano	Attorney	Parliament in Joint Session	2006	2014	
Giuseppe Frigo	Attorney	Parliament in Joint Session	2008		
Alessandro Criscuolo	Magistrate	Court of Cassation	2008	2014–	
Paolo Grossi	Professor of the History of Italian Law	President of the Republic	2009		
Giorgio Lattanzi	Magistrate	Court of Cassation	2010		2014–
Aldo Carosi	Magistrate	Court of Accounts	2011		
Marta Cartabia	Professor of Constitutional Law	President of the Republic	2011		2014–

(Continued)

Judge	Activity Before the Appointment	Appointed By	Year Appointed	President	Vice President
Sergio Mattarella	Attorney; Professor of Parliamentary Law; elected President of the Republic on January 31, 2015	Parliament in Joint Session	2011		
Mario Rosario Morelli	Magistrate	Court of Cassation	2011		
Giancarlo Coraggio	Magistrate	Council of State	2012		
Giuliano Amato	Professor of Comparative Law	President of the Republic	2013		
Silvana Sciarra	Professor of Labor Law	Parliament in Joint Session	2014		
Daria de Petris	Professor of Administrative Law	President of the Republic	2014		
Nicolò Zanon	Professor of Constitutional Law	President of the Republic	2014		

Sources: M. L. Volkansek, *Constitutional Politics in Italy: The Constitutional Court*, New York, St. Martin's Press, 2000; P. Pederzoli, *La Corte costituzionale*, Bologna, Il Mulino, 2008; Italian Constitutional Court website.

Basic Statistics on the Constitutional Court

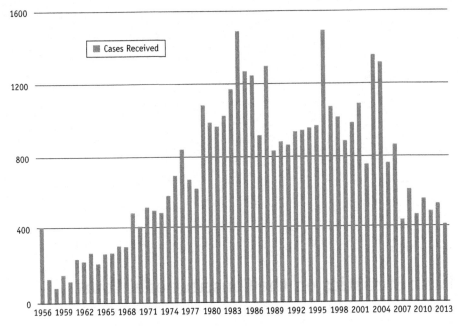

Total Cases Received by the Italian Constitutional Court Per Year.

Year	Cases Received	Year	Cases Received	Year	Cases Received
1956	414	1976	840	1996	1496
1957	132	1977	672	1997	1073
1958	80	1978	624	1998	1016
1959	152	1979	1085	1999	889
1960	119	1980	989	2000	983
1961	241	1981	964	2001	1088
1962	226	1982	1024	2002	757
1963	270	1983	1173	2003	1358
1964	211	1984	1490	2004	1317
1965	266	1985	1271	2005	760
1966	272	1986	1247	2006	861
1967	315	1987	916	2007	447
1968	310	1988	1298	2008	615
1969	489	1989	833	2009	477
1970	420	1990	884	2010	566
1971	525	1991	863	2011	494
1972	507	1992	939	2012	537
1973	490	1993	942	2013	424
1974	587	1994	955		
1975	697	1995	972		

Sources: M. L. Volkansek, *Constitutional Politics in Italy: The Constitutional Court*, New York, St. Martin's Press, 2000; P. Pederzoli, *La Corte costituzionale*, Bologna, Il Mulino, 2008; Italian Constitutional Court website.

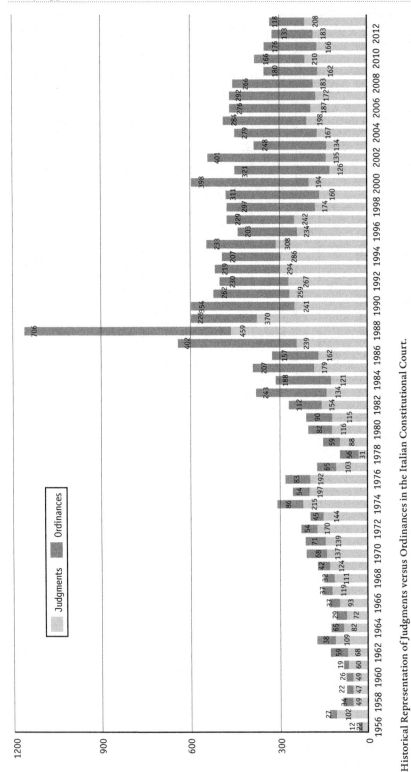

Historical Representation of Judgments versus Ordinances in the Italian Constitutional Court.

Sources: M. L. Volkansek, *Constitutional Politics in Italy: The Constitutional Court*, New York, St. Martin's Press, 2000; P. Pederzoli, *La Corte costituzionale*, Bologna, Il Mulino, 2008; Italian Constitutional Court website.

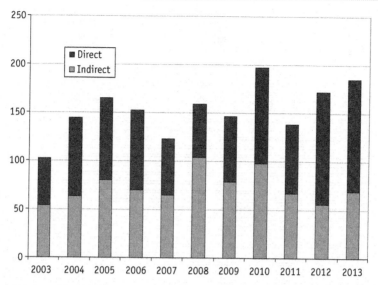

Judgments Reviewed in the Incidental or Indirect Method and Judgments Reviewed in the Direct Method over the Past 10 Years

Judgments		
	Indirect	Direct
2003	54	48
2004	63	81
2005	80	85
2006	70	82

Judgments		
	Indirect	Direct
2007	65	58
2008	104	55
2009	79	67
2010	98	99

Judgments		
	Indirect	Direct
2011	67	71
2012	56	116
2013	69	116
Total	**805**	**878**

Sources: M. L. Volkansek, *Constitutional Politics in Italy: The Constitutional Court*, New York, St. Martin's Press, 2000; P. Pederzoli, *La Corte costituzionale*, Bologna, Il Mulino, 2008; Italian Constitutional Court website.

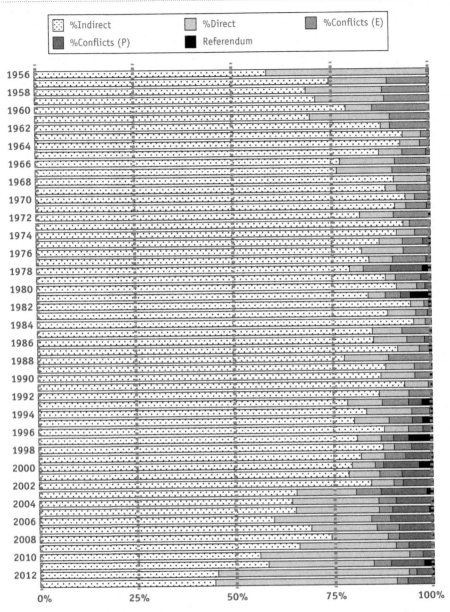

Percentage of All Decisions by the Italian Constitutional Court (Excluding Ordinances of Mere Correction), where P Is the State (*Poteri dello Stato*) and E Is Authorities or Corporations (*Enti*)

Sources: M. L. Volkansek, *Constitutional Politics in Italy: The Constitutional Court*, New York, St. Martin's Press, 2000; P. Pederzoli, *La Corte costituzionale*, Bologna, Il Mulino, 2008; Italian Constitutional Court website.

Table of Cases

---

* Glossary: Decisions – Jurisdiction – Constitutional Parameter
  – *Decisions: Judgement; Order*
  – *Jurisdiction: Incidental; Direct; Conflicts of Attributions among Powers(P); Conflicts of Attributions
    between State and Regions (SR); Admissibility of Referenda*
  – *Constitutional Parameter: Constitution; Charter of Special Region*

ITALIAN COURT OF CASSATION

CONSIGLIO DI STATO

UNITED STATES

COURT OF JUSTICE OF THE EUROPEAN UNION

Index

CPSIA information can be obtained
at www.ICGtesting.com
Printed in the USA
BVOW06s0744280917.
496083BV00001B/1/P